ADVANCE PRAISE FOR *RELIGION AND ITS MONSTERS*

"Ranging from the lair of Leviathan to the mosh pit of The Misfits, Beal's exhumation and dissection of religious monstrosity and monstrous religiosity is as entertaining as it is incisive."

—Stephen D. Moore, author of *God's Gym*

"Timothy Beal has let the monsters out of our cultural and religious basement and allowed them to roam freely—to our great benefit, distress, and delight. His is a detailed, learned, and engrossing book, and our understanding of religious disorientation bounds forward because of it."

—Frederick J. Ruf, author of *The Creation of Chaos*

"Timothy Beal's book fascinates, just as the monsters who inhabit these pages. The author guides us unerringly through a labyrinth whose entry point in the ancient world leads by unexpected turns to contemporary culture. A richly illuminating book, attractively written, which sets the Bible in strange company and thereby makes us rethink the religious in both Bible and culture."

—David M. Gunn, coeditor of *Reading Bibles, Writing Bodies*

"*Religion and Its Monsters* . . . is particularly valuable to biblical scholarship not only as a corrective to a too simplistic reading of the place of the chaotic in ancient Near Eastern religious thought but also as an eye-opening account of the way Western culture has continued to recast the old mythic themes in new forms."

—Carol. A. Newsom, coeditor of *The New Oxford Annotated Bible, Third Edition*

"Tim Beal is a first-rate reader. He knows how to read the Bible in the midst of its complex mythic, symbolic world. He knows how to read popular culture clear to the bottom of its anxiety. He knows how to read at the interface of ancient tradition and current disorder. The outcome is a summons to candor among us, to the best and brightest to face how it is down deep, to the 'keepers' of social order to move past explanation and moralism to the seething where truth boils. Beal as a reader gives us a remarkable, engrossing read."

—Walter Brueggemann, author of *The Prophetic Imagination*

Religion and Its Monsters

TIMOTHY K. BEAL

Routledge New York • London

Published in 2002 by
Routledge
29 West 35th Street
New York, NY 10001

Published in Great Britain by
Routledge
11 New Fetter Lane
London EC4P 4EE

Routledge is an imprint of the Taylor & Francis Group.

The publisher and author gratefully acknowledge permission to reprint the following:

"Bela Lugosi's Dead" reprinted by permission of Bauhaus. Peter Murphy, Daniel Ash, David J. Haskins, Kevin Haskins © 1982 Bauhaus. All rights reserved.

"Dust to Dust" Words and Music by Jerry Caiafa, Michael Emanuel, Daniel Rey © 1999 Zomba Songs Inc., Cyclopian Music, Inc., Zomba Enterprises Inc., Vile of Venom and Daniel Rey (pub. Designee). All rights on behalf of Cyclopian Music, Inc., administered by Zomba Songs Inc. All rights on behalf of Vile of Venom, administered by Zomba Enterprises Inc. All rights reserved. Lyrics reprinted by permission of Warner Bros. Publications.

Library of Congress Cataloging-in-Publication Data

Beal, Timothy K. (Timothy Kandler), 1963-
Religion and its monsters / Timothy K. Beal.
p. cm.
ISBN 0-415-92587-8 – ISBN 0-415-92588-6 (pbk.)
1. Theodicy. I. Title.

BT160 .B35 2001
291.2–dc21 2001019660

CONTENTS

ACKNOWLEDGMENTS

This has been unnerving work. So many horror stories are about professors and researchers going bad. Think of the budding Swiss graduate student Frankenstein in Mary Shelley's novel, the defrocked professor, Dr. Pretorius, in James Whale's *The Bride of Frankenstein*, and the distinguished Semitic languages scholar, Professor Angell, in H.P. Lovecraft's "The Call of Cthulhu," to name just a few. All went over the edge as they followed—or ran from—their monsters into oblivion. Perhaps one reason was that they did not recognize themselves in their monsters. Beyond that, I am betting that a big part of their problem was that they worked in isolation. So I have attempted to secure myself against a similar ruin by surrounding myself with a community of friends and colleagues. I am happy to acknowledge them here.

As ever, I am deeply indebted to those in Tel Mac in Diaspora, especially Bill Perman, Deborah Krause, Tod Linafelt and Brent Plate, who have engaged my work in progress with critical care that stretches beyond friendship and interest. I have also benefited much from the editorial savvy, broad intelligence and patience of my editor, Bill Germano.

Thanks for the criticisms, corrections, references and encouragement offered by many colleagues at Eckerd College, Case

Western Reserve University and elsewhere, especially Carolyn Johnston, Gary Meltzer, Constantina Rhodes Bailly, Chrissy LeBel, David Bryant, Kris Waller, Jan-Lüder Hagens, Jim Flanagan, Bill Deal, Alice Bach, Peter Haas, Tim Murphy, Judith Oster, Tom Bishop and Catherine Scallen of CWRU's Baker-Nord Center for the Humanities, Ted Steinberg, Ed Gemerchak, Geoffrey McVey, Joe Bethancourt, George Aichele, Sue Hanson, Yvonne Sherwood, and Jim Goetsch.

I am also grateful to several teachers and mentors: David Gunn for endlessly insightful questions and comic relief in more ways than one; Elie Wiesel for encouragement and direction in rabbinic literature; Walter Brueggemann for theological insight and "deep vexation" that continue to drive my thinking, even when it comes to monsters; and Carol Newsom, in whose graduate seminars I began getting to know Tiamat, Behemoth and Leviathan in new and provocative ways, and whose own work on Job shapes my interpretation in countless ways.

In many respects this book owes its start and its momentum to the college students whose often wonderfully undisciplined questions led our conversations about biblical and ancient Near Eastern texts into less charted territories. I am especially thankful to students in "Ecology, Chaos, and the Sacred" and "Religion and the Monstrous" at Eckerd College, and to students in "Religion and Horror" at Case Western Reserve University who read and helped revise the book manuscript.

Thanks to my son Seth, who urged me to include the Powerpuff Girls. I probably should have. Thanks to my daughter Sophie, who, after hearing me read the poem on Leviathan in the divine speech from the whirlwind in Job, declared, "That's crazy!" Exactly. And thanks to my partner in marriage, Clover, who intends to smudge the house now that this project is finished, and who warns me, emending Nietzsche, "whoever writes about monsters should see to it that in the process he does not become a monster."

This book is dedicated to the memory of Joel Clayton Hurd (1975–1997). A student of religion and lover of monsters, he never got the opportunity to write his senior thesis comparing the terrifying visions in the Tibetan Book of the Dead with the terrifying visions in the Apocalypse of John.

In Memory of
Joel Clayton Hurd

O nobly-born, the Great Glorious Buddha-Heruka, . . . with three heads, six hands, and four feet firmly postured . . . the body emitting flames of radiance; the nine eyes widely opened, in terrifying gaze; the eyebrows quivering like lightning; the protruding teeth glistening and set over one another; giving vent to sonorous utterances of 'a-la-la' and 'ha-ha'; and piercing whistling sounds . . . will come forth from within thine own brain and shine vividly upon thee. Fear that not.

—Tibetan Book of the Dead (*Bardo Thodol*), I, II
(trans. Lama Kazi Dawa-Samdup)

I saw one like the Son of Man . . . His head and hair were white as white wool . . . his eyes were like a flame of fire, his feet were like burnished bronze . . . and his voice was like the sound of many waters. In his right hand he held seven stars, and from his mouth came a sharp, two-edged sword, and his face was like the sun shining with full force . . . He placed his right hand on me, saying, "Do not be afraid."

—Apocalypse of John 1:12–17

INTRODUCTION

GENESIS 1, TAKE TWO

"To a new world of gods and monsters!" declares Dr. Pretorius in James Whale's 1935 movie *The Bride of Frankenstein*. Pretorius, eager to create a female counterpart for the first monster, is counting himself and his co-creator Henry Frankenstein among the gods, and their creations among the monsters. Pretorius makes his divine aspirations clear in biblical terms, identifying himself with God in the creation story of Genesis 1: "I also have created life, as we say, *in God's own image* . . . Follow the lead of nature, or God . . . *male and female created he them* . . . *be fruitful and multiply*." Pretorius seems to have no problem telling who and what the gods are, and who and what the monsters are.

For the viewers, however, things are not so clear. We tend to identify with the unnamed monster played by Boris Karloff far more than we do with his creators and his killers. We understand the monster in a way that none of the characters in the movie do. When the monster declares, "I love dead, hate living," for example, Pretorius hears only that the Creature wants a companion who is living-dead like himself. We, on the other hand, understand this statement also as a lament in which the Creature expresses his

FIGURE 1. *The Bride of Frankenstein*, Copyright 1935 Universal Studios

loathing of life in this world of gods and monsters and his longing for death. The creator god misses this more profound meaning, but we do not.

Indeed, everyone in *The Bride of Frankenstein* is caricatured *except* the monster. As they chase after him, the frenzied mob of would-be monster killers confirms Nietzsche's warning that "whoever fights monsters should see to it that in the process he does not become a monster."[1] As the monster is raised high on a stake, crucifixion-style, in order to be tried and executed, the camera closes in on his face. We can almost hear him saying, "My God, my God, why have you forsaken me?" (Figure 1). But the monster's creator god, Henry Frankenstein, is a more discomforting divine image than even Pretorius: an indecisive, self-absorbed, grave-robbing fool.

Like his far more eloquent counterpart in Mary Shelley's 1818 novel *Frankenstein or the Modern Prometheus*, Whale's god-forsaken, posthumous monster is something of a theologian. Not a theologian with all the answers but one who raises profound questions, questions that survive their answers. By playing God, does one inadvertently end up playing monster? More radically, does *being* God end up being monstrous? Who is more monstrous, the creatures who must live through this vale of tears, or the creator who put them here? What does it mean to be "monstrous," anyway? Are we not all rendered monstrous under God? Is our monstrosity in the image of God? Where *is* God in all this?

Very quickly we find ourselves in deeply unsettling theological territory, a territory traditionally called theodicy. Theodicy concerns divine justice in the face of unjustifiable suffering. Why do the wicked prosper and the righteous suffer? In a world such as ours, how can we possibly conceive of a just God? Indeed, Shelley's novel begins with an epigraph from the quintessential English theodicy, *Paradise Lost* by John Milton, whose explicit although inevitably unrealized aim is to "justify the ways of God to men." Shelley's epigraph draws us to the theodic question, which echoes far beyond any answer, and which will be posed again and again by the monster to Victor Frankenstein throughout the novel:

> Did I request thee, Maker, from my clay
> To mold Me man? Did I solicit thee
> From darkness to promote me?
>
> —*Paradise Lost* X.743–5[2]

The voice of the monster is the audacious voice of theodicy. It is addressed not only to the creator Frankenstein but also to the creator God. Why did you make me? Why did you put me here? What were you thinking? What kind of a world is this? What kind of divine justice is this? What kind of God are you? The monster in Shelley's novel, as in Whale's movie, stands for these questions and terrifying religious uncertainties. His questions pry at cracks in the world's foundations that open onto abysses of unknowing. In this unhallowed space of theodicy, opened by the creature's tragic appeals to its creator, clear distinctions between gods and monsters get awfully blurry. The horror of *Frankenstein* is a profoundly theological horror.

RELIGION AND ITS MONSTERS, MONSTERS AND THEIR RELIGION

Most of us do not go to monster movies or read Gothic monster tales in search of religion, at least not consciously. Nor do we go to church or temple or ashram in search of monsters. Yet, as Frankenstein's monster has already begun to indicate, religion and monsters have more to do with each other than one might initially assume. Indeed, when it comes to gods and monsters, Pretorius' "new world" is not so new after all.

This is a book about what religion has to do with monsters, and vice versa. Its basic starting point is a two-part proposition: that we can learn something about a religious tradition by getting to know its monsters, and that we can learn something about monsters by looking into their religious backgrounds. Part One of this book, "Religion and Its Monsters," explores representations of the monstrous in Jewish and Christian biblical tradition and in other closely related religious texts from the ancient Near East. Part Two, "Monsters and Their Religion," looks into the religious background of some of our more popular twentieth-century monsters in order to explore relations between religion and the monstrous in today's ever-expanding popular culture of horror. Part One considers religion *as* horror, Part Two horror *as* religion.

PARADOX OF THE MONSTROUS

Monsters are in the world but not of the world. They are paradoxical personifications of *otherness within sameness*. That is, they are threatening figures of anomaly within the well-established and accepted order of things. They represent the outside that has gotten inside, the beyond-the-pale that, much to our horror, has gotten into the pale.

One helpful way of thinking about this paradoxical sense of the monster as a horrific figure of otherness within sameness is by way of Sigmund Freud's concept of the *unheimlich*, that is, the "unhomely" or "uncanny." If *heimlich* refers to that which belongs within the four walls of the house, inspiring feelings of restfulness and security, then *unheimlich* refers to that which threatens one's sense of "at-homeness," not from the outside but from *within* the house.[3] The *unheimlich* is in some sense what is in the house without belonging there, the outside that is inside. The horror of the unhomely experience, then, involves the awareness that something that should be outside the house is in it. It is an experience of otherness within sameness.

For Freud, "home" refers primarily to individual human consciousness. For our purposes, we may extend the sense of "home" in the idea of the *heimlich* to mean anything from self to society to cosmos. That is, this *heimlich* feeling of security and "at-homeness" may refer to one's confidence in the meaning, integrity and well-being of oneself as a subject (the body or self as "house"). Or it may refer to one's confidence in the meaning, integrity and well-being of one's society or culture (the "house of culture," as Herbert Marcuse puts it).[4] Or it may refer to one's confidence in the meaning, integrity and well-being of the entire cosmos (the world ecology as "house"). Taken in this very broad way, the *unheimlich* is that which invades one's sense of personal, social or cosmic order and security—the feeling of being at home in oneself, one's society and one's world. The *unheimlich* is the other within, that which is "there" in the house but cannot be comprehended by it or integrated into it.

Monsters are personifications of the *unheimlich*. They stand for what endangers one's sense of at-homeness, that is, one's sense of security, stability, integrity, well-being, health and meaning. They make one feel *not at home at home*. They are figures of chaos and disorientation *within* order and orientation, revealing deep insecurities in one's faith in oneself, one's society and one's world.

DEMONIZING AND DEIFYING

In his glory days as the vampire in *Dracula*, Bela Lugosi was a celebrity icon, idolized by fans from Broadway to Hollywood. He was not a monster, but he played one on stage and screen. In his last years, the aging star became, as they say, a *monstre sacré*. Still later, after his death and his burial in full Dracula costume and makeup, Goth bands like Bauhaus canonized him as their sacred icon, the ultimate incarnation of Count Dracula for a new generation of monster devotees. Thus Lugosi, like the monster he played, has become a *monstre sacré* in more ways than one.

In what ways can a monster be, or become, sacred?

We humans respond to the monster as a personification of the *unheimlich*, of otherness within sameness, and our responses range from demonization to deification. Often we *demonize* the monster as a threat not only to "our" order but also to the order of the gods or God. In this way the monstrous other who threatens "us" and "our world" is represented as an enemy of God and then is exorcized from the right order of things and sent to some sort of Hell. "Our" order is identified with the sacred order against a diabolically monstrous chaos. Such is the fate of Apophis in Egyptian tradition, and of the sea monster Leviathan in Psalm 74 and Isaiah 27. Think also of the fate of the vampire in Bram Stoker's *Dracula*, as well as of many other monsters from the past century of horror novels and movies. By demonizing our monsters, we keep God on our side.

In other cases, however, the monster is *deified* as a revelation of sacred otherness. Its coming into the world is represented as a *hierophany*, that is, a revelation of the holy. Here the monster is an envoy of the divine or the sacred as radically other than "our" established order of things. It is an invasion of what we might call *sacred chaos* and disorientation within self, society and world. Such is the case with Tiamat in the Babylonian *Enuma Elish*, as well as with Leviathan and Behemoth in the divine speech from the whirlwind in the book of Job. Such is also the case, I propose, with the vampire in F. W. Murnau's film *Nosferatu*, as well as with Cthulhu and other monster gods in the stories of H. P. Lovecraft. If demonizing the monster keeps God on our side, then deifying it often puts us in a world of religious disorientation and horror.

Often what we find is not simply one reaction or the other, but both. The monster if often *both* demonized and deified, revealing a deep sense of ambivalence about the relation between the monstrous and the divine, and intensifying the sense of paradox.

MONSTRUM TREMENDUM, MYSTERIUM TREMENDUM

We are less accustomed to thinking of the monstrous as a figure of divine revelation or an envoy of the sacred than we are to thinking of it as demonic or "evil." Yet the monster's religious import is rooted in the word itself: "monster" derives from the Latin *monstrum*, which is related to the verbs *monstrare* ("show" or "reveal") and *monere* ("warn" or "portend"), and which sometimes refers to a divine portent that reveals the will or judgment of God or the gods. In this sense a *monstrum* is a message that breaks into this world from the realm of the divine. Even in the ancient and cruel notion of "monstrous births" as revelations of divine judgment, the otherness of the monster is considered not only horrifically *unnatural* but also horrifically *supernatural*, charged with religious import.[5]

Likewise, the *experience* of horror in relation to the monstrous is often described in terms reminiscent of religious experience. Both are often characterized as an encounter with mysterious otherness that elicits a vertigo-like combination of both fear and desire, repulsion and attraction. Both religious experience and horror are characterized as encounters with something simultaneously awesome and awful—a feeling captured in the older spelling, "aweful", which still retains its sense of awe. Nowhere is the affinity between horror and religious experience drawn out more fully than in Rudolph Otto's *The Idea of the Holy* (*Das Heilige*, 1917). Working from the idea of the sublime in Immanuel Kant and Edmund Burke, Otto describes religious experience as an encounter with the *mysterium tremendum*, that is, a radically other mystery that brings on a stupefying combination of fascination and terror, wonder and dread. It is "something inherently 'wholly other', whose kind and character are incommensurable with our own, and before which we therefore recoil in a wonder that strikes us chill and numb."[6] For Otto "the monstrous" (*das Ungeheuere*), like the "uncanny" (*unheimlich*), is "a fairly exact expression for the numinous in its aspects of mystery, awefulness, majesty, augustness and 'energy'; nay, even the fascination is dimly felt in it."[7] For him the monster is an aweful *monstrum tremendum*. Indeed, Otto interprets the monsters Leviathan and Behemoth in the book of Job as quintessential representations of the monstrous as a figure for the wholly other.

Of course, Otto (and others who have read horror as religious experience à la Otto) presumes that there is such a transcendent wholly other, a sacred that is not reducible to a cultural or psychological phenomenon. You need not agree. Although Otto, in his introduction to *The Idea of the Holy*, discourages readers from reading his book if they have not had such an experience of the sacred, I do not. This book is not an altar call to the church of the monstrous. The connections we make between the monstrous and the divine, and between horror and religious experience, do not necessarily mean that we have to *confess* monsters as revelations of the divine or the sacred. Because they are sometimes represented as such does not mean that we have to believe in them. Indeed, we may decide instead, following Freud, that the horror inspired by the monstrous, like other experiences of the *unheimlich*, is best explained as the *return of the repressed*. Whereas for Otto the *unheimlich* is an experience of the radically transcendent other, a completely unhomely experience of the *mysterium* that has broken into the home from a wholly other realm, for Freud there is no such thing as wholly otherness or radical transcendence. What Otto calls "wholly other" Freud would call "other" only insofar as it has been repressed. For Freud the *unheimlich* is only "outside the house" (the house of the self, the house of culture, the house of the cosmos) insofar as it is hidden within the house. It is a revelation not of the wholly other but of a repressed otherness within the self.[8] The monster, as personification of the *unheimlich*, stands for that which has broken out of the subterranean basement or the locked closet where it has been banished from consciousness.

My interest here is not in determining what the monstrous *really* is (whether an envoy of the sacred, the returned of the repressed, or both, or something else). Rather I want to explore those places where representations of the monstrous and the religious converge. In those points of convergence, the monstrous becomes a site for religious reflection. I am not so much constructing a theology of the monstrous as I am exploring the monstrous as a form of theological expression. What, for example, can we learn about theological discourse in biblical literature when we approach it through its monsters? By the same token, how does the ostensibly non-religious popular culture of horror often become a venue for doing theology?

Both monsters and religions are always culturally specific. There are only particular religions, and particular monsters, and no one book can hope to be comprehensive of all that gets called religion and all that gets called monstrous. How do monsters and religion converse in other cultural fields? How are they related, for example, in Japanese graphic novels (*mangas*) and animation? My aim is not only to rethink the monstrous in terms of religion, however, but also to rethink religion in terms of the monstrous. It strikes me that exploring religion via its monsters presents a challenge to the common conception of religion as being exclusively about the establishment of order against chaos. This conception was given its classic (that is, normative) formulation in Mircea Eliade's *The Sacred and the Profane,* a book that has exercised powerful influence over many scholars and innumerable college students in Introduction to Religion courses over the past half century. Eliade describes religion as essentially *cosmogonic,* or world creative. Religion is about creating and maintaining a sacred cosmic order against chaos.[9] Religion is about establishing and maintaining sacred space and sacred time against the "formless expanse" of chaos surrounding it.[10]

> The former is the world (more precisely, our world), the cosmos; every thing outside it is no longer a cosmos but a sort of 'other world,' a foreign, chaotic space, peopled by ghosts, demons, 'foreigners' . . . It is not difficult to see why the religious moment [i.e., the manifestation of the sacred] implies the cosmogonic moment. The sacred reveals absolute reality and at the same time makes orientation possible; hence it founds the world in the sense that it fixes the limits and establishes the very order of the world.[11]

Later Eliade reiterates this idea of religion in language that indicates where he sees the monsters in this scenario of sacred order against demonic chaos: "An attack on 'our world' is equivalent to an act of revenge by the mythical dragon, who rebels against the work of the gods, the cosmos, and struggles to annihilate it. 'Our' enemies belong to the powers of chaos."[12] Here religion is about the sacred and the sacred is about order, foundation and orientation over against chaos and disorientation, which are demonized. Certainly this is one aspect of religion in many cultural contexts, and we will see it operative in those instances where the monstrous is demonized as a force of chaos that threatens "our" sacred order. One of those instances is the vision of the great dragon in the Apocalypse of John in the New Testament. In fact, this is the fallen angel turned diabolic dragon to which Eliade is referring in the passage above. Much of contemporary horror functions in just the same way, as a shoring up and consecration of the established order of things (especially social orders that distinguish "us" from "them," self from other). Yet there are other cases in which the monstrous-chaotic is *identified with* the divine or the sacred against cosmic order. So it is in a number of ancient Near Eastern religious texts, as well as in some biblical texts about Leviathan, and throughout contemporary horror literature and film. As we get to know these monsters, what they often reveal is a divinity or a sacredness that is, like many of our religions and like many of ourselves, caught in endless, irreducible tensions between order and chaos, orientation and disorientation, self and other, foundation and abyss.

Religion is never without its monsters. Whether demonized or deified or both, no matter how many times we kill our monsters they keep coming back for more. Not just Dracula but all monsters are undead. Maybe they keep coming back because they still have something to say or show us about our world and ourselves. Maybe that is the scariest part.

PART ONE

Religion and Its Monsters

CHAPTER 1

Chaos Gods

FRAGMENTS FROM THE ANCIENT NEAR EAST

Behind and around the religious traditions of the Hebrew Bible, or Old Testament, is a rich and varied world of gods, monsters and monster gods commonly referred to as the ancient Near East. Covering the region from southwest Asia to northeast Africa and from the invention of writing (c. 3000 BCE) to the rise of Hellenism under Alexander the Great (c. 330 BCE), the ancient Near East includes a very broad range of religions, languages and literary traditions, including Egyptian, Vedic, Sumerian, Babylonian, Canaanite, Assyrian, Phoenician, Israelite and Judean. Yet what we know about them comes mostly from piecing together fragments, relics of what for the most part has not survived. Even when reading more or less whole texts, it is clear that the conceptual landscapes reflected in and generated by them are extremely complex and often unfamiliar to western ideas of self, society and world. Indeed, within a single literary history, such as that of ancient Egypt, there is a tremendous amount of diversity from city to city, from subculture to subculture, and from generation to generation. All this is to make clear from the outset that these stories do not fit together into some single integrated "mythological" whole. Nor can they be reduced to a handful of archetypal struggles and quests. Their gods and monsters are not simply the personae of a god with a thousand faces. Neither are they all surface manifestations of some deep underlying mythological structure that reflects a universal "savage" mind. These sorts of interpretive claims about ancient myths and mythology ultimately deny the particularities of the different stories that are being studied.[1] Yet neither can we deny that the conceptual landscapes reflected in many of these texts are historically related. Clearly there has been a great deal of cultural migration and intermingling among the various traditions of the ancient Near East over the millennia.

TO ORDER AND BACK

One especially common feature among ancient Near Eastern stories of cosmogony (world beginnings) is the motif of *creation out of chaos*. Many ancient Near Eastern cosmogonies envision the world as we know it taking form out of, and sometimes against, a primordial chaos. In some texts, this primordial chaos is imagined as a kind of precosmic soup. In several Egyptian stories, for example, the world begins as a small hill rising out of Nūn, which is the boundless, undifferentiated watery abyss.[2] Likewise the cosmogony of Genesis 1 begins with "the earth being a formless void, with darkness over the face of the deep and a wind of God sweeping across the waters." The words translated "formless void" (*tohu wabohu*), "deep" (*tehom*), and "the waters" (*hammayim*) combine to suggest an amorphous, watery chaos from which God will speak the world in all its complexity into existence. Later, in Genesis 6–8, God will try to undo the very same creation by opening the floodgates in the heavens above the earth and the deeps beneath it, thereby allowing these primordial chaos waters to return in drowning torrents. In this story world, then, the primordial chaos waters are identified with both creation and destruction, cosmic birth and death: on the one hand, it is the *materia prima*, the original material from which all life emerges; on the other hand, it is the deadly flood, whose violent inbreaking would mean death and the end of a livable world ecology. Already in this double meaning of the primordial chaos waters (as source of, and threat to, creation), we see how cosmogonic beginnings and apocalyptic endings resemble one another: both take place on the edge of the world as we know it. Both involve a transition between cosmos and chaos, cosmogony being about cosmos *emerging out of* chaos and apocalypse being about cosmos *returning to* chaos in order that a new cosmos may emerge. Both cosmogonic beginnings and apocalyptic endings are visions of the edge of the world.

These days we are familiar with the idea of order emerging out of chaos and returning to it, thanks to chaos and complexity theory. Granted that entropy, the Second Law of Thermodynamics, holds true for the long run of things. Our now middle-aged cosmos is steadily running out of energy and its structures are dissipating into chaos—a concept many of us can understand from personal experience. Yet along this irreversible road to heat death, we keep discovering chance movement in the opposite direction: new complex structures are emerging *out of* chaos.[3] Indeed, that is what our livable world is. That is what an ecosystem is. That is what life is. Entropy is not only the end of the world but also its source. Chaos is both deadly and fecund.

Less familiar but nonetheless fascinating to those of us attuned to the sciences of chaos is the idea that primordial chaos might take the form of divinity, or rather divine monstrosity. In many ancient Near Eastern stories, the chaos out of and against which the world is created is personified as a "chaos god" or "chaos monster" who must be defeated by another god in order to create or maintain cosmic order. These monstrous chaos gods are paradoxical representations of radical otherness appearing within the order of things, the otherworldly within the worldly, the primordial within the ordial. They lurk on the thresholds of the known, at the edges of the cosmological map, revealing deep insecurities within a cosmos that trembles in the balance between order and chaos. Indeed, by personifying chaos in the form of a chaos god, these texts suggest that this sense of cosmic insecurity is rooted within divinity itself. Beneath faithful assertions in these stories that the cosmos is hospitable, secure and meaningfully ordered—in a word, *heimlich*—one senses the presence of a lurking *unheimlich* chaos within the divine that at any moment might come flooding back over everything.

CHAOS MOTHER

This is the story of the chaos god Tiamat, primordial mother of all gods, even of the creator god Marduk who kills her in order to form the world out of her corpse. Her story is told in the Babylonian *Enuma Elish*, one of the fullest and most complex surviving creation stories of the ancient Near East.[4]

The story begins before the creation of earth and heavens, even before the birth of the great Babylonian god Marduk, and even before the birth of his begetter Ea, with the first divine couple, Tiamat and Apsu. The name Apsu, related to the Sumerian Abzu, suggests "watery deep" or "sweet water ocean."[5] Tiamat means "sea," and in the opening lines of the story she is called Mummu Tiamat, that is, "mother" or "maker" Tiamat. Together they represent a dual personification of the primordial chaos waters out of which all else will be born. In this beginning, very unlike Genesis 1, there is no solitary creator god speaking the world into existence with the opening line "Let there be light." Here it all begins with the intimate intermingling of the primordial pair: as Tiamat and Apsu "mix their waters" together, the "gods were born within them."

But with the birth of this second generation of gods, the honeymoon is over. Almost immediately, the divine children begin troubling their parents, especially their mother Tiamat. So much so, in fact, that Apsu determines to kill them off. Before he can do so, however, the young gods learn of his intention and beat him to the punch: the wise god Ea puts Apsu to sleep with a spell and then kills him, setting up his own dwelling place in Apsu's body. There, "inside pure Apsu," Ea then creates Marduk, who soon gains preeminence among the gods. The elder god Anu gives Marduk the four winds, which he uses to stir up Tiamat further.

Upon hearing of Apsu's murder, Tiamat is convinced by those gods still loyal to her to attack Ea and the rival gods who are dwelling in his corpse. Cloaked in radiant, godlike dragons and surrounded by a horned serpent, another dragon, a rabid dog and a number of other animal-human combinations, Tiamat rages out of control. Terrified, the rival gods search for one among them who can face her and her armies. Marduk rises to the occasion, and the other gods, overjoyed, ordain him their champion and king. They send him off to battle and commence getting drunk.

In the battle that ensues, Marduk ultimately defeats Tiamat in a rather gory, even gratuitous face-to-face battle. As they close in on one another, Marduk dispatches a fierce storm wind against her. When she opens her mouth to swallow it, she is unable to close her lips, and the wind begins to distend her like an over-filled balloon. Seizing the opportunity, Marduk shoots an arrow into her belly, and she explodes into two pieces. He then throws down her corpse, tramples her lower part, smashes her skull with his mace, cuts her arteries, and has the North Wind carry the smell of her death "as good news" to his compatriot gods back home in Apsu's corpse.[6]

While the other gods catch the whiff and begin the victory celebration (remember that they have been drinking for some time already), Marduk proceeds to use her body to create the world. He slices her, "like a fish for drying," and makes half of her into a roof for the sky. With the other half he forms the earth. He channels her chaotic primordial waters into springs and rivers, opening the Tigris and Euphrates from her eyes, and making her spittle into clouds. Marduk then turns his attention to other, less ecological and more religious-political matters. He establishes a religious order and rituals devoted to him, and makes Babylon the center of the universe and "home of the great gods." Thus we see how the divine establishment and maintenance of cosmic order are intimately related to the divine establishment and maintenance of political and social order (as microcosmos). Babylon is the *axis mundi,* the center of the universe, the navel of the cosmic body. In fact, there is good evidence that the *Enuma Elish* was used in rituals related to the Babylonian *Akitu* new year festival, which served to reaffirm the divinely ordained and guaranteed order not only of creation but also of Babylon as the center of creation.[7]

Cosmic and political order are established and guaranteed through the overcoming and containment of primordial chaos, here embodied in the figure of Tiamat. The cosmos is imagined as her filleted corpse. On the one hand, the chaos god Tiamat is clearly conceived as a monstrous threat to both cosmic and social-political order, and the survival of the world as well as the survival of the state depend on the creator god Marduk defeating her *and* keeping her from returning. On the other hand, that which threatens cosmic and political order is also the source of that order.

The fact that the primordial chaos is personified and monstrocized not only as feminine but as maternal (*Mummu Tiamat*, "Mother Tiamat," mother of the gods and source of all creation) seems to beg for psychoanalysis. Indeed, Tiamat might be considered a prototype of what Barbara Creed has called the "monstrous-feminine" in modern horror.[8] Tiamat is both *materia prima* and *mater prima*, original matter and original mother, and the story can be read as a story of the birth of her children and their subsequent denial of their—and the world's—original fusion with her. Read from this angle, the story is not only about Babylon's champion god subduing the chaos monster god in order to create a livable world; it is about the creation of the cosmos as a violent denial of its original fusion with and continued (but largely repressed) dependence on the chaos mother.

Notice, moreover, that the one who defeats the chaos monster in this story is also the one who most resembles her. Like Tiamat, Marduk is associated with images of cosmic turbulence: he uses a flood wave "to stir up Tiamat," he wields an "unfaceable" flood weapon, a tempest, a tornado, and a whirlwind. In fact, Marduk's own description is monstrously and awesomely unnatural, defying the imagination. His limbs are said to be "beyond comprehension, impossible to understand, too difficult to perceive," he has four eyes and four ears, and fire blazes forth from his mouth whenever he moves his lips.[9] Perhaps it takes a chaos monster to kill a chaos monster.

Marduk's defeat of Tiamat in the story may appear to be final. Yet on a deeper level there is a lurking sense that the watery monster of primordial chaos might stir and rage out of control yet again if not continually kept under Marduk's lordly control. Tiamat is killed but might not stay that way. Living on the (undead?) slaughtered body of the chaos god who bore you produces at least a little anxiety. In the ancient world, as in the modern monster tale, it is difficult to keep a good monster down. They have a tendency to reawaken, reassemble their dismembered parts, and return for a sequel. Therefore Marduk is called upon toward the end of the final tablet to keep up the good work of maintaining the order and stability of the cosmos as well as the order and stability of Babylon.

Employing a kind of realized eschatology of "already-but-not-yet," the text calls on Marduk to keep defeating the already defeated Tiamat:

> Let him defeat Tiamat, constrict her breath and shorten
> her life,
> So that for future people, till time grows old,
> She shall be far removed, not kept here, distant forever.[10]

The desire of those literally living on Tiamat's body to keep her "far removed" and "distant forever" is deeply ironic, and suggests, once again, the *paradox of the monstrous* as the other within. Tiamat, the radically other, the anti-cosmic and anti-Babylonian, is also the most immanent. Her body is the cosmos. Human and divine life come from it and return to it. Here, paradoxically, is an intimacy and immanence that induces horror.

THE CLOUDRIDER AND THE WARRIOR GODDESS

The cosmic horror that looms over the world in the *Enuma Elish* pervades other ancient Near Eastern stories of monstrous chaos gods as well. In the Sanskrit hymns from the Indian *Rig Veda*, for example, the creator god Indra must slay the chaos demon Vṛtra in order to release its primordial chaos waters as life source, thereby creating and establishing a livable cosmos, the order of which is integrally related to Vedic understanding of social order.[11] And in Egyptian tradition, the sun god Re's battle against the dragon-like chaos god Apophis is a daily drama of world re-creation. Apophis is a god of darkness that threatens the sun's coming and going and, therefore, cosmic regularity. He must be confronted by Re at the cosmic threshold moments of dawn and dusk. An eyeless, earless, screaming embodiment of primordial chaos, Apophis stands for the return of the cosmologically repressed.[12]

This sense of cosmic horror is especially pervasive in the cycle of stories about Baal and Anat in Ugaritic narrative poetry, a body of literature closely related to the Hebrew Bible.[13] The central theme in the Baal-Anat Cycle is *theomachy*, that is, the struggle of various gods within the Ugaritic pantheon for ascendancy under the supreme but rather passive father god, El.[14] The champion in the story cycle is the cloud-riding rain god Baal ("Lord"), who is often aided in his efforts to be enthroned over the other gods by the independent, wild-spirited warrior goddess Anat.

The first adversary is Prince Yamm (= Hebrew *yam*, "sea"), a divine personification of the primordial chaos waters who is called "beloved of El," and who appears to be favored over Baal by the divine mother Athirat.[15] He is an enemy of Baal and Anat, then, but not of the divine parents. Yamm demands that El hand Baal over to him, and El does, which leads to a battle in which Baal is victorious, thanks to a special weapon which leaps from Baal's hands "like a raptor" and strikes Yamm between the eyes. Yamm collapses and his convulsing body falls to the earth, where Baal dismembers him and is proclaimed king.[16] At another point in the story cycle Anat, too, claims to have slain Yamm. "Surely I fought Yamm, the Beloved of El," she asserts, "Surely I bound Tunnan and destroyed him. / I fought the Twisty Serpent, / The Potentate with Seven Heads."[17] Apparently Yamm has been slain more than once, but keeps coming back for more. It is hard to keep a chaos monster down.

The second adversary is Divine Mot (= Hebrew *mawet*, "death"), also beloved of El. Mot is the voracious god of death and the underworld whose gaping mouth reaches up to heaven and down to hell. Upon hearing of Baal's earlier victory and enthronement, he threatens to rip Baal to pieces and then eat his flanks, innards and forearms. "Surely you will descend into Divine Mot's throat," he vows, "Into the gullet of El's Beloved."[18] In the fight that ensues, Mot kills Baal, taking him "like a lamb in my mouth, like a kid crushed in the chasm of my throat." But then Anat rises in a vengeful rage. She seizes Mot, splits him in two with her sword, grinds him to powder with millstones, and sows him in an open field so that birds devour him.[19] With Mot defeated, Baal is resurrected and returns to the throne, an event that the story associates with the return of life and fertility (perhaps signifying the coming of autumn rains). As the chaos god who threatens cosmic order is overcome, the world ecology is restored. But this is not the end of the story. Later, Mot returns to battle Baal again. After a long, evenly matched struggle, El intervenes on Baal's behalf and Mot surrenders. Thus Baal maintains his throne, at least for the time being. By the end of the cycle, the sense is that Baal's preeminence and the related well-being of the world ecology are not entirely secure. There is always the possibility of a rematch.

As in the *Enuma Elish*, moreover, both chaos monster slayers, Baal and Anat, are themselves often figures of chaos more than order. Baal brings not only rains but also storms and lightning, which represent cosmic chaos more than they do peace, harmony and fertility. And just before Baal's messengers arrive at Anat's palace, she is depicted battling in the valley between two towns, "the people of the seashore" and "the populace of the sunrise," which may be metaphors for the transition between day and night (i.e., when the sun meets the sea on the horizon). Whether metaphorical or literal, her passion for the chaos of war is striking, as she adorns herself with severed heads and arms and revels in neck-deep gore:

> Under her, like balls, are heads,
> Above her, like locusts, hands,
> Like locusts, heaps of warrior-hands.
> She fixes heads to her back,
> Fastens hands to her belt.
> Knee-deep she gleans in warrior blood,
> Neck-deep in the gore of soldiers.[20]

The "adolescent" warrior goddess Anat is turbulent, chaotic and anomalous. As Neil Walls has made clear, moreover, her liminal identity represents a threat to established patriarchal gender norms. Neither mother nor daughter nor wife, a violent warrior goddess with her own palace, she may have represented "social chaos," eliciting "androcentric fear of uncontrolled women."[21] Yet in the Baal-Anat Cycle she is also a champion of the chaos battle who is credited with the slaying of a figure whose ascendancy would have been the ultimate ecological catastrophe. Here again, as with Marduk versus Tiamat, it appears that in some sense it takes one to kill one.

NO REST

Baal's and Anat's victories over Yamm and Mot are, like Marduk's victory over Tiamat, entirely inconclusive, and therefore so is Baal's lordship, and therefore so is the security of the world ecology. Taken collectively, there is in this story cycle a profound and abiding sense of precariousness and insecurity built into the order of things. This insecurity is personified most vividly in the figures of Mot and Yamm, who, like Baal, never seem to stay dead for long. Mot kills Baal. Then Anat kills Mot. Baal comes back to life. Then Mot returns. Mot and Baal battle once more, and Mot surrenders. But for how long? Likewise, the fact that Anat and Baal have each killed Yamm at least once suggests that it is impossible to keep a good chaos monster, or for that matter a good chaos monster killer, down. If Baal can come back, and if Yamm and Mot have been killed more than once, then clearly the battle for ascendency and stability within the divine family is endless. As J. C. L. Gibson writes, this text "faces up the powers that be with both irony and circumspection, aware of the knife-edge that separates harmony from chaos and life from death."[22]

Recall, moreover, that Yamm and Mot are both "beloved of El," and that Yamm is allied with El's divine consort "Athirat of the Sea." Here again, the anti-cosmic, monstrous forces of chaos in this narrative cycle, as in the *Enuma Elish*, are not anti-divinity or "evil" in some dualistic sense. Rather, these chaos monster gods are part of a divinity that is deeply divided within itself about the future viability of the cosmos and of life as humankind knows it. Religion, in this context, is not simply cosmic, as is often asserted by modern theorists of religion. Rather it is a locus for negotiating between the cosmic and the chaotic, which are, paradoxically, both interdependent and mutually exclusive. In these stories, cosmic horror is profoundly theological. The precariousness of the world as a livable abode for humankind is believed to be rooted in a divinity in which creation and chaos are in perpetual and ultimately unresolvable tension with one another.

CHAPTER 2

The Bible and Horror

BIBLICAL MONSTERS AND MAD PROFESSORS

Every fall, the conservative watchdog Young America's Foundation publishes a predictably damning assessment of the current state of higher education, based on its yearly survey of current courses listed in college and university bulletins and catalogs. Timed to play on the anxieties of first-year college students and their parents and to coincide with the special college issues of major magazines, the reports and related press releases are dominated by terms of the bizarre, the outrageous and the horrific, highlighting "shocking and revealing courses" which supposedly indicate the "appalling nature of the curriculum" in America's best schools. The rhetorical strategy employed here is that of making monsters out of political and intellectual opponents. The YAF depicts these "outrageous" and "bizarre" courses as the awful brain-children of the monstrous fantasies of leftist professors bent on destroying "traditional values," specified in terms of "Western culture, the United States of America, the free market, and [conservative Christian] religion."

Along with the programs of study typically targeted by conservative critics of higher education (women's and gender studies, gay and lesbian studies, African-American studies), the 2000 report pays particular attention to courses in religion. It bewails, for example, the increasing number of courses on folklore and magic. Never mind that these have been central research and teaching topics in religion departments since the mid-1800s. In a special section called "The Disease Spreads," moreover, it focuses on how this lamentable trend in the teaching of religion has contaminated even religion and theology departments in top-ranked Catholic colleges and universities.

The report's focus on religion is indicative of the special place that the academic study and teaching of religion holds in the latest rounds of the culture wars over the state and direction of higher education. What is at stake is no less than the legitimate place of the study of religion in American higher education. In fact, the YAF's report is symptomatic of a very broad and general expectation, among both conservatives and liberals, in and out of the academy, that a religion department ought to be the soul and moral conscience of its institution. Religion professors are often expected somehow to represent religious traditions and serve as apologists for them—to profess religion rather than the study of it. To pronounce the state of religion departments in our best church-affiliated colleges and universities as contaminated and diseased, therefore, is to declare that the very soul of higher education is sick.

For those like the YAF who want to make these courses and their professors into monsters, the real horror of teaching religion in an academic context is not that the courses are "trendy," "bizarre" or "intellectually vacuous." Wishful thinking. The real horror is in the proposition that religious traditions considered normative be studied alongside other ideas, practices and institutions in such a way that the normative will be contaminated by critical comparison, revealing similarities and differences that are not always orthodox.

One of the courses presented in the 2000 report and the related "Dirty Dozen" press release as a most telling symptom of the dreadful state of higher education generally and religion studies specifically is a course called "The Bible and Horror," taught by Tod Linafelt at Georgetown University. In fact, this course topped the list in *The Washington Times*'s article based on the YAF press release. That article begins, "Students at Georgetown University this year can take a class called 'The Bible and Horror,' which seeks to answer the question: 'What might religion and horror (or the monstrous) have in common?'" As the lead-off course in the article, and as a highlighted course in the larger YAF report and press release, it is assumed that "The Bible and Horror" will immediately impress readers not only as absurd but downright offensive, even blasphemous, the dreadful offspring of a mad professor's monstrous imagination.

No doubt a little thinking, perhaps with the help of a knowledgeable student, would provide ample justification for the vast majority of courses in the YAF list. More often than not, an academic question or topic strikes us as absurd when we have not thought ourselves into it far enough, either because we are not sure how to or because we refuse to. This is certainly the case in regard to the YAF's vilification of "The Bible and Horror." Indeed, advocating for the "biblical" in today's culture wars has little to do with anything that is actually *in* the Jewish or Christian biblical canons. The "traditional values" that pass as "biblical" in the rhetoric of groups like the YAF do so primarily on the gamble that almost no one actually *reads* biblical texts these days, and that when someone does, it is under the watchful eye of the right kind of theological and ecclesiastical authority.

Given the YAF report's general tone of defensiveness about Christianity and the Christian Bible, its apparent biblical illiteracy on this point is nonetheless ironic. There are indeed monsters in the Bible, inspiring not a little horror. Indeed, one might say that the Bible is literally *riddled* with monsters. Riddled, because there are many stories, psalms and prophetic visions in which they appear, their names and epithets often giving them away as close Hebrew relatives to the Ugaritic monster gods of the Baal-Anat Cycle (including Yam [Ugaritic Yamm], *tannin* or "sea monster" [Ugaritic Tunnan], and Leviathan [Ugaritic Litan]).[1] But also riddled because the biblical canon as a whole does not seem to know quite what to do with them. Indeed, the relation between the biblical God and these monsters is particularly riddling and disturbing.

WATER PLAY OR WATER FIGHT

This biblical problem of what to do with monsters vis-à-vis God is made acutely apparent when we consider two very different visions from the Psalms of the sea monster Leviathan. In Psalm 104,

Leviathan is imagined as a playful part of God's wondrous creation, whereas in Psalm 74, Leviathan is imagined as a monstrous threat to the social and cosmic order and an archenemy of the God who establishes both.

Psalm 104 is a holistic ecological vision of creation, praising the creator God who establishes and maintains an intricately balanced and integrated world ecology, laying its foundations over the watery abyss "so that it will never totter," stretching the heavens like a tent, establishing mountains and valleys, and appointing the right places and times for every living creature, including humans. Within this vision of nature's inspired economy, the psalmist highlights Leviathan as a frolicsome creature of divine delight.

> How many things you have made, LORD!
> All of them, in your wisdom, you made.
> The earth is full with your creations.
> This is the sea, great and vast.
> There are its creeping things beyond counting,
> living beings, small and great.
> There the ships go.
> Leviathan—this you formed to play with.
> All of them look to you
> to give them food in their time. (Psalm 104:24–27)[2]

The beautiful interrelatedness of sea ecology, and its total dependence on its divine artisan-creator for sustenance, is powerfully reflected in the literary craft and integrity of this passage. Within it, Leviathan is presented as a centerpiece among the "many things" of God's creation. Far from posing a threat to God or God's created order, Leviathan has been created by God precisely for playful sparring. Here Leviathan is cause for rejoicing and praise.

This Psalm is closely related to the creation theology represented in the first creation story in Genesis, in which God simply speaks and the various details of the world emerge out of the primordial chaos waters without resistance. Indeed, in that story God creates "the great sea monsters [*tanninim*]" along with all other sea life on the fifth day of creation (1:21). The word translated here as "sea monster" (*tannin*) is the Hebrew equivalent for Tunnan, a name associated with the chaos monster Yamm in the Baal-Anat

Cycle. Here in Genesis, however, as with Leviathan in Psalm 104, the *tannin* is no chaos monster. It may be "monstrous" in size, but it is clearly part of God's divinely ordained world ecology, not opposed to it. Both this creation story and Psalm 104 insist that there are no such things as monsters. All is part of creation, and all is easily governed by the creative and law-giving word of God. In the beginning was *not* the chaos monster.[3]

We get a very different picture of Leviathan in Psalm 74. In this psalm, Leviathan and a cohort of related monsters are personifications of primordial chaos, menacing both the order of creation and its creator God.

Psalm 74 is a lament spoken out of political and theological crisis, namely the desecration and destruction of the Jerusalem Temple by the invading Babylonians in 587 BCE. In fact, it is this crisis that is most formative for the final form of the Hebrew Bible. Insofar as Jerusalem is understood as the very center of the cosmos, the *axis mundi,* moreover, this theological crisis is not only political but also cosmic. If the microcosmic center of creation can be desecrated, then the order and stability of the cosmos as a whole are teetering if not already collapsing into chaos. It is in this context of national and cosmological disorientation that the psalmist recalls God's creation of the world in terms of a chaos battle, and it is in this context that Leviathan, Yam, and the sea monsters (*tanninim*) are recollected not as part of creation but as God's uncreative archenemies:

> You yourself drove back Yam with your strength.
> You broke the heads of the sea monsters in the waters
> You yourself crushed the heads of Leviathan.
> You gave it as food for the seafaring people.[4]
> You yourself cut openings for springs and torrents.
> You made great rivers run dry.
> Yours is the day, and yours is the night.
> You yourself established light and the sun.
> You yourself fixed all the boundaries of the earth.
> Summer and winter you yourself made.

In this passage, Leviathan, Yam and the sea monsters are all personifications of the primordial forces of chaos that God destroyed in order to create the cosmos. In sharp contrast with Psalm 104, this psalm of lament represents these figures—especially Leviathan, whose demise is described in the most graphic detail—as chaos monsters that once threatened both creation and the creator God. In describing God's work of creation, the psalmist faithfully remembers, and insists that God faithfully remember, God's violent triumph over these anti-cosmic monstrosities. In reminding God of this former chaos battle, the psalmist aims to motivate God once again to quash the monstrous heads of chaos, which are now rearing up in the form of a new monstrous enemy. Just as you did not allow chaos monsters to destroy your creation in the beginning, the psalmist is saying, so you must not allow this newly awakened chaos monster, Babylon, to destroy your people, your city and your temple, which together represent the social, political and religious center of that creation.

DISORIENTATION AND THEOLOGICAL HORROR

Psalm 104 is a prime example of what Walter Brueggeman calls a "psalm of orientation."[5] In psalms of orientation, the voice of the psalmist is firmly grounded and oriented, utterly confident in the order and sense of the world and thriving within that order. The counter-voice to these psalms of orientation is found in the psalms of lament and complaint, or "psalms of disorientation." These psalms, which are radically incommensurable to the psalms of orientation, give voice to the experience of radical cosmic, political and psychological—always theological—breakdown and crisis. In them, the sense of orientation with regard to God's reliable command over the cosmic, political and moral order of the universe expressed in psalms like 104 no longer makes any sense. Solid ground crumbles away, and the flood waters return.

> Save me God,
> for the waters have come up to my neck.
> I am sinking into the deep mire,
> without foothold.
> I have come into watery depths,
> and the flood overtakes me. (Psalm 69:1–2)

The voice of disorientation sees the primordial flood waters returning, and along with them often come monsters who are by no means harmonious with the divine order of creation. So it is in Psalm 74.

Indeed, we might well describe the voice of disorientation in the Hebrew Scriptures as the voice of horror—psychological, political, cosmic horror—in which the order of things that is elsewhere asserted to be well established and steadfastly maintained by the God of creation and justice appears to be falling apart at the seams. "God sits enthroned over the flood," declares Psalm 29:10, but the horrified voice of disorientation can no longer afford such confidence. Might the floods be returning? Is the watery chaos monster really just a big water toy? Is God a chaos tamer or a chaos monster? Or both? These are the questions that are stammered out, in fear and trembling, by the voice of disorientation.

When it comes to God and monsters, Psalm 74 shares less with the creation theology of orientation expressed in Psalm 104 and more with the chaos battle motifs of other ancient Near Eastern texts, such as the Baal-Anat Cycle and the *Enuma Elish*, in which a deity identified with the order of creation and the well-being of humankind defeats, at least for the time being, the forces of cosmic and political horror embodied by a chaos monster or chaos god. The references in Psalm 74 to God's slaying of Yam, Leviathan and the sea monsters are strongly reminiscent of references in the Baal-Anat Cycle to the slayings of Yamm, Litan and Tunnan. The brief description of God's victorious battle with Leviathan, moreover, recalls the cosmic and political champion Marduk's defeat of Tiamat, in which Marduk crushes Tiamat's skull and arranges her waters into streams and rivers.

Without looking any further than Psalms 104 and 74, we can see that the Hebrew Bible is no more univocal when it comes to monsters than it is on any other theologically substantial topic. In the beginning was not the chaos monster (Genesis 1:21; Psalm 104; cf. Psalm 148). In the beginning was the chaos monster, and it appears to be reviving (Psalm 74). Leviathan is God's partner for water sports (Psalm 104). God crushed the heads of Leviathan, along with Yam and the sea monsters who stood as primordial threats to God and God's creation (Psalm 74). These ambiguities with regard to chaos monsters and God's relation to them are unresolvable, revealing a religious tradition whose inherent tensions between orientation and disorientation, between order and chaos, between ecological holism and ecological horror, go to the very core of its one God.

MONSTROUS ENEMIES

One way in which the Young America's Foundation is consistent with biblical tradition is in its practice of making enemies into monsters. As we have already begun to see in Psalm 74, biblical texts often make chaos monsters out of enemy nations. Behind this is an understanding that God's people, who are constituted and defined as a nation by their liberation from Egypt and by their adherence to divine law, are a social-political microcosm of the order of creation, a sociology of the cosmology. Therefore a threat against God's people may be construed as a monstrous threat against the entire cosmos and its creator God.[6]

There are numerous biblical passages in which enemy nations, past or present, are represented as chaos monsters. Some texts, for example, represent Egypt as a chaos monster whom God defeated by means of the Exodus. In Psalm 89, God's crushing and scattering of the monster Rahab ("proud" or "haughty," considered by many scholars to be another name for Leviathan) represents both the defeat of the primordial chaos monster at creation and the defeat of Egypt: "You yourself crushed Rahab like a corpse. With your powerful arm you scattered your enemies." And in Isaiah 51, a text dating late in the Babylonian exile, the prophet recalls God's deliverance of Israel from Egypt in terms of a victorious chaos battle against Rahab, the sea monster (*tannin*), and Yam, in hopes of rousing God against a new monstrous enemy.

> Awake, awake, clothe yourself in strength,
> arm of the LORD!
> Awake as in the old days,
> as in previous generations.
> Was it not you who hacked Rahab to pieces,
> who pierced the sea monster?
> Was it not you who dried up Yam,
> the waters of the great deep,
> who made the depths of Yam

a crosswalk for the redeemed?
So will the redeemed of the LORD return,
and come to Zion with shouting. (Isaiah 51:9–11a)

In this bold, almost taunting passage, the prophet's recollection of God's former might—in contrast with what is experienced as God's current slumber in weaker clothing—fuses the cosmogonic language of God's victorious battle (cutting, piercing, subduing) against personified chaos (hacking Rahab, piercing the sea monster, subduing Yam) with the language of the Exodus (parting or drying the Reed Sea so that the people could cross).[7] In both of these texts, moreover, God's victorious *cosmogonic* (cosmos-creating) battle against the primordial chaos monster and God's victorious *poligonic* (nation-creating) battle against the monstrously oppressive Egypt are inextricably related. God's cosmic order, which is established and maintained against the chaos monster, is inextricably linked to God's social order, which is established and maintained against the people's experience of oppression under the law of the monstrous Egypt.

In the prophet Ezekiel's oracles against other nations (chapters 25–32, dating immediately after the fall of Jerusalem in 587 BCE), it is not the defeated Egypt of days gone by but the present-day Egypt and its Pharaoh that the prophet represents as "the mighty sea monster." In this passage, however, Egypt's status as monster is less a sign of its horrible threat and more an indication of its certain doom, because it did not come to Judah's aid against Babylon. Here the prophet has God announce a gory death sentence for Pharaoh, king of Egypt, who is depicted as a sprawling and thrashing sea monster. God vows to put hooks in its jaws, to haul it up in dragnets and fling it into an open field, covering the mountains and filling the valleys with its rotting flesh and drenching the earth with its flowing blood (29:3–6; 32:2–6). This Pharaonic sea monster is about to be turned into just one more filet of fish, while God, like the warrior Anat in the Baal-Anat Cycle, revels in the blood and guts. In Ezekiel's gory prophetic imagination, to call a nation by the name of a chaos monster is to pronounce its death sentence.

More often, however, to make a monster out of an enemy is to endow it with otherworldly power, thereby eliciting a sense of persistent, unstoppable, un-killable horror. Isaiah 27, for example, imagines a day when "the LORD, with his cruel, great, and mighty sword, will punish Leviathan the fleeing serpent, Leviathan the twisting serpent. He will slaughter the sea monster in the sea" (27:1). In this passage the prophet associates an enemy nation, presumably Babylon, with a broad repertoire of names and epithets for the chaos monster, all of which appear as anti-cosmic adversaries (or different names for the same anti-cosmic adversary) in the Baal-Anat Cycle and in Psalm 74.[8] What distinguishes this text from the others, however, is that here the battle is *anticipated* rather than remembered. Crucial to the psalmist's point in Psalm 74 is the claim that Yam, Leviathan and the sea monsters have already been slain by the creator God; indeed, the psalmist's present hope is based on this claim. Here, however, Leviathan remains alive and kicking.

Similarly, Jeremiah 51 describes the Babylonian King Nebuchadrezzar as a chaos monster devouring the inhabitants of Jerusalem: "He devoured me, he crushed me . . . he made me like an empty dish. He swallowed me as would a sea monster. He filled his belly with my precious ones," perhaps a reference to slain children. In response to this lament, God promises to make the Babylonian monster king "disgorge what he has swallowed." Whether the monster's victims will come back up in one piece, and whether the world will ever be the same again, is far less certain.

Although the enemy has yet to be overcome in these texts, there is at least some consolation in the insistence that God is siding with Judah rather than sporting or raging against them with the monster. Elsewhere, however, there is no such consolation. In Isaiah 8, for example, Assyria is imagined as God's monstrous means of pronouncing judgment on Judah: "Behold, my Lord will bring up against them the mighty and massive waters of the River, the king of Assyria and all his glory. It will rise over all its banks, and it will sweep into Judah like a flash flood, reaching up to the neck." Here the king of Assyria, who by this time has already obliterated the northern kingdom of Israel, is personified as the flood waters of the great river Euphrates, which is associated with primordial chaos waters. Isaiah's audacious and horrifying claim is that God is raising up these mighty and massive flood waters against Judah. God is taking sides with the monstrous enemy against Judah.[9]

CONJURING

Behind all these biblical representations of enemy nations as chaos monsters is the assumption that cosmic and social-political order and chaos are intimately related to one another. The world's ecology and the nation's sociology are entirely interdependent, so that the invasion of chaos within the nation is also the invasion of chaos within the cosmos. This understanding of the interrelation of cosmic and political order is not unique to biblical tradition within the ancient Near East, nor is the strategy of representing one's enemies as chaos monsters. Marduk's defeat of Tiamat in the *Enuma Elish*, for example, led to the creation of the world as well as of Babylon as its cosmic center. The ever-looming possibility that Tiamat might reawaken and play havoc is a source of cosmic as well as political horror.

Making enemies into monsters is a kind of conjuring, and conjuring is always anxious and risky, because it is always more than one bargains for. To make another nation into a monster does more than simply mark it as a clear enemy. Insofar as chaos monsters are the otherworldly within the worldly, such conjuring also endows the enemy with a kind of supernatural, primordial, mysterious otherness, an agency that resists being reduced to an easy target, and that never stays down for long. To name an enemy after a chaos monster, especially when the same name is used for a chaos god in a closely related tradition (e.g., Yam/Yamm and Leviathan/Litan), is to risk imbuing it with a kind of sacred chaos—a sacred chaos with which God may even be allied, much to Israel's and Judah's horror.

FIGURE 2. Job's night of terrors (Job 7:14), an engraving by William Blake, *Illustrations of the Book of Job* (London: William Blake and J. Linnell, 1826; New York: G. Putnam's Sons, 1902), plate 11, Kelvin Smith Library, Special Collections, Case Western Reserve University.

CHAPTER 3

The Sleep of Wisdom

JOB AND THE ABYSS OF SUFFERING

"All suffering is an abyss," wrote the twenty-three-year-old Romanian philosopher E. M. Cioran in a 1934 essay which he later described as slander against the universe, born out of a desperate insomnia.[1] Suffering is chaos that infiltrates my body, disorienting my sense of self, and shattering my world. "Suffering separates and dissociates; like a centrifugal force it pulls you away from the center of life, the hub of the universe where all things tend toward unity."[2] It alienates me from my established moorings, blurring what was once clear discernment of the order of things. As the microcosm of the body crumbles in pain, so does the cosmos itself. The world that once made sense, that was once meaningfully whole, founded and guaranteed by a God who sits enthroned over chaos, suddenly crumbles under overwhelming torrents. Suffering is radically uncreative. It undoes the world.[3]

Pain is an abyss. To be *in pain* is to be in the abyss. And indeed, when I am in it, even when I am with another who is in it, it is as though the abyss of suffering is overtaking the entire world. "The venom drawn out from suffering would be enough to poison the whole world in a bloody eruption, bursting out of the volcano of our being."[4] This suggests an intimate relation between one's individual body and one's experience and understanding of the world as a whole. The breakdown of one's subjectivity through suffering is a breakdown of one's entire world. If suffering is an abyss, then the body in pain is an embodiment of chaos, a chaos monster, whose chaos spreads like poison from the individual body to the entire universe.

> You never suspected what lay hidden in yourself and in the world, you were living contentedly at the periphery of things, when suddenly those feelings of suffering which are second only to death itself take hold of you and transport you into a region of infinite complexity, where your subjectivity tosses about in a maelstrom.[5]

This is the story of Job. In the biblical book of Job, the voice of pain is an eruption of chaos within the order of creation so carefully mapped out elsewhere in biblical literature, especially in texts identified with wisdom and Torah piety. Wisdom thinking in biblical literature emphasizes discernment of the meaning, integrity and structure—in short, the *wisdom*—of God's creation through close observation of daily life. The wisdom of the creator inheres within the intricate and ingenious order of creation itself, and can be discovered through study of it. Such wisdom teachings, found especially in Proverbs and in a number of the Psalms, find their orientation in earlier biblical traditions of creation and Torah piety, which understand the divinely ordained order of creation to be stable, reliable and reasonable, and which understand the divinely ordained order of society to be closely related to it.[6] Keep God's Torah and you, your society and your world will be blessed and thrive; disobey and you, your society and your world will break down and return to chaos. The sleep of wisdom produces chaos monsters. Or rather, the sleep of wisdom leaves no one to guard against their *return*.

In the book of Job, it is precisely wisdom's guard that breaks down. The story of Job is the story of the *exhaustion of wisdom*. In this story, wisdom's best and most vigilant watchmen, Job's so-called "friends" are worn out by Job's disorienting voice of pain.

His undeserved and unjustifiable suffering presents a crisis of cosmic proportions, outlasting and exhausting wisdom in a night of theological unknowing, and putting Job in the company of chaos monsters.

Nowhere else in the Hebrew Bible, indeed nowhere else in the known literature of the ancient Near East, is the particularity of the face of pain, and the theological horror written across it, so carefully attended to than in the book of Job. Nowhere else is the voice of utter disorientation, and the theological horror shrieking through it, so carefully sustained than in the book of Job. The book of Job is a giant breach in the biblical corpus, sending cracks through the rest of Scripture, interrogating the systems and strategies of Torah and wisdom for making theological sense out of pain.[7] "Face me and be devastated," Job declares to wisdom's guardians, who insist that there must be some reason in God's good universe for Job's pain and loss. "Put your hand over your mouth!" (Job 21:5).

ABSENCE OF ALL REFUGE

The philosopher and Talmudic scholar Emmanuel Levinas writes that "in suffering, there is an absence of all refuge. . . . The whole acuity of suffering lies in the impossibility of retreat. . . . In this sense suffering is the impossibility of nothingness."[8] This experience of the impossibility of retreat is powerfully and acutely expressed by Job. There is no rest and no refuge for Job, especially from the oppressive, panoptic gaze of God. Job says,

> Why did I not die at birth? . . .
> Now I would be lying down in peace.
> I would be sleeping. I would be at rest. . . .
> Why is light given to the miserable,
> and life to the bitter-souled,
> who long for death when it is not there,
> and dig for it more than for hidden treasure,
> who are extremely joyful
> and glad when they find the grave?
> Why is light given to one who cannot see the way,
> whom God has hedged in? . . .

> Truly that which I fear is overcoming me,
> and what I dread is befalling me.
> I am not at ease, nor am I quiet.
> I have no rest, but trouble comes. (Job 3:11, 13,
> 20–23, 25–26)

Job's restless terror under the divine gaze, which he experiences as a sort of divine panopticon, is far from the guiding, comforting gaze of God in Psalm 139. There the psalmist declares,

> You shut me in behind and before,
> and put your hand on me.
> Such knowledge is beyond me.
> It is so high I cannot attain it.
> Where can I escape from your spirit?
> Where can I flee from your presence?
> If I go up to heaven, there you are.
> If I go down to Sheol, you are there too.
> If I take wing with the morning,
> and settle at the far limits of the sea,
> even there your hand will lead me;
> your right hand will hold me tight.
> If I say, "Surely darkness will hide me,
> and the light around me will become night,"
> even the darkness is not dark to you.
> Night is as the daylight.
> Darkness and light are the same. (Psalm 139:5–12)

In a rabbinic discussion in the Talmud about the creation of humankind, the psalmist's joyful declaration that "you shut me in behind and before" is cited in support of the idea that the original human (in Genesis 2:7) was formed with two faces. That is, it had one face in front and one in back.[9] God, the rabbi suggests, faces the human both coming and going. In a lecture on this passage from the Talmud, Levinas offers this meditation:

> It is impossible to escape from God, not to be present before his sleepless gaze. A gaze which is not experienced

> as a calamity . . . In the biblical passage, certainly God's presence means: to be besieged by God or obsessed by God. An obsession which is experienced as a chosenness . . . Everything is open . . . With only a single face, I have a place in the rear of the head, the occiput, in which my hidden thoughts and my mental reservations accumulate. Refuge which can hold my entire thought. But here, instead of the occiput, a second face! Everything is exposed . . . *You are always exposed! But in this spirited psalm you are discovered with joy; it is the exaltation of divine proximity that this psalm sings: a being exposed without the least hint of shadow.*[10]

The voice in Psalm 139 is the voice of wonder and praise from one living in an all-embracing divine panopticon, entirely exposed and entirely known. For the psalmist, the sleepless gaze of God arouses an insomnia without the least trace of restlessness or fear. For Job, by contrast, divine omnipresence means creaturely terror. Job experiences it as ceaseless pursuit, exposure and torment, leaving him longing for sleep, even a final sleep. For Job, unlike the psalmist, death is refuge from divine besiegement and divine obsession. In Job's vexed realm, you are discovered with terror; it is the dread of divine proximity that Job screams: a being exposed without the least hint of shadow.

The difference between the psalmist and Job, of course, is that Job has been singled out as the subject of a wager between God and "the accuser," or *haśśaṭan* (with a definite article, not the proper name Satan), who is something like the prosecuting attorney on God's divine council.[11] Job is singled out, moreover, precisely because of his righteousness. God says to the accuser, "Have you noticed my servant Job? There is no one else like him on the earth, blameless and upright, fearing God and turning away from evil" (1:8). The accuser replies, "Have you not put a fence around him and his house and all that he has on every side?" How hard is it to be righteous when all you know is blessing? Of course, the accuser makes a good point, and leaves God with the burden of proving that Job's righteousness is not the result of blessing rather than vice-versa. So it is Job's perfectly law-abiding *righteousness* that singles him out for testing. Contrary to the way God's justice is supposed to work, then, the most righteous one is chosen not for blessing but for curse.

In the first round of devastation, his property is lost and his children are killed. When he still holds fast to his piety, the accuser declares, "Skin for skin! A man will give up all he has for his own life. But touch his bones and flesh, . . . " (2:4–5). Job is then "inflicted . . . with terrible boils from the sole of his foot to the top of his head" (2:7). Ironically, in Deuteronomy 28:35, this affliction is precisely what Moses declares God will use to punish the Israelites when they do not obey God's justice: "If you do not obey the LORD your God . . . *the LORD will inflict you* at the knees and thighs *with terrible boils* from which you will never recover, *from the sole of your foot to the top of your head.*" This passage uses the same Hebrew verb for "inflict" (*nakah*) that Job 2:7 does, and the language describing the terrible boils from the sole of the foot to the top of the head is identical (except, of course, that Job 2:7 refers to "his" foot and head and Deuteronomy 28:35 refers to "your" foot and head). Likely the description of Job's cursed affliction is drawn from the description in Deuteronomy. But whereas in Deuteronomy the curse is supposed to be the result of unrighteousness and disobedience, in the book of Job it is the result of Job's exemplary righteousness. It is as though his goodness in God's eyes has painted a giant bullseye on his forehead. In Job's story, the moral universe affirmed elsewhere in biblical tradition, according to which righteousness equals blessed well-being and disobedience equals cursed suffering, is turned inside out and upside down.

"Skin for skin!" As Job's skin, his hide, cracks and peels away, so does his theological hide. There is no more hiding, an absence of all refuge. The old answers no longer hold water, or rather no longer hold back the chaos waters. As his trusty old theological hide cracks and peels away, he finds himself dreadfully exposed.

DESIRING CHAOS

At several points in the dialogues (chapters 3–37), Job cries for help. He cries out to be saved from the floods that are overtaking his world, born out of his own suffering. He longs in vain for an answer, a word of God or from God that would justify his suffering, that would reinstate order against chaos. He longs in vain for a word that would make theological sense of his pain, and that would thereby reorient him within God's moral universe. Like the voice of disorientation in the psalms of lament, he cries out to be saved from the abyss and its monsters.

At other points, however, Job's voice is far more radical and deeply disturbing, *identifying with the monstrous forces of uncreation against the creator God.* In such deeply disturbed and disturbing moments, Job desires an unmaking of the world, a *chaogony,* a return of chaos against cosmos. The most striking example is found in Job's opening curse of "his day," which he blurts out after seven days of silence, scraping his sores with potsherds.

> Job opened his mouth and cursed his day. And Job said:
> "Annihilate the day on which I was born,
> the evening a male-child was announced.
> That day . . . let there be darkness." (3:3–4a)

Although Job's curse is explicitly aimed only at "his day" (which refers to both the day of his birth and the night of his conception), the language deployed in it is clearly aimed at undoing all of God's creation. Job's embittered declaration "let there be darkness" (*yehi ḥoshek*) is a literal inversion of God's own initial world-creative words in Genesis 1:3, "let there be light" (*yehi 'or*), with which God spoke the first day into being and began creating order out of chaos. God's first act of creation called forth light (*'or*) from darkness (*ḥoshek*). Job draws it back into darkness, undoing the first creative distinction God had made out of the formless void. As Job calls for the undoing of "his day" with the pronouncement "let there be darkness," then, he is also calling for the undoing of God's first day, that is, the birthday of creation. He continues, elaborating extensively on this desire for such an unworldly, formless void of terror and gloom.

> Let God above not seek it [that day].
> Let daylight not shine on it.

Let darkness and deathshadow reclaim it.
Let a cloud settle on it.
Let the darkening terrify it.
That night, let gloom take it away.
Let it not be counted among the days of the year,
Let it not enter into the counting of months.
Behold that night, let there be no life.
May no exulting be heard in it. (3:4b-7)

Job's language is dense with the vocabulary of abysmal darkness. It is important to note, moreover, that many of these words also include connotations of destruction, the collapse of order and the invasion of chaos. The word translated as "gloom" (*'ofel*), for example, is frequently associated with calamity and cosmic breakdown; the word translated "deathshadow" (*ṣalmawet*), furthermore, is literally a compound of nouns for "darkness" and "death"; and the verb *ga'al* ("reclaim"), in some late Hebrew texts, carries the meaning of "defile" or "pollute." Anthropologist Mary Douglas has shown how systems of purity in the priestly codes of the Torah are rooted in a particular understanding of the order of creation. Therefore, that which defiles purity endangers not only the person or the community but the entire cosmos.[12] Finally, the phrase "let there be no life" or "let it be lifeless" (*yehi galmud*) echoes the earlier declaration "let there be darkness" (*yehi ḥoshek*), once again subverting God's own language of creation in Genesis 1. In all this Job is calling forth chaos against cosmos in a way that is directly subversive of God's work as creator. God's language in Genesis is cosmogonic. Job's here is *chaogonic*.

At this point in his summoning of chaos against cosmos, Job seeks the company of the chaos monsters Yam and Leviathan. Although Job himself does not presume to be able to rouse these monsters, he calls on those who can. "Let those who cast spells on Yam damn it [that day]," he declares, "those who are skilled at rousing Leviathan" (Job 3:8).[13] In the context of Job's curse, Yam and Leviathan represent primordial threats against the order of creation and against the creator God, much as they did in Psalm 74:13–14, where the psalmist declares to God that "you yourself drove back Yam with your strength. You broke the heads of the sea monsters in the waters. You yourself crushed the heads of Leviathan." In Psalm 74, however, and in every other biblical text in which chaos monsters are enemies of God, they are also enemies of God's people. Not so with Job, who in this passage is sicking them on his day and, indirectly, on God's entire order of creation. Whereas other texts dread these chaos monsters, and either remember or hope for their destruction by God, Job *desires* them, even *identifies with* them, conjuring them as a destructive force against creation.

Later, in chapter 7, Job reinforces his identification with chaos monsters, though with some trepidation, when he wonders aloud whether God is inflicting so much suffering on him because God thinks that *he* is a chaos monster that needs to be subdued. He cries out to God, "Am I Yam or a sea monster [*tannin*], that you set guard over me?" (7:12; cf. 26:12–13). Here again Job considers himself to be *aligned with the chaos monsters against God*. There is, of course, at least one major difference between Job's identification with chaos monsters here and his identification with them in chapter 3. At this point, Job is not choosing to take sides with the monsters, as he was before; rather, he is suggesting that God has mistaken him for a monstrous opponent, and that is why God is crushing him. Nonetheless, in both cases, whether by choice or by mistaken identity, Job perceives himself to be aligned with chaos monsters against God.

Still later, while complaining about his hopeless situation in which the defendant in his case (God) is also the judge, jury and police, Job says, "God does not hold back his anger. Under him Rahab's helpers are bought down. How then can I answer him, or choose my arguments against him?" (9:13–14). Here again, the suggestion is that Job's opposition to God is like that of a chaos monster. His challenge to God, doomed though it is, represents a potential invasion of monstrous chaos in God's world.

LYRICISM OF TERROR

Suffering is an abyss. And to suffer, to be in pain, is to be in the abyss. Sometimes the sufferer cries out for help, for an answer that will justify or make sense of the pain. In such moments, the sufferer cries out for a word of *reorientation* within God's universe, a word that can exorcize the monsters and restore the right order of things. Sometimes this is Job's cry. At other times, however, the chaos of suffering leads Job to identify with primordial, uncreative chaos.

Cioran's suffering transported him, he felt, to a "region of infinite complexity, where your subjectivity tosses about in a maelstrom," and this in turn opened up a new poetics for him, what he called "the lyricism of suffering . . . a song of the blood, the flesh, and the nerves . . . blooming in vital dislocations."[14] As the abyss of suffering erupted within Cioran's body, his slandering of the universe, like Job's opening curses, became a lyricism of chaos:

> Let us return to original chaos! Let us imagine the primordial din, the original vortex! Let us throw ourselves into the whirlwind which has preceded the creation of form. Let our being tremble with effort and madness in the fiery abyss! Let everything be wiped out so that, surrounded by confusion and disequilibrium, we participate fully in the general delirium, retracing our way back from cosmos to chaos, from form to swirling gyres . . . How great my terror and my joy at the thought of being dragged into the vortex of initial chaos. . . . [15]

Cioran's lyricism is ultimately hopeful, for he envisions the return to chaos as a necessary prelude to a new, yet-unrealized creation: "In every whirlwind hides a potential form, just as in chaos there is a potential cosmos. Let me possess an infinite number of unrealized, potential forms! Let everything vibrate in me with the universal anxiety of the beginning, just awakening from nothingness!"[16] His is an apocalyptic imagination. He longs to see this world, now alien to him as the result of his suffering, return to primordial chaos in order that a new world may be born. For Cioran, reversing creation is not an end in itself but an end that creates the potential for a new beginning.

In its shrillest moments, Job's lyricism of suffering is more radical than Cioran's, though by the same token less sustainable. In his uncreative outbursts, I dare say that there is no detectable undercurrent of hope that the return to chaos will be a prelude to a new creation. In his subversively uncreative pronouncement "let there be darkness," in his expressions of a longing for deathshadow and calamity to overtake his day, in his summoning of chaos monsters to aid in the accursed work, there is a lyricism of terror without retreat, without hope and without rest. And wisdom, whether waking or sleeping, is knocked off guard.

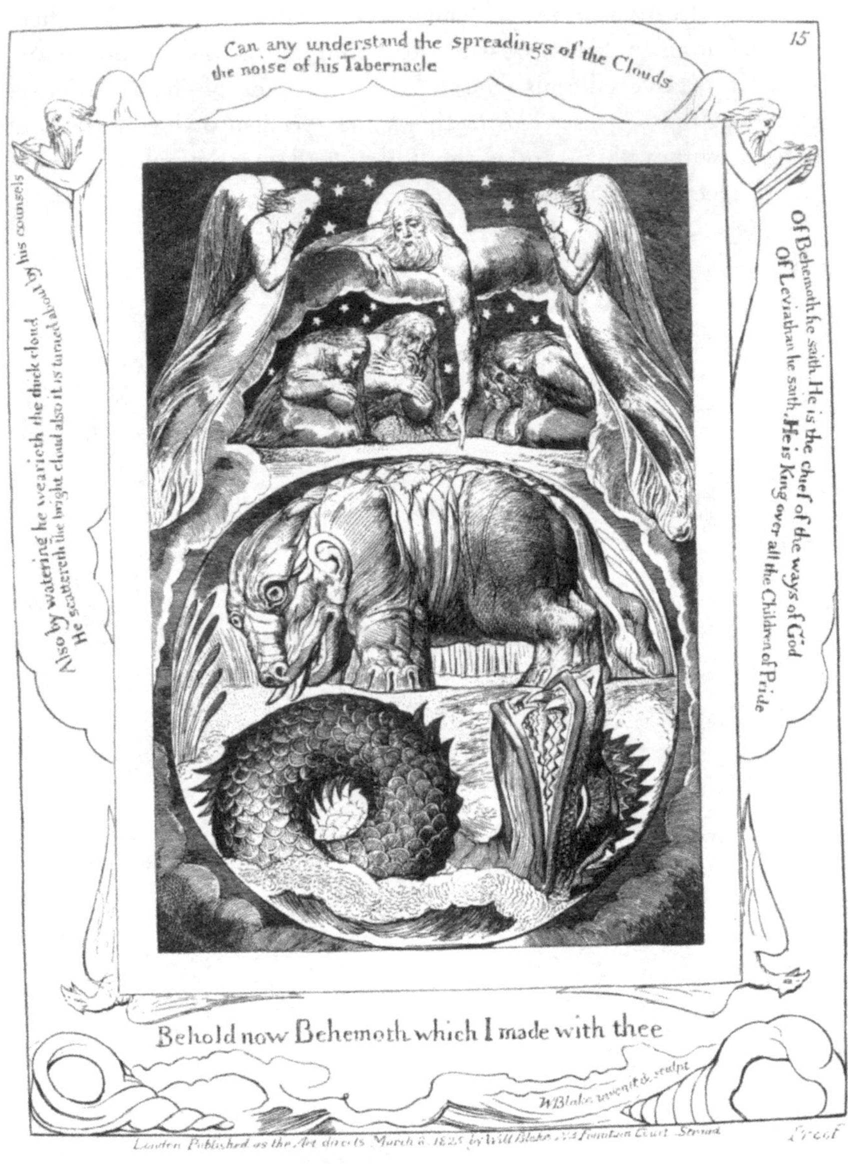

FIGURE 3. Behemoth and Leviathan (Job 40-41), an engraving by William Blake, *Illustrations of the Book of Job* (London: William Blake and J. Linnell, 1826; New York: G. Putnam's Sons, 1902), plate 15, Kelvin Smith Library, Special Collections, Case Western Reserve University.

CHAPTER 4

From the Whirlwind

ROUSING GOD ROUSING LEVIATHAN

The book of Job is like a great fissure running across the biblical landscape. When we follow it we find that it travels from the world-unmaking pain of Job to an aweful vision of God, whose terrible glory is most sublimely revealed through the monstrous Leviathan.

At his lowest points, Job's abysmal suffering leads him to desire chaos against God's cosmos, even identifying with the chaos monsters Yam and Leviathan, whom he assumes to be God's anti-cosmic archenemies. In pain, without rest or retreat, under a divine gaze that he experiences as a torturer's surveillance, Job is drawn to the monstrous as a violent invasion of unaccountable excess within God's established order of creation. These monsters are forces of uncreation and, as such, potential threats to the creator. Still, Job has little hope of seriously challenging the creator God with or without their help. Although he identifies with chaos monsters, even representing his voice of pain as a monstrous embodiment of chaos within God's world, he fully expects that God will smash him down just as God has smashed down other chaos monsters who threatened divine rule (7:12; 9:13–17; 26:12–13). Job identifies himself among the monsters but sees God as the ultimate monster killer.

When God is finally roused to respond to Job from the whirlwind (chapters 38–41), however, Job's expectations are blown away. Job's conception of himself as a monstrous threat against the divinely ordained order of things is overwhelmed by a simultaneously wonderful and terrifying revelation of a God who does not slay or banish the chaos monster but glories in it and identifies with it as an embodiment of cosmic horror. Job's identification with the monstrous against God leads ultimately to God's identification with the monstrous against Job. God out-monsters Job, pushing the theological horror one monster step beyond Job's wildest expectations.

DIAPERED MONSTER

The first part of the divine speech from the whirlwind (38:1–40:2) emphasizes God's supremacy as powerful creator and intimate caretaker of all the overwhelmingly vast and wonderful details of the world's ecology, from the deepest foundations of the earth to the heavenly vaults of hail and snow, from the birth cycles of the mountain goat to the hunting patterns of the eagle. God opens by barraging Job with a series of rhetorical questions centering on the theme of creation out of chaos: "Where were you when I laid the foundations of the earth? . . . Who set its dimensions? On what were its bases sunk? Who set its cornerstone?" To which the obvious answers from an overwhelmed Job would be "No, I was not there and you were" and "I have no idea and you know it all." As the barrage of questions continues, the creator God's relation to primordial chaos, personified as Yam, comes to the fore:

> Who shut Yam behind doors
> when it burst forth from the womb,
> when I made clouds its clothing,
> and dense clouds its swaddling?
> I made breakers as my boundary for it,
> and set a bar and doors.
> I said, "This far you may come, but no farther.
> Here your proud waves will stop." (Job 38:5–11)[1]

Recall that, in his opening curse, Job called upon those who cast spells on Yam to help him slander God's universe. A little later, in chapter 7, he wondered aloud whether God was perhaps taking him to be a chaos monster: "Am I Yam or a sea monster that you set guard over me?" (7:12). God's opening questions effectively put Job back in his place, which is not among chaos monsters. The message to Job is that he was not there and that he is not Yam. Not close.

Although God claims to have rebuked and restrained Yam, moreover, there is no sense in this passage that their conflict was violent or that Yam was killed. Rather, the image here is of God scolding Yam the way a parent would scold a raucous and unruly toddler, after which it is swaddled in a fresh cosmic diaper. The adversarial Yam may think it is a monstrous threat, but it is really something closer to Max in his wolf suit in *Where the Wild Things Are*, that is, God's child who is acting monstrous and needs scolding but also swaddling.

Indeed, the image of Yam diapered in clouds suggests that this primordial, chaotic force has been integrated into the present world ecology, like chaos clothed in cosmos. And the image of the creator God doing the diapering may even suggest that God and Yam are something like family (remember that Yamm is El's child, "beloved of El," in the Ugaritic Baal-Anat cycle). In our present, turn-of-the-century culture of psychotherapy, oriented toward reflection on family dynamics, some might go so far as to ask whether Yam is in some sense an expression of another, more chaotic aspect within the godhead (i.e., divine family), or whether Yam is a revelation of God's inner child. We need not go that far, however, to see that in this passage the chaos monster Yam is not completely eradicated from the world, nor is it completely dissociated from the creator God. It is a personification of primordial chaos *within* cosmos, intimately related to the divine.

BEHOLD BEHEMOTH

Following Job's predictably subordinate midway response (40:3–5), the divine speech comes to its grand finale, which reveals the aweful glory of God through the aweful glory of two monsters of divine favor, Behemoth (40:15–24) and Leviathan (40:25–26; or, in some versions of the Old Testament, 41:1–34).[2] As centerpieces of the speech, these two monsters, especially Leviathan, constitute God's ultimate self-revelation to Job.[3]

The first, Behemoth (literally the plural form of the Hebrew *behemah*, "cattle"), is clearly part of God's creation: "Behold now Behemoth, whom I made as I did you" (40:15). Behemoth is a creature. Indeed, it is preeminent within creation, "the first of God's ways." This could mean that Behemoth is the greatest of God's creatures or that it is the first thing that God created, or both. Although clearly located within creation, however, the description of it inspires more dread than wonder at God's ways in the world. The emphasis is placed on its incredible strength and potency, and the final image is of it stopping the river's flood waters, "confident that the Jordan will burst forth into its mouth" (40:23). The verb translated here as "burst forth" (*nagaḥ*) was used earlier to describe God's restraining of Yam "when it burst forth from the womb" (38:8). The subtle suggestion is that Behemoth's haughty strength might even rival the bursting, chaotic Yam. Although a creature and not a primordial chaos monster, then, Behemoth is not exactly an image of the order and harmony of the world ecology. It is not outside creation, but like Yam it represents a kind of dangerous otherness within creation.

DRAWING OUT LEVIATHAN

Behemoth is the last precarious stepping stone in God's increasingly frightful world before Job is transported into the chaotic waters of Leviathan, who is the ultimate focus of God's speech. In fact, when God stops talking about Leviathan, God stops talking. It is as though the divine voice from the whirlwind is literally carried away in Leviathan's chaotic glory.

Leviathan, like Behemoth, is described as having been "made." But whereas God claims to have made Behemoth "as I did you," that is, a creature among other creatures (albeit fantastic), God describes Leviathan as a creation like no other, a creation that is, in a sense, outside creation. Indeed, at one point God declares that even other gods fear Leviathan: "At its rising, gods are afraid. At its breaking they are beside themselves" (41:17 [or 41:25]). This Leviathan is a chaos monster who threatens other gods.

We have seen how different biblical texts represent Leviathan in a variety of mutually exclusive ways. On one extreme, Psalm 104 describes Leviathan as part of the order of creation, a sea beast whom God "formed to play with" (cf. Psalm 148). On the other extreme, Psalm 74 and Isaiah 27 envision Leviathan as radically outside the order of creation, a dreadful chaos monster who opposes the creator God and must be destroyed. This latter conception of Leviathan is shared by Job in his opening curse, in which he desires that Leviathan be stirred up against creation. Here, in the divine speech from the whirlwind, we find a disturbing combination of these two extremes. On the one hand, as in Psalm 74 and Isaiah 27, Leviathan is an embodiment of primordial chaos within creation. On the other hand, as in Psalm 104, God identifies with it.

God's incantation of this monstrous plaything begins with a series of direct challenges, in the form of rhetorical questions, addressed to Job (40:25–32 [or 41:1–8]). "Can you draw out Leviathan with a fishhook? Can you press down its tongue with a rope?" (40:25 [or 41:1]). "Can you fill its skin with harpoons and its head with fishing-spears? Place your hand on it. Think of the battle. You will not do it again" (40:31–32 [or 41:7–8]). The rhetorical effect of these questions and this last challenge is to convert Job's desire to rouse Leviathan into repulsion, causing him to draw back from the vertiginous edge of the abyss.

Yet God is not similarly repelled. As the speech continues, the challenge of taking on Leviathan merges with the challenge of taking on God. Notice how the first-person divine subject ("I," "me") merges with its third-person monstrous object ("it"):

> See! Any expectation of *it* will be disappointed.
> One is overwhelmed even at the sight of *it*.
> There is no one fierce enough to rouse *it*.
> Who can take a stand before *me*?
> Who will confront *me*? *I* will repay him!
> Under all the heavens, *it* is *mine*. (41:1–3a [or 41:9–11a])[4]

As the subject of the poem shifts suddenly from "it" (Leviathan) to "me" (God), the identity of the monstrous blurs with that of God, and vice versa. God identifies with the monster over against all challengers. The last line here, "under all the heavens, it is mine," may be understood two different ways. It may be read as God's claim on all of creation, that is, "everything in the world is mine." But the more literal reading, which is also more consistent with the exclusive focus on Leviathan throughout this passage, takes it as God's claim on Leviathan, that is, "it is mine" or "for me" (*lî hû'*). Taken this way, God is here laying claim to Leviathan against all other claims, and thereby is remonstrating against Job for his earlier desire to conjure Leviathan.

By this point God appears to be caught up in the incantation, unable to stop singing Leviathan's praises, declaring "I will not keep silence concerning its parts . . . " (41:4 [or 41:12]). Following another series of rhetorical questions—"Who can strip off its outer garment? Who can penetrate its double coat of armor? Who can open the doors of its face?"—God begins an extravagant description of the monster that continues through the remainder of the whirlwind speech (41:5–26 [or 41:13–34]). This description overwhelms the imagination, piling feature upon feature to create an impossible image, thereby conceiving an inconceivable monstrosity: its coat of mail . . . the doors of its face . . . terror surrounds its teeth . . . its back is made from fusing together rows of shields . . . it sneezes light . . . its eyes glow like the dawn . . . flames and sparks spew forth from its mouth . . . smoke billows from its nostrils . . . terror dances before it . . . it is clad in immovable, hard-cast folds of flesh . . . its heart is hard as a stone . . . its belly is covered with sharp potsherds. This description of Leviathan is an impossibly over-determined amalgam of features (fire, water, smoke, armor, weaponry, animalia, etc.) stitched together into one monstrous body. As such the monstrosity of Leviathan is an example of what Noël Carroll calls "category-jamming," or "classificatory obfuscation."[5] Its descriptive language combines different elements that are categorically exclusive of one another, and thereby jams the imagination's ability to form a complete picture of the monster. As God declares toward the end of the speech, "on earth there is not its likeness" (41:25 [or 41:33]). The word translated here as "likeness" (*mashal*) can also mean "parallel," "parable" or "representation."[6] That is, there is no language for it, no way to represent it. Failing to find adequate words to describe the monster, this text uses language to go beyond language, to conjure something beyond imagining.

As Leviathan trails off, leaving a churning mass of exhausted analogies in its hoary wake, so does the divine voice from the whirlwind, leaving in its wake a world boiling over with chaos.

WHOLLY OTHER

In *The Idea of the Holy*, Rudolph Otto finds in this divine whirlwind speech a prime example of religious experience as aweful encounter with monstrous otherness. Against the typical modern western identification of "the holy" (*das Heilige*) with moral goodness or purity, Otto characterizes religious experience as a non-rational encounter with a wholly other *mysterium tremendum* that is beyond reason and imagination and that elicits, simultaneously and irreducibly, an oscillation between terror and fascination, fear and desire. In many cases, his descriptions of this kind of religious experience could just as easily describe the experience of horror in the face of the monstrous. In "the truly 'mysterious' object," he writes, "we come upon something inherently 'wholly other', whose kind and character are incommensurable with our own, and before which we therefore recoil in a wonder that strikes us chill and numb."[7] It "may appear to the mind an object of horror and dread, but at the same time it is no less something that allures with a potent charm, and the creature, who trembles before it, utterly cowed and cast down, has always at the same time the impulse to turn to it, nay even to make it somehow his own."[8] Indeed, at one point Otto refers to "the monstrous" (*das Ungeheuere*) as "a fairly exact expression for the numinous in its aspects of mystery, awefulness, majesty, augustness and 'energy'; nay, even the fascination is dimly felt in it."[9]

In the divine speech from the whirlwind as a whole, Otto finds a "sheer absolute wondrousness that transcends thought . . . the mysterium."[10] Indeed, far from a rational answer to Job's questions about divine justice, and far from an explanation of the ingenious ecology of God's creation, Otto reads the entire speech as what he calls a "dysteleology," that is, an anti-explanation or anti-justification, a "negation of purposiveness."[11] Within that speech, moreover, he sees Behemoth and Leviathan as the ultimate figures of the *mysterium*. All that come before them are "portents only," whereas here the poem "gives us 'monsters'—but 'the monstrous' is just the 'mysterious' in a gross form. Assuredly these beasts would be the most unfortunate examples that one could hit upon if searching for evidences of the purposiveness of the divine 'wisdom.'"[12] Behemoth and Leviathan are the "grossest expression" of a wholly other divine mystery.

DIVINE ABYSS

In the creation theology of Psalm 104, God and Leviathan were found frolicking together in the sea. There Leviathan is not a chaos monster but rather part of the divinely ordered and beautifully interrelated ecology of creation. In the chaos battles depicted in Psalm 74, on the other hand, God and Leviathan appear in deadly conflict. There Leviathan is a chaos monster who radically threatens the order and well-being of creation as well as its creator God. What has not been encountered until now, however, is God reveling in and identifying with Leviathan *as* chaos monster.

Stephen King writes that horror "arises from a pervasive sense of disestablishment, that things are in the unmaking."[13] This has certainly been the case since Job first opened his mouth to curse his day. The unmaking of Job through abject suffering leads him to an unhallowed vision of the unmaking of the entire order of creation. Indeed, as Roger C. Schlobin points out, the peak of horror in Job goes beyond this sense of disestablishment and unmaking into a radical inversion of meaning: "the 'unmaking' is followed by an unnatural and unholy *making* that no one, reader or character, can understand or coerce."[14] And the peak of this unmaking and inversion of meaning in the book of Job is the divine self-revelation from the whirlwind. We might call it a holy unholy making, a divine self-revelation made in the demolished ruins of the twin foundations of wisdom and Torah. Job's voice declared the unmaking of the world as he and his friends knew it. God's voice declares the horrific theology that comes in its wake.

Nietzsche warned that "when you look long into the abyss, the abyss also looks into you."[15] That would be terror enough—to lose oneself in the deep dark eyes of the abyss. But in Job the terror is also theological: when you look long into the abyss, you may find *God* looking back at you.

The divine speech from the whirlwind forcefully subjugates Job's chaotic, even monstrous voice of pain. But this subjugation is not accomplished by reimposing or superimposing divine order and authority; rather it is accomplished by overwhelming him with divine chaos. Job expected that his own chaotic outbursts and desires to rouse Yam and Leviathan would get him smashed just as God had smashed other threatening chaos monsters. But God does not squash Job like a monster. Rather, God *out-monsters* him, pushing the theological crisis brought on by Job's unjustifiable suffering to new, horrifying extremes, opening up a vision of the world and its creator God on the edge. In the divine speech from the whirlwind, Leviathan is a spectacle not of the grandeur of God's well-ordered world ecology, but of the awesome and awful chaos that churns just beneath the surface. Likewise, it is a spectacle not of a God who sits enthroned over chaos, not of a God who subdues chaos, but of a God who rouses it, who stirs it up, who revels in it. The epiphany of Leviathan in the climactic verses of the speech from the whirlwind elicits a sense of mystery in God's creation, surely, but it is a mystery that is radically disorienting and ungrounding, an *unheimlich* encounter with chaos that touches on the divine.

Wisdom, waking or sleeping, cannot guard against the welling up of the abyss of suffering and the return of monsters. The wisdom of Job's friends can neither deny nor mend the crack in their theological foundations that is opened up by voice of undeserved, unjustifiable suffering, as God readily acknowledges when addressing the lead friend Eliphaz at the end of the story: "I am enraged at you and your friends, for you have not spoken rightly about [or "to"] me as my servant Job has" (Job 42:7). On the one hand, there is some consolation here, in that God licenses rage against God in the face of undeserved pain. God licenses theodicy as a questioning and challenging of God's justice against the friends' defensive justifications of God. On the other hand, there is some terror here, insofar as the challenging and questioning that God encourages is a soliciting of chaos against order. Does the child who rages out of control necessarily want the parent to encourage the rage or even to outdo her or him in it? This is a terrifying freedom and a terrifying revelation, affirming Job's theodic questions that open up abysses and awaken monsters, who turn out to be beloved of God, against the friends' theodic answers that attempt to shut them up and put them back in their place. We are left, like Job, in a world that at any moment may crumble into primordial chaos, even at God's bidding.

CHAPTER 5

Dinner and a Show

WATCHING AND EATING MONSTERS IN RABBINIC TRADITION

Clearly the Hebrew Bible is not in agreement with itself about what to do with its monsters. As a result it canonizes their ambiguity. The amalgamation of mutually incompatible meanings embodied even in one monstrous name, such as Leviathan, is beyond sorting out or resolving in a way that takes account of all the different texts in which it appears: Leviathan is part of creation; Leviathan is outside creation and a threat to it; Leviathan is the enemy nation; God crushed Leviathan's heads and killed it long ago; God will pierce Leviathan and kill it in the future; God plays with Leviathan; God sings Leviathan's praises. Biblical monsters bear no single meaning, no overall unity or wholeness. They are theologically unwholesome. As such they stand for the haunting sense of precariousness and uncertainty that looms along the edges of the world, the edges of society, the edges of consciousness, and the edges of religious understanding and faith.

Different post-biblical traditions try to sort all this ambiguity out in different ways, though always inconclusively. If we are looking for the text that has had the greatest influence on western cultural history, including modern horror, the prize must go to the vision of the devil-dragon in the Christian Apocalypse of John, also known as the book of Revelation. But if we are looking for the most ingenious and spectacular vision, nothing beats the rabbis' plans for a final dinner and show featuring Leviathan and Behemoth in the Talmud and Midrash.

SEAFARING TALES OF THE RABBIS

The Babylonian Talmud, which was compiled around the end of the sixth century CE, is a series of extended rabbinic discussions centered around the text of the Mishnah, a compilation of commentary on the Torah that was completed around 200 CE. Although compiled from a variety of rabbinic sources spanning several centuries, the final form of the Babylonian Talmud, like that of the earlier Palestinian Talmud (completed around the end of the fifth century CE), often reads like a series of narrative accounts of conversations among rabbis. As with most conversations, they often move far afield of their designated subject. So it is in the discussion of a Mishnah text concerning the business of selling ships in Tractate Baba Bathra (73a–77b). The initial Mishnah simply clarifies the fact that when one sells a ship, the deal includes the ship's mast, sail, anchor and other implements needed for directing it, but does not necessarily include its crew or other things that the seller is storing in it (73a). Very quickly, however, the rabbinic discussion (Gemara) of this Mishnah loses its mooring in the business details of selling and buying ships and drifts into the less familiar and more fantastic straits of seafaring and monster tales, winding up eventually with a vision of a future banquet for the righteous in which Leviathan and Behemoth play a spectacular part.

Rabbah bar Bar Hana makes the first move in this direction: "Seafarers told me: The wave that sinks a ship appears with a white fringe of fire at its crest, and when stricken with clubs on which is engraven, 'I am that I am, Yah, the Lord of Hosts, Amen, Amen, Selah,' it subsides" (73a).[1] The phrase "I am that I am" is what God says to Moses from the burning bush when Moses asks who is sending him and his people against Pharaoh of Egypt in Exodus 3. Very subtly, then, this seafaring legend is picking up on the biblical tradition that associates Egypt and its Pharaoh with chaos waters and chaos monsters (e.g., Psalm 89, Isaiah 51, Ezekiel 29 and 32). The divine word that went with Moses against Pharaoh is the word that subdues the deadly wave. This text assumes, moreover, that this is no ordinary wave, but a wave that has agency and personality, that seeks to sink ships, that understands Hebrew and knows its Torah.

Bar Bar Hana then tells the story of a conversation between two giant waves. It was witnessed by seafarers who were lifted by a wave so high that they saw the resting place of the smallest star in the heavens. "If it had lifted us up any higher we would have been burned by its heat." While up there, they heard one wave ask another of equal size if it had left anything in the world to destroy, so that it could go and wash it away. The other wave answered, "Go and see the power of the master [by whose command] I must not pass the sand [by] the breadth of a thread" (73a). This text picks up on the description of God setting limits for Yam or "sea" in Job 38, discussed earlier ("You may come so far and no farther"). Here, as in bar Bar Hana's first comment, the waves are not quite monsters, but they are nonetheless personifications of vast, potentially destructive power that is kept in check, chaos battle style, by the creator God or by invoking the name of that God.

At this point attention turns more directly to monster tales. Bar Bar Hana begins by recounting his many first-hand encounters both at sea and on land (73b–74a). He once saw a giant antelope the size of Mount Tabor who cast a dung ball so big that it clogged the River Jordan. He once saw a giant frog, as big as sixty houses. It was swallowed by a sea monster (Aramaic *tannina'* = Hebrew *tannin*),[2] and the sea monster was then swallowed by a raven. After swallowing the sea monster that swallowed the frog, the raven then perched itself on a massive tree. "Come and see how strong was the tree," he declares, by way of proof of the size of the raven that allegedly perched on it. To which Rab Papa bar Samuel adds, "Had I not been there I would not have believed it."

Another time, bar Bar Hana saw a fish so big that when it was cast upon the shore it destroyed sixty towns and provided food for sixty others. A year later, when he returned to the area, he saw that the townspeople were cutting rafters from its skeleton in order to rebuild the towns that had been destroyed.

On another occasion they encountered a fish so big that it took them three days and nights in a fast ship to travel from one of its fins to the next with it going one way and them going the other. And just in case anyone suspects that the ship was slow, bar Bar Hana adds that when a horseman shot an arrow the ship outstripped it. Rab Ashi concludes that this fish must have been one of the *small* sea monsters.

Then there was the giant fish whose back was covered with sand and grass. Thinking it was solid ground, bar Bar Hana and his shipmates disembarked and began cooking their food. The heat from their cooking made the fish roll over and they jumped back aboard their ship in the nick of time.

On another occasion, bar Bar Hana recounts, they met a giant bird, called the Ziz, whose ankles were in the sea and whose head was in the heavens. Assuming that the water must be shallow, they decided to take a swim. But before they entered the water, a Bath Kol (divine voice) called out, "Do not go down here, for a carpenter's axe was dropped [into this water] seven years ago and it has not reached the bottom. And this, not [only] because the water is deep but [also] because it is rapid."

The wilderness, like the sea, can be a place of fantastic mystery. Bar Bar Hana tells wilderness tales along with his seafaring tales. Once, for example, an Arab merchant took him to see the Dead of the Wilderness, that is, those Israelites who died during the wandering in the wilderness without ever seeing the promised land. They slept on their backs, and they were so gigantic that the Arab rode his camel under the raised knee of one of them. Bar Bar Hana cut a corner of purple-blue fabric from one of their garments, and they found that they were unable to move away. The Arab explained that if one takes anything from any of them one cannot move away.

Following bar Bar Hana, and picking up his preoccupation with the fantastically large, Rab Safra brings the conversation around to an encounter with the monster Leviathan itself: "Once we were traveling on board a ship and we saw a fish that raised its head out of the sea. It had horns on which was engraven: 'I am a minor creature of the sea. I am three hundred parasangs [over 900 miles long] and I am now going into the mouth of Leviathan'" (74a).

The stories told thus far, including this last one about Leviathan, are monster legends that aim to inspire awe and dread, much like the kind of monster tales that might be told around a campfire. The main vehicle for the fear in them is overwhelming size. In what follows, however, the conversation begins to move away from the emphasis on size, and at the same time begins to focus on the purposiveness of certain monsters. That is, the focus begins to shift from monsters as figures of what Rudolph Otto called "dysteleology," or the negation of purpose, to monsters who exist to fulfill some larger divine will.

This shift begins with two stories in which divers try to gain treasure but are thwarted by sea monsters. In the first story a Karisa tries to stop them from taking a treasure chest of purple-blue for the righteous in the world to come. In the second story a sea monster tries to swallow a ship when one of its divers takes the precious stone it protects. When a giant raven severs the sea monster's head for the second time, the salted birds that are on the ship come to life and fly away with it (74a–74b). In both these stories, sea monsters serve as protectors of treasures that are being saved by God for a time to come. They guard against humans and other creatures who would otherwise steal them away and thereby pervert their cosmic purpose. These monsters are opposed to human will but aligned with divine will.

Next, a second-hand story about Rabbi Joshua's encounter with Leviathan is passed along:

> Our rabbis taught: R. Eliezer and R. Joshua were travelling on board a ship. R. Eliezer was sleeping and R. Joshua was awake. R. Joshua shuddered and R. Eliezer awoke. He said to him: "What is the matter, Joshua? What has caused you to tremble?" He said unto him, "I have seen a great light in the sea." He said unto him: "You may have seen the eyes of Leviathan, for it is written: His eyes are like the eyelids of the morning."

The scriptural passage "his eyes are like the eyelids of the morning" is from Job 41:10 (or 41:18), in which, as discussed in the previous chapter, God is singing the praises of Leviathan. In this story, an experience of horror in which a great light appears where it should not appear is interpreted using a text from the Hebrew Bible. At the same time, the Hebrew Bible is interpreted using a text from seafaring lore: Joshua's shuddering at the sight suggests that the description of Leviathan in Job 41 is at least as terrifying as it is fascinating.

FRESH, FROZEN OR SALT-CURED

This story of Joshua's encounter with the luminous eyes of Leviathan brings biblical interpretation into more direct relation to the telling of monster tales, and inaugurates a series of discussions that draw in several other biblical texts referring to Leviathan or "sea monsters" (*tanninim*). In the process, several different biblical texts are stitched together as a canvas for depicting Leviathan's part in a grand, indeed monstrous banquet for the righteous in the world to come.

First, the scripture on the creation of sea monsters in Genesis 1:21 is quoted: "And God created the great sea monsters." Here the sea monsters are not primordial chaos monsters that oppose God and God's creation, but are asserted to be part of the order of creation and in keeping with divine intention (compare Psalm 104:7). Of course there are a number of other biblical passages that envision a much more hostile relationship between God and such monsters. Interestingly, the next rabbi to speak, Johanan, immediately turns attention to just such a passage, namely Isaiah 27:1, in which the sea monster, the twisting and fleeing serpent, and Leviathan are identified as different names for God's and Judah's cosmic and political archenemy Babylon. But Johanan does not identify this sea monster with Babylon or any other archenemy. He begins to envision a strikingly different meaning and purpose for the future slaying of Leviathan anticipated by Isaiah:

> R. Johanan said: This [Genesis 1:21] refers to Leviathan the fleeing serpent and Leviathan the twisting serpent, for it is written: In that day the Lord with his cruel [and great and strong] sword will punish . . . [Leviathan the fleeing serpent and Leviathan the twisting serpent, and he will kill the sea monster that is in the sea (Isaiah 27:1)].[3]

Thus Johanan places one text, Genesis 1:21, in which great sea monsters are part of God's created order, next to another text, Isaiah

27:1, in which a particular sea monster, Leviathan, is a *hostile opponent to* that created order. In this way he places an apparent biblical contradiction about Leviathan and the sea monster front and center, as though the one text obviously refers to the other. How can this be? According to this interpretation, Leviathan is a great sea monster (*tannin*), created on the fifth day (Genesis 1:21), whose ultimate purpose will be fulfilled when it is killed by God in a time to come. Then why does Genesis say that great sea monsters, *plural*, were created? Rab Judah provides the answer, and in the process brings another monster into the picture, namely Behemoth, whom God describes along with Leviathan in the final whirlwind speech of Job:

> All that the Holy One, blessed be He, created in his world he created male and female. Likewise, Leviathan the fleeing serpent and Leviathan the twisting serpent he created male and female; and had they mated with one another they would have destroyed the whole world. What [then] did the Holy One, blessed be He, do? He castrated the male and killed the female preserving it in salt for the righteous in the world to come; for it is written: And he will slay the sea monster that is in the sea [Isaiah 27:1]. And also Behemoth on a thousand hills were created male and female, and had they mated with one another they would have destroyed the whole world.[4] What did the Holy One, blessed be He, do? He castrated the male and cooled the female and preserved it for the righteous for the world to come; for it is written: Behold now its strength is in its loins [Job 40:16a]—this refers to the male; and its might is in the muscles of its belly [Job 40:16b][5]—this refers to the female. There also, [in the case of Leviathan], he should have castrated the male and cooled the female [why then did he kill the female]?—Fishes are dissolute. Why did he not reverse the process?—If you wish, say: [It is because a] female [fish] preserved in salt is tastier. If you prefer, say: Because it is written: There is Leviathan whom Thou hast formed to sport with, and with a female this is not proper. Then here also [in the case of Behemoth] he should have preserved

> the female in salt?—Salted fish is palatable, salted flesh is not. (Baba Bathra 74b)

Alluding again to the creation story in Genesis 1, Judah here explains that God created all creatures female and male, including Leviathan, "the twisting serpent . . . the fleeing serpent . . . the sea monster that is in the sea." So God had actually created two Leviathans in the beginning, one female and one male, and these are the "great sea monsters" referred to in Genesis 1:21. But as soon as the words "be fruitful and multiply, fill the waters of the sea" were uttered, God realized that there would be trouble. For if Leviathan were allowed to reproduce, it would destroy the world. Leviathan, in this sense, is a part of the order of creation that, with God's blessing to thrive in the world, would *become* a chaos monster, destroying everything else. Leviathan is within the world ecology even while being potentially destructive to it. The cosmos is an ecology of order and chaos, apparently to the dismay of the creator God.

In response to this dilemma, according to Judah, God castrated the male and killed the female, preserving her in salt (why is she preserved? keep reading). Judah then ties the text of Isaiah 27:1 into the conversation: "and God will slay the sea monster that is in the sea." The castrated male Leviathan is still alive and kicking in the world, but not forever. God will slay him in the future. God has killed Leviathan (the female) *and* God will kill Leviathan (male).

So also, says Judah, with Behemoth, which he refers to in tandem with Leviathan just as God does in Job 40–41. The two lines quoted from Job 40:16, according to Judah, refer to the male and female Behemoths, respectively, apparently taking the reference to strong loins in the first part of that verse as a reference to male strength. Thus castration would appropriately diminish the male Behemoth's strength. And the female Behemoth got the same raw deal as the female Leviathan. Except that the female Behemoth required a different method of preservation, that is, cooling instead of salting. Salting would not have been very tasty for the beefy Behemoth (why does it need to be tasty? read on). And given that a fish might still be able to reproduce in cold temperatures, cooling would not have worked for the female Leviathan. Perhaps God could have killed the male instead of the female? Quoting from Psalm 104:26, in which Leviathan is presented as a play partner for

God, the rabbi insists that such a relationship would not have been appropriate. A (presumably male) God should not be splashing around with a female sea monster.

Sexual discrimination aside for the moment, we are left with the rabbis sharing the world with a male Behemoth and a male Leviathan. The female Behemoth is in the cooler and the female Leviathan is curing in salt. Drawing from Isaiah 27:1, it is expected that God will eventually slay the male Leviathan, that is, "the sea monster that is in the sea." Continuing this same train of thought about a future slaying of Leviathan, another rabbi, Rab Demi, begins to explain how this will come about. In the future the angel Gabriel will arrange a "wild beast contest" involving Leviathan, that is, a Roman coliseum-style spectacle in which Leviathan will presumably be killed (74b–75a).[6] As the conversation turns in this direction, we begin to get some sense for why it matters that the flavor of the female monsters be well preserved.

Drawing extensively, and most ingeniously, from the long description of Leviathan in the divine whirlwind speech in Job, bar Bar Hana provides several details concerning a banquet that will accompany the wild beast contest. First, based on Job 40:30 (or 41:6),[7] he says that the flesh of Leviathan will be given as food for the righteous at said banquet in the world to come (75a). At this feast of Leviathan, he explains further, God will make a tabernacle, or *sukkah*, from Leviathan's skin for every righteous person who is worthy of such an honor. As a basis for this claim, he quotes from Job 40:31, but with a twist: Bar Hana quotes the passage as "Can you fill tabernacles [*besukkot*] with his skin?" rather than "Can you fill his head with darts?" reading the homonym *besukkot* (with the letter *samek*), "in tabernacles," rather than the standard Masoretic Hebrew text's *beśukkot* (with the letter *sin*), "with darts"! Bar Bar Hana goes on to explain that guests deemed not righteous enough to receive whole genuine Leviathan hide tabernacles will receive, instead, head coverings made of the same material. This is based on the second line of Job 40:31 (or 41:7), which bar Bar Hana reads as "a covering of fish [for] his head" (reading *ṣilṣal dagim* as "a covering of fish" rather than "fishing spear"). Guests deemed unworthy of such fish hats will receive Leviathan hide necklaces, and guests unworthy even of those will receive, at least, amulets made from the same monster fabric. All the leftover skin from Leviathan, bar Bar Hana explains, will be used to decorate the walls of the banquet hall.

At this point, attention turns from Leviathan to various other matters concerning the final banquet, and eventually even returns to the business of buying and selling ships (75b–77b). But as the conversation moves on, we are left for the time being with a number of loose ends and monstrous leftovers. We have a female Leviathan in salt, a female Behemoth in the cooler, and their respective male partners roving earth and sea for some undetermined time to come. We expect that Leviathan, "the sea monster of the sea," will be killed eventually, and that this will involve some kind of spectacular contest arranged by Gabriel. Furthermore, the righteous will enjoy a banquet, related to the wild beast contest, in which the main course will be Leviathan (perhaps both fresh and salted varieties). But how, specifically, is the contest related to the banquet? Is that where Leviathan will be killed? By God, Gabriel or someone else? And where does Behemoth (dead and alive) fit into all this? For some answers and a fuller picture of the spectacle to come, we must politely slip out of this Talmudic conversation and go elsewhere in rabbinic tradition, to Midrash Leviticus Rabbah.

IS THIS MONSTER KOSHER?

Midrash Leviticus Rabbah is an early (fifth-, sixth- or seventh-century CE) Palestinian compilation of midrashic commentary based on select passages from Leviticus. The discussions of the rabbis in Leviticus Rabbah often involve extended interpretive discussions that build outward through the incorporation of more and more biblical texts. In one such discussion (XIII.3), concerning the dietary restrictions (kosher laws) in Leviticus 11, Judah and Simeon provide additional details about the wild beast contest involving Leviathan mentioned by Demi and Bar Hana in Bavli Talmud Baba Bathra: the spectacle is to be held for the righteous, they explain, as a reward for refusing to watch the Roman spectacles, and it will involve both Leviathan and Behemoth, who will kill one another in battle. In addition to providing these helpful details, however, they introduce a problem concerning the *method* by which Behemoth and Leviathan will be slaughtered at this final spectacle and banquet for the righteous: will this monster meat be kosher? Will the slaughter be done in a kosher manner? If not, how will the righteous be allowed to eat it?

> Behemoth and Leviathan are to engage in a wild-beast contest before the righteous in the Time to Come, and whoever has not been a spectator at the wild-beast contests of the heathen nations in this world [or "nations of this world"] will be accorded the boon of seeing one in the World to Come. How will they be slaughtered? Behemoth will, with its horns, pull Leviathan down and rend it, and Leviathan will, with its fins, pull Behemoth down and pierce it through.—The Sages said: And is this a valid method of slaughter? Have we not learnt the following in a Mishnah: All may slaughter, and one may slaughter at all times [of the day], and with any instrument except with a scythe, or a saw, or with teeth [i.e., with a jaw cut out of a dead animal], because they cause pain as if by choking, or with a nail [of a living body]? (XIII.3)

The expectation here is that Leviathan and Behemoth will slaughter one another in the same instant, since they have no other worldly rivals. Behemoth will use its horns to pull down and tear apart Leviathan, while Leviathan will use its fins to slay Behemoth by "piercing" it (from the verb *naḥar,* related to "nostril" and referring to piercing the windpipe). Even before the sage responds, the terminology in this description invokes priestly concerns about whether or not their mutual slaughter in this manner fulfills kosher requirements. The term used by the rabbis in reference to their mutual "slaughter" is a form of the verb *shaḥaṭ,* which appears primarily in ritual contexts such as Leviticus 1–7 to describe the proper slaughter of animals for sacrifice. The sages' question makes the concern explicit: "Is this slaughter valid," or more literally, "is this slaughter *kosher*?" Is it ritually permitted? If not, how will the righteous be allowed to eat of it? Insofar as the Mishnah (Talmud Hullin I.2) says that anyone can perform the slaughter on any given day, it is acceptable that they kill each other at this time. The problem lies in the *method* of killing, for Leviathan's fins are serrated, and therefore something like a saw, which is one of the instruments not permitted for slaughtering animals.

Assumed here, of course, is that what is kosher for the routine killing of everyday animals should also apply in such an extravagantly spectacular scene as the final battle between Behemoth and Leviathan. Beyond that, it is fascinating to note that the reason given for prohibiting the use of these particular slaughtering instruments is that they cause undue pain. To be killed with one of these instruments would feel like being choked or clawed to death. Perhaps even a monster should not be slaughtered in such a cruel and unusual manner.

In response to this question from the sages, however, Abin ben Kahana explains that this is an exceptional case, and therefore these extraordinary methods of slaughter are permitted. He begins with a quotation, drawn from Isaiah 51:4, "a new law [*torah ḥadashah*] shall go forth from me," which he reads as, "a novel interpretation of the law [*ḥiddush torah*] will go forth from me."[8] That is, this entirely novel case of slaughter calls for a novel interpretation of the pertinent law, one which will allow Leviathan's slaughter of Behemoth with its saw-like fin to be kosher. The righteous will taste Behemoth.

In this same spirit of exception, Rabbi Berekiah pushes both the kosher issue and the exceptional character of this case even further. Beyond the saw-like nature of Leviathan's killing tool, he points out, the prohibition in Leviticus 7:24 against eating any dead animal (*nebelah*) that has been killed or torn by other animals would suggest that *neither* Behemoth nor Leviathan will be kosher.[9] As Berekiah insists, however, "whoever has not eaten *nebelah* in this world will have the privilege of enjoying it in the World to Come." Just as the self-restraint of the righteous in refusing to participate in the Roman spectacles of human and animal contests means that they will enjoy a far more spectacular monster contest, so their self-restraint in refusing to eat torn animals in this world means that they will enjoy torn monster in the world to come.[10] So save room.

JONAH'S UNDERSEA ADVENTURE

Another midrashic text, the eighth- or ninth-century *Pirke de Rabbi Eliezer*, offers an alternative to the mutual killing anticipated by the rabbis in Leviticus Rabbah. It imagines that God has other plans for Leviathan in which Jonah will be the hero.[11] This text offers an imaginative retelling of the Jonah story that focuses on what happens to him during his stay in the belly of the great fish that swallows him.

The fish that swallows Jonah, the text explains, was not just any old giant fish who happened to be swimming by when the seamen threw Jonah overboard. It had been ordained to do so since creation. Jonah enters into it as though he is entering a synagogue. Inside, the fish's two eyes are like windows and a great pearl hangs in the belly, shining like the sun at noontime—a kind of "tactfully lit, *schul*-submarine," as Yvonne Sherwood puts it.[12] After showing Jonah many things in the sea and in the abysses, the fish explains to him that the day has arrived for it to be eaten by Leviathan.

Terrible timing? Not at all. As soon as Jonah hears that this is the fish's day to be monster meal, he realizes why God has sent him on this undersea adventure. Without pause he demands that the fish take him to Leviathan. When they arrive, Jonah declares to Leviathan that the reason he has come is to discover Leviathan's dwelling place. For he is the one who will put a rope through Leviathan's tongue, haul it out of the sea, and slaughter it for the great banquet in the world to come. God had taunted Job, "Can you draw out Leviathan with a fishhook? Can you press down its tongue with a rope?" (Job 40:25 [or 41:1]). Jonah would have answered, "Yes I can and yes I will!"

After declaring his ultimate purpose, Jonah then exposes his "seal of Abraham," that is, his circumcised penis, and that frightens the monster away. With Leviathan gone for the time being, Jonah and the fish continue their underwater sightseeing tour, including stops at the pillars of the earth, the deepest underworld of Sheol, the palace of God, and below it the Shetiyyah Stone, which is the initial foundation stone sunk by God at the time of creation.

The fish tells Jonah that this would be a good time to pray. Jonah agrees and does so, praying that God will now return him to life above sea level. God does not seem to be listening until Jonah vows that he will indeed return for Leviathan, and will haul it up for slaughter for the banquet in the world to come. As soon as the words leave Jonah's mouth, God gives a sign to the fish, and the fish spits Jonah out on dry land. Thus Jonah's ultimate purpose as Leviathan butcher for the final banquet receives divine confirmation.

Although they do not fit together into a single, seamless vision, the general impression given in all these rabbinic stories and discussions is that the world, especially the sea, is literally teeming with monsters. Although clearly part of creation, created by God and intended by God for particular purposes, these monsters nonetheless represent a certain uneasy fragility and instability within the order of things—what I earlier called cosmic horror. They represent an otherworldliness within the world. The fact that the chaotic forces of Leviathan and Behemoth, if left on their own to procreate, could have destroyed God's creation suggests a world ecology in which order and chaos intertwine, often unpredictably, sometimes surprising even God. Yet within these rabbinic discussions in Talmud and Midrash there is, along with a certain fear and trembling, an undercurrent of excitement and fascination in the monster tales and in the expectation of the final dinner and show. Not so in the early Christian text of the Apocalypse of John, to which we now turn.

CHAPTER 6

To the Devil

APOCALYPSE

"An apocalypse," or "revelation of Jesus Christ which God gave him to show his servants what must soon take place; he made it known to his servant John, who testified to the word of God and to the testimony of Jesus Christ, even to all that he saw" (Apocalypse of John [a.k.a. Revelation] 1:1).[1] "Apocalypse" is from the Greek verb *apokalupto*: *apo*, "from" or "out of," and *kalupto*, "hide" or "cover." Apocalypse: out of hiding; that which is revealed when the covering, the hide, the skin is peeled away; unhiding.

The visions of the world to come in rabbinic tradition reveal a final dinner and show in which the only one to lose his hide will be Leviathan, and this to adorn the righteous guests and deck the halls. In the early Christian New Testament vision of the Apocalypse of John, on the other hand, it looks like the skin of world itself is cracking and peeling away, opening an abyss just below its surface that teems with monsters who rise up against God and God's righteous ones in a bloody final battle of political and cosmic proportions. This text was likely composed late in the Roman Emperor Domitian's reign (around 95 CE), and is haunted by the earlier persecutions of the Jesus movement under Nero in the late 60s and by the destruction of the Jerusalem Temple in 70.[2] Rooted in this context of oppression, the Apocalypse of John peels back the hide of *Pax Romana*, the "Peace of Rome" that is also the imperial order of Rome, revealing an alternative vision of it as the new Babylon, personified in the form of reawakening chaos monsters. One of these chaos monsters, the great red dragon who appears at the beginning of a long series of visions of the final chaos battle (chapters 12–22), bears a striking resemblance to representations of Leviathan and the sea monster in the Hebrew Bible. Yet according to this new vision, in a new religious context in which there is a pronounced cosmic dualism of good versus evil, this chaos monster is presented as an ultimate personification of evil, also known as the Devil or Satan. In the Apocalypse of John, it is to the Devil with Leviathan and the sea monster, inaugurating a new and long-lasting diabolical career for the biblical chaos monster.

IT'S THE EDGE OF THE WORLD AS WE KNOW IT

In many respects, the Apocalypse of John has defined "apocalypticism" for popular culture as well as for scholarship. The genre of apocalyptic literature is commonly defined as a revelation from a god, to a seer, through a mediator, concerning immanent events. This definition is basically a synopsis of the first verse of the Apocalypse of John, which is the first known visionary text to describe itself as an apocalypse: it is introduced as "an *apokalupsis* of Jesus Christ which God gave him," that is, a revelation from God through the mediator Jesus Christ, concerning "what must soon take place," which Jesus "made known to his servant John," who is now making known to his readers and hearers "all that he saw."

Yet in many ways "all that he saw" runs counter to what contemporary culture has come to expect from apocalypticism. This text does not envision the *end* of the world so much as its *edge*. Viewed through John's apocalyptic spectacles, the world is revealed as profoundly out of joint, off kilter, teetering on the threshold between birth and death, beginning and end. In this apocalyptic spectacle, the cosmogonic beginning becomes the chaogonic ending. Unlike many of the apocalyptic visions of our day, the spectacular chaogony in the Apocalypse of John is not an end in itself. In it, the world is retaken by primordial chaos in order that a radically new heaven and earth may be born (21:1).

The horror of the Apocalypse of John is, as Tina Pippin astutely puts it, "both intimate and global" in a way that contemporary apocalypses often fail to capture.[3] The cosmic horror in this text is intensely personal, even palpable. One of the reasons for the intimacy of the horrors conveyed here is that they seem to have invaded the very subjectivity of the seer, John of Patmos. One has the sense that as John sees the world falling to pieces before his eyes, he is also experiencing his own selfhood falling to pieces. His is a vision *of* the edge, but also a vision *on* the edge—the cosmic edge, the political edge, but also John's own psychic edge. Indeed, some would say that he, like his predecessor the prophet Ezekiel, is way over the edge. "I, John, your brother, who share with you the persecution and kingdom and the patient endurance, was on the island called Patmos on account of the word of God and testimony to Jesus. I was in the spirit . . . " (Apocalypse 1:9–10). "After this I looked and there in heaven a door stood open . . . " (4:1). "Then I was given a measuring rod like a staff, and I was told, 'Come and measure the temple of God . . . ' (11:1). "The first horror is over; there are still two horrors to come" (9:12); "the second horror is over; the third will come soon" (11:14). "Then I took a stand on the sand of the seashore. And I saw a beast rising out of the sea . . . " (12:18–13:1). "I, John, am the one who heard and saw these things. And when I heard and saw them, I fell down to worship at the feet of the angel who showed them to me" (22:8). Out of place (in exile, in heaven, on the seashore, in the temple), out of kilter, out of joint, sometimes out of body (in the spirit), John is perpetually dislocated and disoriented. John is politically, physically and psychically ungrounded, unhomed, watching the horrors unfold from the primordial shoreline.

In this state of disorientation it is often difficult to distinguish god from monster, that is, to determine who is on whose side in the battle. Consider the first actual "apocalypse of Jesus Christ" given to John, which is not only an apocalypse *from* Jesus Christ or mediated *by* him, but an aweful revelation *of* him, one that is radically unlike any other in the New Testament, and one that John himself is at a loss how to read:

> Then I turned to see whose voice it was that spoke to me, and on turning I saw seven golden lampstands, and in the midst of the lampstands I saw one like the Son of Man, clothed with a long robe and with a golden sash across his chest. His head and his hair were white as white wool, white as snow; his eyes were like a flame of fire, his feet were like burnished bronze, refined as in a furnace, and his voice was like the sound of many waters. In his right hand he held seven stars, and from his mouth came a sharp, two-edged sword, and his face was like the sun shining with full force. (Apocalypse 1:12–16)

This initial vision of the risen Jesus draws much of its imagery and vocabulary from Daniel's vision of a divine messenger clothed in linen and gold, who has eyes like lamps of fire, limbs like burnished brass and a voice like the voice of a multitude (Daniel 10:5–6). But the fact that John's vision is built in part from this earlier biblical image of a divine messenger does not diminish the sense of terror embodied here.[4] Indeed, when the apparition had come to Daniel, none of the people near him saw it yet they were all overwhelmed with terror and ran away to hide. Then Daniel, doubly isolated (seeing what others cannot see and remaining while all the others flee), lost all strength, went deathly pale and fell face-first to the ground in a trance (Daniel 10:7–9). Though the messenger soon brings Daniel around, the initial epiphany is one of isolating terror. So also for John at this new revelation of Jesus. In response to it he falls on his face "as though dead" (1:17). Indeed, this image of the risen Jesus draws from Daniel not to identify or make sense of what John sees, but to compound and accentuate the sense of disorientation.

Much like Daniel's description of the messenger, and much like God's description of Leviathan in Job, moreover, this text provides a written description of something that defies visual depiction. It is a writing of the unimaginable, combining a series of mutually incompatible elements (images, sounds) in such a way that one simply cannot compose a picture, in the mind or on paper, that does not leave something out, as numerous illustrations of this vision since the Middle Ages clearly attest (e.g., the fourteenth-century Cloisters Apocalypse, Figure 4). It is a revelation of something that

FIGURE 4. *The Cloisters Apocalypse* (early fourteenth century), folio 3 verso, John's vision of Jesus Christ (Apocalypse 1:12–20), The Metropolitan Museum of Art.

defies its own revelation. The parts add up to more than any comprehensible whole.

John's initial uncertainty, infused with both dread and fascination in response to this overwhelming spectacle of the risen Christ, is similar to the responses of many first-time readers to the various epiphanies of God, monsters and angels throughout the great cosmic battle that takes place in the latter part of the book (chapters 12–22). Each new vision, each new monstrous portent, disturbs whatever certainty might have been achieved up to that point. Is that one of "us" or one of "them"? It does not help matters that at least as much cosmic devastation and human suffering is being meted out by God and God's angels as by God's monstrous opponents. In chapter 14, for example, two angels appear with sharp sickles, swinging them across the earth, throwing the victims into the "wine press of the wrath of God," treading their bodies so that "blood flowed from the wine press, as high as a horse's bridle, for a distance of about two hundred miles" (14:19–20); and in chapter 16 seven angels pour seven bowls of wrath on the earth, causing great human suffering and death as well as ecological disaster. As with the four-eyed, giant-eared, "incomprehensible" Marduk, and as with the blood-and-gore-steeped Anat adorned in the severed heads and limbs of her enemies, the balance between terror and fascination tips with our conscious awareness of whose side we are on.

DIABOLICAL DRAGON

With regard to the great red dragon in Apocalypse 12, however, whose coming inaugurates a cosmic battle that will rage through chapter 20, the text allows for very little ambiguity.

The scene opens with a "great portent appearing in heaven: a woman clothed with the sun, with the moon under her feet, and on her head a crown of twelve stars. She was pregnant and was crying out in birthpangs, in the agony of giving birth" (12:1–2). This is a vision of both cosmic and political rebirth and rejuvenation. That the woman is clothed in the sun identifies her with other positive cosmic images (Jesus's face like the sun in 1:16; the herald angel ascending from the rising sun in 7:2; and the angel with a face like the sun in 10:1). Her crown signals royal status, and the twelve stars in it identify that royal status with the twelve tribes of Israel. Twelve is also a product of three, which symbolizes the spiritual world, and four, which symbolizes the order of creation. Thus she simultaneously embodies the divine order of creation and of Israel. She is an image of God's cosmopolis against Rome's. While embodying that order herself, moreover, she is also giving birth to it on earth. For the child she bears, the text explains, will rule (or "shepherd") all the nations with an iron rod as part of the divine plan. At the same time, the description of her crying out in the midst of labor pains indicates that this is a liminal moment, in which the new birth is precarious and vulnerable.[5]

Enter the dragon. "Then another portent appeared in heaven: a great red dragon, with seven heads and ten horns, and seven diadems on its heads" (12:3). This dragon is immediately identified as a chaos monster who threatens all that is represented by the woman clothed in the sun: with one sweep of its giant tail, it knocks down a third of the stars in heaven, throwing them to earth, and then it positions itself in front of the woman in order to devour the child as soon as it is born. It is anti-cosmic, anti-Israel and therefore anti-God.

Its desire to devour the newborn child, however, is soon frustrated. As the child is born, it is snatched from the dragon's waiting mouth and taken immediately up to God. The woman quickly flees into the wilderness "where she has a place prepared by God, so that there she can be nourished" (12:5–6).

Immediately after the woman and her child are taken into divine refuge, the dragon and its angels engage in a battle against the archangel Michael and his angels. Michael defeats the dragon and casts it down to earth. It then chases after the woman in the wilderness, pouring forth a flood of water from its mouth in order to wash her away. At this point the earth itself comes to the aid of the woman, opening its mouth and swallowing the dragon's flood waters. Infuriated, the dragon gives up on her and goes after her children, who are identified as all those "who keep the commandments of God and hold to the testimony of Jesus" (12:17). In what follows, he delegates authority over the unrighteous masses to the beasts who emerge in his wake, one from the sea and one from the earth. This reign comes to an end when the dragon is locked into the abyss for a thousand years and finally thrown into the lake of fire along with its beastly cohorts (chapter 20), after which a new heaven, a new earth and a new Jerusalem are born (chapter 21).

Thus the great red dragon in the Apocalypse of John is presented as a chaos monster that threatens divine order on every level. It is a personification of cosmic and political horror, a chaotic threat to creation and to the divine plan for a new counter-Roman empire. It sweeps down stars, thus uncreating what God had created in Genesis 1. It threatens the woman clothed with the sun, who embodies divinely ordained cosmic and political order. Primordial flood waters pour forth from its belly. Both earth and heaven fight against it. Its red color stands for war and bloodshed. It wants nothing more than to devour the one who is meant to shepherd all the nations, and when that desire is frustrated, it wreaks havoc among the righteous followers of Jesus. It spends a thousand years in the abyss. And its destruction leads immediately to the creation of the new heaven and earth with Jerusalem as its cosmic and political center.

In this early Christian context of cosmic dualism, moreover, this chaos monster is identified with Satan, or the Devil, a fallen angel who comes to personify cosmic evil against God in a way that is unprecedented in earlier biblical texts. The dragon's diabolic identity is made explicit at two points, once toward the beginning of the cosmic battle, when it is thrown out of heaven by Michael, and the other toward the battle's end, when it is locked up in the abyss:

> The dragon and his angels fought back, but they were defeated, and there was no longer any place for them in heaven. The great dragon was thrown down, that ancient serpent, who is called the Devil and Satan, the deceiver of the world—he was thrown down to earth, and his angels were thrown down with him. (Apocalypse 12:7b-9)

> He [an angel] seized the dragon, that ancient serpent, who is the Devil and Satan, and bound him for a thousand years, and threw him into the pit [or 'abyss'], and locked and sealed it over him so that he would deceive the nations no more . . . (Apocalypse 20:2–3a)

The dragon in the Apocalypse of John is the Devil incarnate, God's quintessential Other, in a cosmic battle between the forces of good and the forces of evil.

THE MONSTER-MAKER'S BIBLE'S BIBLE

Horror writer, director and producer Clive Barker said that there are at least two books in every American household: "one of them is the Bible and the other one is probably Stephen King."[6] It is interesting that he considers the presence of a Stephen King book to be *probable* whereas the presence of a Bible is *certain*. In fact, he is surely wrong to expect that either book is quite so pervasive, in America or anywhere else. But if there is a Bible in Stephen King's home, or in Clive Barker's for that matter, it is likely a Christian Bible (including a New Testament), and it probably falls open to the Apocalypse of John. Many things to many people, this text is a veritable manual for monster-making.

John's apocalyptic imagination is the wellspring of an overwhelming, primordial flood of monstrosities, climbing in and out of heaven, in and out of the abyss, in and out of the world, as the boundaries between cosmos and chaos, heaven and hell, sacred and profane are washed away in blood, gore, and bowls of plague and abomination. As such it is the sourcebook for innumerable monsters in subsequent Christian tradition as well as in today's ostensibly irreligious popular cultures of horror.[7] The Apocalypse of John is indeed The Monster-maker's Bible.

But the Apocalypse of John does not conjure its monsters out of nothing. In fact, their images are drawn from a wide background of stories about chaos monsters, especially dragons and serpents, who threaten the cosmic and social order and who are slain by hero gods. Look into the abysmal mouth of John's great red dragon, and you might see a number of ancient monsters and monster gods milling about in the chaos waters of its belly: the Greek dragons Hydra, slain by Hercules, and Python, who threatens Leto's son Apollo (and whom Apollo eventually slays); perhaps also the Vedic serpent-demon Vṛtra;[8] perhaps the Babylonian chaos mother Tiamat; and the anomalous Egyptian chaos god Seth of the Red Land, who is defeated in battle by Horus; and Ugaritic Yamm or Tunnan or Litan, the "Potentate with the Seven Heads." But most prominent among them will be Leviathan and the "sea monster" (*tannin*) from Jewish biblical tradition. Indeed, John's primary source for making monsters—The Monster-maker's Bible's Bible—is the Old Testament, especially those so-called "proto-apocalyptic" texts such as Ezekiel, Isaiah (esp. chapters 24–27), Joel and Daniel, which themselves are saturated with disturbing visions of God and monsters.

John's vision of the great dragon draws explicitly from earlier biblical references to chaos monsters, especially Leviathan and the "sea monster," both of which are consistently translated as *drakon* in the Septuagint (Greek) version of the Old Testament. In the Septuagint text of Ezekiel 29, for example, the Hebrew "great sea monster" (*hattanim haggadol*; 29:3) is translated into Greek as "the great dragon" (*ton drakonta ton megan*), whom God will "cast down" (*katabalo*, from the verb *ballo*, "cast"). Likewise, the Apocalypse of John twice refers to this monster as "the great dragon" (*ho drakon ho megas* in12:9; also12:3), and describes him being "cast out" (*eblethe*, also from *ballo*) of heaven by God (12:9). In the Septuagint version of Psalm 74:12–14, furthermore, both Leviathan and the "sea monster" (*tannin*) are translated into Greek as *drakon*. This psalm, moreover, describes the dragon with multiple heads (*tas kephalas tou drakontos*, "the dragon's heads"), and so does Apocalypse 12:3 (*tas kephalas outou*, "his heads").[9] The Septuagint text of Isaiah 27:1 also translates both Leviathan and the "sea monster" (*tannin*), whom God will kill on a future day of judgment, as *drakon*.[10] In that text, moreover, the Hebrew epithet for Leviathan, *naḥash* ("serpent," as in "twisting serpent" and "fleeing serpent"), is translated into Greek as *ophis* ("serpent"). And the Apocalypse of John twice refers to the great dragon with the epithet "the archaic serpent" (*ho ophis ho archaios*; 12:9; 20:2).

So John's dragon is a transfiguration of earlier biblical traditions concerning chaos monsters. It stitches together a new monster from old skins, a new "ancient serpent" for a new cosmic, political, always theological crisis, that of Roman persecution of the early Jesus movement at the end of the first century, some twenty-five years after the destruction of the Jerusalem Temple. This, of course, is a familiar biblical move, and the prophets Isaiah and Ezekiel are masters of it. It is no accident that John's dragon is closest to the earlier biblical chaos monsters of Psalm 74, Isaiah 27 and Ezekiel 29, because they, too, represented threats not only to the cosmic order but also to the political order of Judah, which is supposed to be a microcosmos of God's creation. In Psalm 74, God's victory over Leviathan was reason to hope for God's future victory over Babylon; in Isaiah 27, Leviathan is a personification of Babylon; and in Ezekiel 29, the sea monster personifies Egypt. In the latter two cases, the monster still lives, but the prophet anticipates that God will kill it on a future judgment day. Ezekiel's vision of this demise is especially gory, a feature which must have been a particular draw for John of Patmos, whose text is similarly inclined. In the Apocalypse of John, these ancient monsters and the former enemies they personify (especially Babylon, which destroyed the first Jerusalem temple centuries earlier) emerge as personifications of a new battle-red monster of destruction and persecution, namely late first-century Rome, its emperors and its armies.

Yet the chaos monster's transfiguration as "the Devil or Satan" is completely unprecedented in light of earlier biblical tradition. In the Hebrew Bible, neither Leviathan nor the sea monster nor any other monster is ever identified with the Devil or Satan, a figure who does not acquire the identity of ultimate anti-God until later, post-biblical Christian thought.

As elsewhere in the Apocalypse, John's spectacle of the great red dragon sorts through various fragments of biblical and Greco-Roman tradition in order to piece together a new version of the monster. In the process, it attempts to *sort out* the biblical canon's deep theological ambivalence with regard to this "ancient serpent" in terms of a theologically tidier, more systematic scenario of good versus evil, God versus Devil.

In other texts from the Hebrew Bible, especially in the book of Job, we have encountered visions of the world and of God in which chaos and order intertwine. In those texts, the chaos monster (Leviathan, *tannin*, etc.) emerges as a means of expressing that intertwining, engendering a sense of uncertainty and cosmic horror that is deeply theological, going to the very core of the character of God within biblical monotheism. The Apocalypse of John works against such an intertwining, peeling Leviathan-the twisting serpent off the character of God and sending it to the Devil.

This post-biblical Christian apocalyptic vision of the dragon has some things in common with the rabbinic expectations of a final battle and banquet in the world to come. Both visions are largely collective male fantasies that do not seem to imagine the women in their communities as major participants. Both reveal a world to come that is radically other than the present world, and in which it is good to be among the righteous "us." Both visions estrange hearers and readers from "this world," and make them long for another, even if that longing is accompanied occasionally by a cold shudder. And for both traditions, "this world" is the world of Roman domination. That is, both text traditions represent marginal religious ideas and practices within the Roman Empire, and both are profoundly haunted by personal and collective traumas meted out in the name of the *Pax Romana*, including severe persecutions and the destruction of the Jerusalem Temple. Out of this situation of oppression, moreover, both envision an ultimate restoration of God's people and of God's city Jerusalem as the center of the new creation. And last but not least, both envision a spectacular final battle that involves the return engagement of biblical chaos monsters.

But there are two particularly striking differences. The first has to do with the dualism that operates in the Apocalypse of John. In the rabbinic vision of the return of chaos monsters, as in other rabbinic monster tales, one has the clear sense that these monsters are not opposed to God, even when they threaten humans, as when the sea monster attacks the seafarers who try to steal its treasure. In the Apocalypse, on the other hand, the biblical chaos monster returns as the Devil or Satan, personifying ultimate evil against God.

The second difference has to do with the kind of violence these two different traditions imagine. On the one hand, the end-of-the-world spectacle imagined in the Talmud and Midrash involves no human carnage whatsoever. There the final battle ends in a nice dinner, and the only ones who get killed are Leviathan and Behemoth. Indeed, the Midrash even shows some concern that these monsters not suffer undue pain in the process of killing one another. The Apocalypse of John, on the other hand, is neck deep in human blood, much of it spilled by God and God's sickle-swinging, plague-bearing angels. In its vision, the rise of the new Jerusalem and the joyful gathering of the righteous few within it can take place only after the present world is washed away in torrents of blood and plague. The ultimate well-being of the righteous, who were chosen by God from the foundation of the world (13:8; 17:8), is imagined against the ultimate suffering of the unrighteous, whose fate likewise must have been set since the beginning.

FROM BEOWULF TO DRACULA TO HARRY POTTER

As Christianity gains increasing cultural and imperial hegemony by the fourth century, and as the Apocalypse of John is gradually recognized as canonical Scripture within a slowly solidifying Christian New Testament, the spectacular vision of the great red dragon in Apocalypse 12 helps to launch a new diabolical career for the biblical chaos monster. Images of it as a figure of the Devil pervade the apocalyptic imagination of Christian visual culture throughout the Middle Ages and into our day. As we will see, it also becomes a figure for European colonialist representations of the deities of other religions as monstrously diabolical. And those monstrous representations will, in turn, feed the emerging popular cultures of the Gothic and horror.

Likewise, the story of Michael defeating the great dragon in battle and thereby saving the woman clothed in the sun has inspired many other legends of saints slaying dragons in order to save towns and/or damsels in distress. Certainly it is an important narrative background for the *Beowulf* poet's presentation of the hero slaying the abysmal fire-breathing "earth dragon" (*eorð-draca*, also called *wyrm*, "serpent") in order to save the people it was tormenting.[11] Although this story is set in fifth- or sixth-century pre-Christian Germania, its poet is well steeped in Christian thought and biblical tradition.[12] While the story's pagan characters use their own local pre-Christian terms to describe the various monsters, the Christian poet uses a biblical vocabulary.[13] The Grendelkin, for example, are said to descend from a line of monsters going back to Cain in Genesis 4.[14] So also the dragon, who is clearly related to the Christian Bible's most famous dragon of the Apocalypse (and whose "heathen hoard" also identifies it with accursed pagan religion). By the same token, the heroic Beowulf, although undeniably pagan, is subtly identified with the dragon-slaying archangel Michael and God's armies.

A more prominent example of a revamping of Michael versus the dragon is the legend of Saint George, dating back to the sixth century, in which the hero kills a dragon, thereby saving a princess and securing a promise from her father that all his subjects would be baptized. In this story, the dragon is a threat to patriarchy, to the nation and to eternal salvation. Early visual depictions of George defeating the dragon are often strongly reminiscent of visual depictions of the archangel Michael driving the dragon from heaven (Figure 5). As George becomes patron saint of England, moreover, the dragon comes to represent a diabolically monstrous threat against England, especially against its Christianity and its patriarchy. In this light we will want to explore family resemblances between biblical chaos monsters like Leviathan, the dragon of the Apocalypse, the gold-hoarding dragon of *Beowulf*, the dragon of the Saint George legend and Bram Stoker's *Dracula*. Dracula, whose name comes from the Romanian *dracul*, "the dragon" or "devil," represents a monstrous invasion of England that especially threatens its religious faith and its women. He must be slain by the story's patriarchal heroes in order to save not only the fatherland but the entire world.

FIGURE 5. *The Cloisters Apocalypse* (early fourteenth century), folio 20 verso, Michael and his angels defeat the great dragon and his angels, who are cast to earth (Apocalypse 12:7–12), The Metropolitan Museum of Art.

Finally, one must wonder about Draco Malfoy, the diabolical bad boy in J. K. Rowling's tremendously popular Harry Potter novel series. With a name like Draco, and living in a house called Slytherin that has a basilisk lurking under its foundations, surely there must be a bit of the dragon of the Apocalypse in him. (Is Harry Potter on its way to becoming a new British national myth—one that, like so many others, millions of Americans hold dear?)

Although we must acknowledge the great success and many successors of John's great dragon of the Apocalypse in subsequent monster-making traditions, it would be a mistake to assume that this dragon has undone the deep religious ambiguity of biblical monsters forever. John's dragon does not erase or replace other less diabolical epiphanies of the monstrous in biblical tradition, but rather compounds with them. Indeed, there can be no final revela-

FIGURE 6. *The Cloisters Apocalypse* (early fourteenth century), folio 35, the dragon and the beasts are cast into the lake of fire (Apocalypse 20:9–10), The Metropolitan Museum of Art.

tion or resolution of the monstrous in the biblical traditions of Judaism or Christianity. Those other monstrous figures remain there, pressing in from the margins of the biblical map, in those dreadfully unknown and infirm territories where one's theological grounding becomes disconcertingly shaky.

PART TWO

Monsters and Their Religion

CHAPTER 7

New Monsters in Old Skins

When monsters go to bed at night, or at sunrise as the case may be, to whom do they say their bedtime prayers?

Monsters seem to be particularly fond of religious spaces and decor, especially the kind that has not been modernized: decrepit graveyards full of crumbling tombstones, dusty candlelit cathedrals strewn with crosses and communion goblets. Why do they seem so comfortable there? And why do these same sacred spaces so often give us moderns the creeps?

So far we have been seeing what we can learn about religion by getting to know its monsters. Now we will see what we can learn about monsters, especially the monsters of modern horror, by getting to know their religious backgrounds. This will take us as far from Part One as Genesis is from Mary Shelley's *Frankenstein*, as far as Leviticus is from Bram Stoker's *Dracula*, and as far as Job is from Clive Barker's *Hellraiser* movies. Which is not so far as one might suspect.

MODERN CHAOS BATTLES

As we have seen, biblical tradition is fraught with tensions that go to the very core of its conceptions of the world and its creator God.

On the one hand, it is confident in the stable, reasonable order of the cosmos, confident in our ability to articulate that order and live according to it, and confident in God as founder and guarantor of that order; on the other hand, it is haunted by monstrous forms of profound disjunction and disorder, shadowy revelations on the edge between creation and uncreation, cosmos and chaos, and haunted by the lurking anxiety that God, like the world God created, is fraught with the same tensions. The biblical tradition is endlessly caught between cosmogonic visions of the stable moral universe, in which God has crushed the monsters and sits enthroned over chaos, and chaogonic visions of a world on the edge of collapse, in which the monsters are alive and well and it is not always clear whether God is with them or against them.

In many respects, modern horror is caught in the same tensions, and its monsters often stand for the same theological questions and anxieties. Some monster tales and latter-day monster enthusiasts identify with their monsters, embracing them as figures of chaos against cosmos. In most cases, however, they appear in something like a modern version of the ancient chaos battle motif. As with the diabolical dragon in the Apocalypse of John, they are roused and brought to light in order to be killed, thereby resanctifying cosmos, society and self, and reinstating faith in a monster-free world in which God smiles down upon us in the rainbow.

This chaos battle motif, in which sacred order is pitted against the diabolically monstrous forces of chaos, is deeply rooted in western culture. In his essay on the rise of modern western consciousness during the seventeenth century, Stephen Toulmin shows how the hidden agenda of modernity was to reestablish cosmic and political order against chaos by establishing a new vision of *cosmopolis*, that is, a new vision of the total coherence of all things in which "the divinely created Order of Nature and the humanly created Order of Society were once again illuminating one another."[1] This new vision was established in the aftermath of the old vision, which had been reduced to chaos under the weight of assassinations, executions, the Thirty Years' War and other seventeenth-century crises. This new cosmopolis was not simply social-economic, moreover, but religious, a *theological* response to a *theological crisis*.[2] It offered society a way of imposing order against chaos, of staving off the flood waters that threatened to overwhelm it. It was an awakening of reason that was intent on keeping the chaos monsters down. In this sense, we might say that the more or less hidden agenda of modernity is the same as the not so hidden agenda of the chaos battles found in biblical and other ancient Near Eastern stories: to establish and sacralize order against chaos, from heavenly bodies to individual bodies and everything in between.

HOBBES' MORTALL GOD

Thomas Hobbes' theory of the commonwealth in his treatise *Leviathan* (1651), written in the wake of the Thirty Years' War (ending 1648) while Hobbes was in Paris during England's own Civil War, may be read as an example of this modern battle for sacred order against monstrous chaos in the political arena. For Hobbes, the primordial chaos that precedes the establishment of political order is the teeming pandemonium of individual wills, which, left to their own powers, tend toward a living nightmare of atomization, a state of war in which life is, as he famously put it, "solitary, poor, nasty, brutish and short." The commonwealth he envisions is a means of subordinating all that chaos of the state of nature, which is a state of war, to a single sovereign authority which would embody and speak for all individuals. Leviathan is the name Hobbes gives to this imagined sovereign lord to which all other chaotic, particular voices must submit. Its authority signifies the lack of authority of all civil subjects. Without Leviathan, their fragmenting, atomizing individualities pull inevitably in the direction of anarchic chaos. Hobbes' commonwealth is imagined as an embodiment of collective political order established against the specter of political chaos.

Hobbes' political theory, then, imagines the creation of the political order of the commonwealth in a way that parallels the cosmogonic narratives of biblical and other ancient Near Eastern traditions. Just as those narratives imagine the cosmos emerging out of or against primordial chaos, so here the political order of the commonwealth emerges out of and against a primordial social chaos. Hobbes' theory is poligonic in the same way those narratives are cosmogonic.

In fact, Hobbes' description of the procedure for creating a commonwealth in his opening paragraph is clearly drawn from the language of biblical cosmogony in Genesis 1, especially the creation of human life. Indeed, in this light he appears to be an early modern precursor to another unwitting monster creator, Victor Frankenstein. The human art of creating "artificiall life" in the form of an engine or a watch is, he writes, an imitation of "NATURE (the Art whereby God has made and governes the world)."[3] That is, the creations of modern technology parallel God's own work not only as creator but also as sustainer of the cosmic order. So also, Hobbes continues, in the realm of politics, human artifice is able to create an "Artificiall Man" which he names Leviathan, a political body made up of the individual parts of society.

> *Art* goes yet further, imitating that Rationall and most excellent worke of Nature, *Man*. For by Art is created that great LEVIATHAN called a COMMON-WEALTH, or STATE, (in Latin CIVITAS) which is but an Artificiall Man; though of greater stature and strength than the Naturall, for whose protection and defence it was intended.

Hobbes then presents something of an anatomy lesson on this Leviathan creature, the conclusion to which makes most explicit the parallel between God's creation of humankind in Genesis 1:27–28 and the modern human creation of a super-human political body which he calls Leviathan:

> the *Soveraignty* is an Artificiall *Soul*, as giving life and motion to the whole body; The *Magistrates*, and other *Officers* of Judicature and Execution, artificiall *Joynts*; *Reward* and *Punishment* (by which fastned to the seate of the Soveraignty, every joynt and member is moved to performe his duty) are the *Nerves*, that do the same in the Body Naturall; The *Wealth* and *Riches* of all the particular members, are the *Strength*; *Salus Populi* (the *peoples safety*) its *Businesse*; *Counsellors*, by whom all things needfull for it to know, are suggested unto it, are the *Memory*; *Equity* and *Lawes*, an artificiall *Reason* and *Will*; *Concord*, *Health*; *Sedition*, *Sicknesse*; and *Civill War*, *Death*. Lastly, the *Pacts* and *Covenants*, by which the parts of this Body Politique were at first made, set together, and united, resemble that

> *Fiat*, or the *Let us make man*, pronounced by God in the Creation.[4]

He uses the biblical language of covenant-making, moreover, to describe the method by which this great "Artificall Man" will be created: "This is more than Consent, or Concord; it is a reall Unitie of them all [all individuals], in one and the same Person, made by Covenant of every man with every man."[5] Hobbes is clearly aware of the biblical linkage of God's creation of the world and God's creation of Israel through covenant. Indeed, for Hobbes, this cutting of a covenant is the longhand for "that *Fiat*, or the *Let us make man*, pronounced by God in the Creation":

> *I Authorise and give up my Right of Governing my selfe, to this Man, or to this Assembly of men, on this condition, that thou give up thy Right to him, and Authorise all his Actions in like manner.* This done, the Multitude so united in one Person, is called a COMMON-WEALTH, in latine CIVITAS. This is the Generation of that great LEVIATHAN, or rather (to speake more reverently) of that Mortall God, to which wee owe under the Immortal God, our peace and defence. For by this Authoritie, given him by every particular man in the Common-Wealth, he hath the use of so much Power and Strength conferred on him, that by terror thereof, he is inabled to conforme the wills of them all to Peace at home, and mutuall ayd against their enemies abroad.

Hobbes thus conceives the commonwealth as a human creation, through covenant, of a sovereign "Body Politique" under which all particular human wills are subordinated. Indeed, it gets its power by absorbing all individual power, thereby becoming the singular author and governor of state order.

Hobbes expects, moreover, that this sovereign body politic, Leviathan, which stands for the order of the whole against the terror of individuals in the state of nature, will be an object of religious reverence, a "Mortall God" who is above all except the immortal creator God. And his power as mortal god is a kind of sublime power. What Hobbes conjures is an image of the *political sublime*, who rules by terror. "Peace" in this scenario is the absence of war at home and abroad, brought about by a justice that is synonymous with the imposition of social order at any cost. The terror of social chaos is overcome only by the greater terror of this one sovereign lord.

THEOPHANY

The title page for Hobbes' treatise provides a visual rendering of his sovereign Leviathan (Figure 7).[6] Insofar as Leviathan is to be a "Mortall God," we might go so far as call this picture a *theophany*, that is, a revelation of the divine body politic that Hobbes envisions in his political theory. Behold the crowned head of the great and sovereign Leviathan. He is gigantic, no doubt shaking the earth and trampling down the mountains as he walks, his arms spanning and his eyes gazing over town and country. His arms also span the series of symbols of church and state which run down the left and right sides of the lower half of the page, indicating his complete dominion over both spheres, from matters of war to matters of religious orthodoxy and divine judgment. This is an image of the political sublime which lords over military as well as religious authority and power.

On closer inspection we notice that the body of this great "Mortall God" is actually made from the bodies of those who give up their individual wills and rights in order that their power may conform to him. Leviathan is literally a "Body Politique," a single figure that embodies all members of the polis. The bodies of those very individuals who are prone to anarchy when left to their own desires are stitched together into the single body of the sovereign lord. Through the suture of all individual subjects, this body politic rules out anarchy.

This lord is, moreover, an unseen seer. He oversees all, yet none of those who are stitched into his body can see either him or the world he oversees. Their faces are turned inward, pressed so closely against one another and against Leviathan's splendid frame that they can see nothing. They comprise its very surface, its body armor, its *hide*. They live together as members of one political body by faith that he is there, watching over things for them, assured of things hoped for, convicted of things not seen. In an earlier drawing for Hobbes' title page, which served as the title page for the

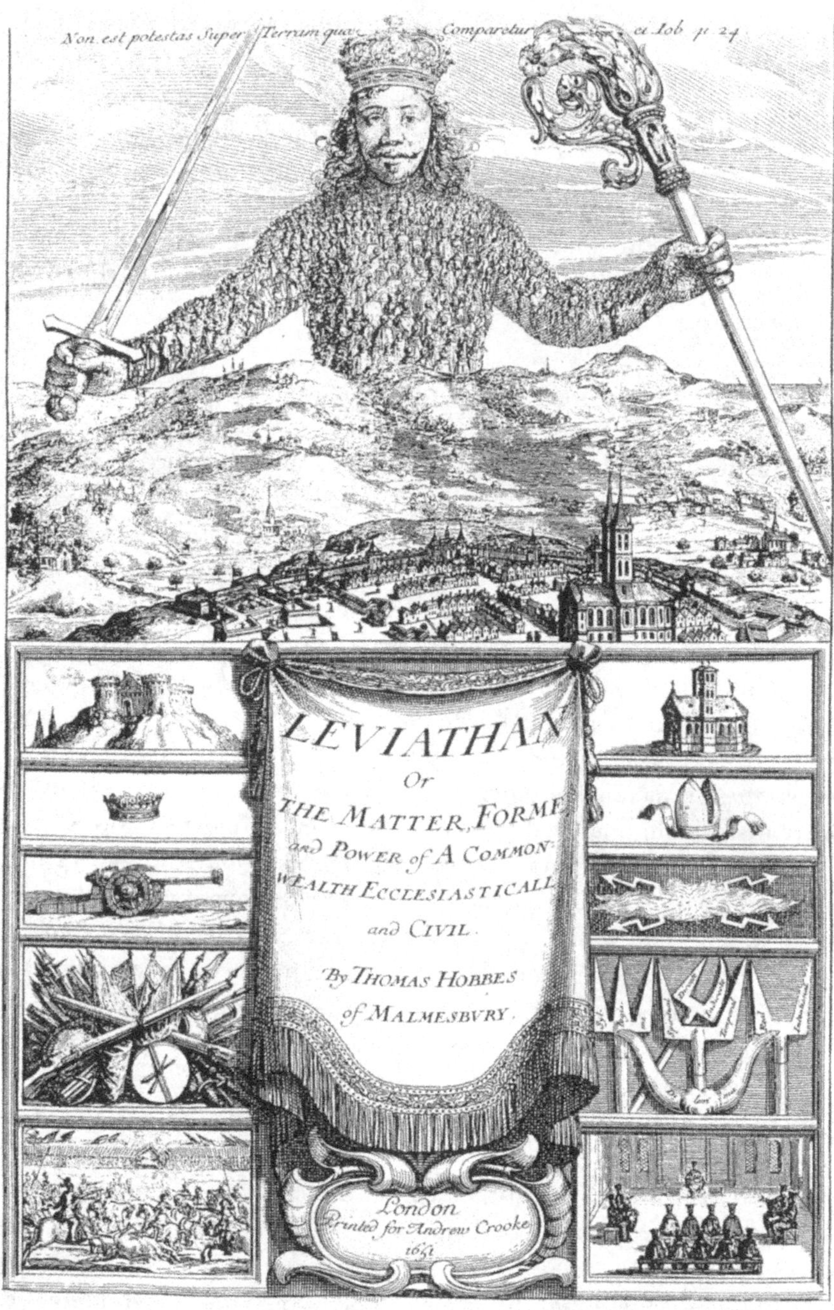

FIGURE 7. Original title page to Thomas Hobbes' *Leviathan* (London: Andrew Crooke, 1651), Kelvin Smith Library, Special Collections, Case Western Reserve University.

vellum prepublication copy which Hobbes sent to Charles II (but which was blocked by his advisor, Edward Hyde, Earl of Clarendon[7]), the heads are several times larger and they, like Leviathan, face outward. Their faces overlook the landscape *along with* Leviathan. This representation lends the individual members of the commonwealth a degree of agency that is altogether absent in the final frontispiece image, in which they are tiny and faceless, turned away from all oversight and absorbed into the body of Leviathan.

BUT WHY LEVIATHAN?

Why on earth did Hobbes name this sovereign overlord of political order against chaos after Leviathan? Leviathan is anything but an image of political order in biblical tradition, even when it is represented as part of God's creation. Indeed, in most biblical texts Leviathan is a chaos monster, sometimes even a monstrous personification of the enemy as chaotic threat to political order (Isaiah 27, Psalm 74). Why, then, does Hobbes choose this as a name for his "Mortall God" of political order?

It is not a matter of biblical illiteracy. In fact, Hobbes's *Leviathan* is as much a biblical-theological treatise as it is a political treatise, including well over six hundred biblical citations, and making several groundbreaking arguments about the nature and authority of Scripture. It comes as a surprise to many that Hobbes' *Leviathan*, like Benedict Spinoza's *Tractatus Theologico-Politicus* (1670), is an important early influence on modern biblical criticism as well as modern political theory and philosophy.[8] Arguing from the internal evidence of the biblical texts, for example, Hobbes points out that parts of the Torah, or the book of Moses, could not have been written by Moses (e.g., the account of his death in Deuteronomy 34). Indeed, Hobbes anticipated that his critics would attack his biblical-theological interpretations more than his political theories. In his dedication of *Leviathan* to the brother of his deceased colleague Sidney Godolphin, who "was pleas'd to think my studies something," he writes, "That which may most offend are certain Texts of Holy Scripture, alleged by me to other purpose than ordinarily they use to be by others."[9] Clearly, Hobbes understood that there were political stakes in biblical interpretation. But for him doing political theory meant doing biblical interpretation as well. The two were inseparable.

Why, then, if he knew his Bible, did he name this lord of political order against chaos Leviathan?

A clue is found in the text that runs across the top of the book's frontispiece. It is a quote from one of the last verses of the divine speech from the whirlwind in the Latin Vulgate version of the book of Job (41:24). There God is praising the incomparable power and glory of Leviathan: "*Non est potestas Super Terram quae Comparetur ei*," that is, "there is nothing on earth to be compared with him."[10] In fact, although Hobbes refers to his commonwealth by the name of Leviathan from the first page onward, this biblical quotation on the frontispiece is the only indication of what Hobbes means by his use of this name until we are well into the book. No biblical explication is given until the end of chapter 28, as a conclusion to his discussion of reward and punishment (which, you may recall, are the nerves and tendons of this great Body Politique), and as a lead-in to Leviathan's susceptibility to certain diseases (including sedition, the desire to decide for oneself concerning good and evil, and the subjection of the sovereign to civil laws). There, he includes a translation of the last two verses of the Latin text of Job 41, and explains how these verses are the basis for his use of the name Leviathan:

> Hitherto I have set forth the nature of Man, (whose Pride and other Passions have compelled him to submit himselfe to Government;) together with the great power of his Governour, whom I compare to *Leviathan*, taking that comparison out of the two last verses of the one and fourtieth of *Job*; where God having set forth the great power of *Leviathan*, calleth him King of the Proud. *There is nothing*, saith he, *on earth, to be compared with him. He is made so as not to be afraid. Hee seeth every high thing below him; and is King of all the children of pride*. But because he is mortall, and subject to decay, as all other Earthly creatures are; and because there is that in heaven, (though not on earth) that he should stand in fear of, and whose Lawes he ought to obey; I shall in the next following Chapters speak of his Diseases, and the causes of his Mortality; and of what Lawes of Nature he is bound to obey.[11]

The Leviathan that Hobbes has in mind, then, is the one God praises from the whirlwind, a Leviathan whose *fearless power* is superior to the rest of God's creation, including humankind. Fire-breathing, sea-boiling and other monstrous qualities aside, it is Leviathan's incomparable, terrifying and awe-inspiring power that Hobbes finds so compelling as a figure for his sovereign political body. In this text from Job, Leviathan is declared by God to be above all except God. So too, explains Hobbes, with his political Leviathan.

Hobbes reads the book of Job as a treatise on theodicy, which questions God's justice in the face of Job's unjustified and unjustifiable suffering. The divine answer from the whirlwind, according to Hobbes, is less an answer to Job's questioning than it is an overwhelming and silencing of Job by force. The question of theodicy in the book of Job, Hobbes writes, "is decided by God himselfe, not by arguments derived from *Job*'s Sinne, but his own Power. For whereas the friends of *Job* drew their arguments from his Affliction to his Sinne, and he defended himselfe by the conscience of his Innocence, God himselfe . . . justified the Affliction by arguments drawn from his Power, such as this, *Where were you when I layd the foundations of the earth*."[12] Job's questions concerning divine justice, or lack thereof, are not answered but obliterated by God. Recall that the quotation Hobbes gives as an example ("Where were you when I laid the foundations of the earth?") comes at the beginning of that overwhelming and subject-obliterating speech from the whirlwind. God's long poem in praise of Leviathan comes at the very end, as the climax of that speech. Leviathan, then, as Hobbes reads it, is the climactic figure of overwhelming and terrifying *divine power against justice*. It is an imposition of order without justice that puts the insubordinate, even subversive questioning of the individual to rest. Placed in the context of Hobbes' reading of the book of Job, his political Leviathan stands for the awful and awesome imposition of peace with or without justice.

AWE AND ORDER

So Hobbes hooks Leviathan by the snout and draws it out of the book of Job and into a new political arena, where it becomes the privileged figure for his "Mortall God" who would, by terror as necessary, subdue and conform the potential chaos of individuals in the state of nature under the rule of its sovereign head.

Hobbes thereby launches a new life for Leviathan in politics. Not that this was Leviathan's first time on the political scene, but it certainly was a radical departure from earlier appearances. Leviathan has made appearances as the monstrous representative of the enemy nation Babylon, whose destruction of Judah was conceived not only as a threat to the existence of God's people as a nation but also as a threat to the very order of God's creation (Psalm 74 and Isaiah 27). On those occasions Leviathan was the furthest thing from political order. In Hobbes' text, by contrast, Leviathan is not a chaos monster but the champion of political order against chaos. In this sense, Leviathan the "Mortall God" is envisioned in the role typically identified with the creator God in biblical tradition. This god maintains political order by subduing all chaotic forces under its rule.

The monster Hobbes fears most is an unruly populace, given over to chaos by their conflicting individual wills. For others, however, the real political monster is none other than Hobbes' Leviathan itself, whose primary means of rule is top-down power, often without regard for questions of justice. In fact, the idea that Hobbes' Leviathan is the real monster, whose rule will lead to political breakdown and chaos, goes back to Hobbes' own earliest critics, who are often as biblically literate as Hobbes and who do not miss the more chaotic and monstrous dimensions of Leviathan in biblical literature. George Lawson (1657), for example, argues against Hobbes that a commonwealth ought to be "a multitude of reasonable Men, not a Leviathan, which is an irrational brute," and later characterizes Hobbes' Leviathan as "the great monstrous animal . . . found to consist of an absolute power, and absolute slavery" who keeps the populace in "awe and order" by the sheer terror of its power alone.[13] Picking up on the tradition that understands Leviathan to be a biblical name for a whale, another contemporary, Bishop John Bramhall (1658), organizes his critique as a kind of chaos battle against Hobbes' Leviathan, in which he first pierces its heart (its religion), then its chin (its idea of the commonwealth) and finally its head (its rationality). Bramhall considers that the political "order" Leviathan would maintain would be a nightmarish reign of terror under the rule of a monstrous sovereign who "may lawfully kill a thousand innocents every morning for his breakfast."[14]

Indeed, in contemporary political discourse, one rarely comes across a positive, Hobbesian use of the name Leviathan, as godlike champion of order against chaos. Rather, as in the works of Hobbes' earliest critics, Leviathan has become synonymous with totalitarian state power that rules out all particular voices of dissent or difference by terrible force. Leviathan has come to represent the monster of hegemony.

HELLRAISER

This post-Hobbesian image of Leviathan as a monster of political hegemony has found its way not only into contemporary political discourse but also into contemporary horror. In Clive Barker's *Hellbound: Hellraiser II* (1988), the sequel to the extremely popular *Hellraiser* (1987), Leviathan is the name of the lord of the Labyrinth of Hell.[15] It is a figure of monstrous awe and order. Like the image of Leviathan on the frontispiece of Hobbes' book, this sovereign Leviathan hovers over its subjects who wander its mazy halls like lab rats (Figure 8). Its geometric diamond shape, its steely hardness, and its industrial machinelike appearance contrast sharply against these weak, disorderly, fleshy human subjects. Indeed, the apparently impenetrable hardness of this "God of flesh, hunger and desire" exposes what everyone else lacks and desires. And it does so in the most physical way, by messing with their skin, that is, their *hide*, peeling back sections of their faces and tummies, pinning them to other spots, and exposing the soft vulnerable flesh inside. The terror of Leviathan within the story world of *Hellraiser* lies in its power to expose, to *un-hide* the dreadful mortal weaknesses of its subordinate subjects. In the labyrinth of Leviathan's Hell, there is no hiding. Yet in the end, like the great Wizard of Oz, Leviathan and the underworld it rules turn out to be all in the mind. There is nothing hiding beneath Leviathan's own steely surfaces. It gains its power and its terror only from those subjects who subordinate themselves to it.

The Leviathan of *Hellbound* is anything but a chaos monster in the tradition of biblical and postbiblical tradition. Rather, its precursor is Hobbes' Leviathan, a monster of hegemony. This

FIGURE 8. Leviathan, Lord of the Labyrinth, in Clive Barker's *Hellbound: Hellraiser II*, Copyright 1988 New World Pictures.

Leviathan is a modern industrial monstrosity of awe and order within which soft-skinned humans get caught and torn apart. It is not a monstrous figure of chaos but a monstrous figure of order.

Hobbes believed that his *Leviathan* turned politics into a science in service of what Richard Tuck calls "the grand Hobbesian enterprise of liberating men from terror."[16] In other words, *Leviathan* was intended to be an awakening of reason to stop the production of monsters. Leviathan was not supposed to be a chaos monster but a chaos tamer, a mortal god of political order against chaos. For others, however, on the other end of modernity, this awakening of reason has awakened a new monster in old biblical skins: Leviathan the order monster.

CHAPTER 8

Other Gods

ORIENTALISM AND ITS MONSTERS

Banqueting plans of the ancient rabbis notwithstanding, most of us do not knowingly invite monsters to dinner. Generally speaking they are not very good guests. Not only are their table manners and diets often atrocious, but they never seem quite able to avoid mixing religion and politics.

Sewn together from various cultural and political images of the unknowable and unthinkable, the monster often appears as an index of all that a particular culture projects as beyond its pale.[1] Monsters are conglomerations of many different forms of otherness—cosmological, political, psychological and religious otherness.

So it is that one culture's gods can become another culture's monsters. This is one way to look at the history of western colonialism, making monsters out of other people's gods. Americans and western Europeans often have made their monsters from other people's gods, that is, from the gods of unfamiliar, "other" religious traditions. The fact that their travel narratives employ a vocabulary of the monstrous that is strikingly close to that of Gothic horror films and literature is no coincidence. It indicates a deep historical relationship in modern western culture between religion, orientalism and the popular culture of horror. In fact, monsters on the silver screen often reflect a long history of western European reactions to religious ideas and practices that diverge from the familiar and normative.

Let me begin with the Winged Monkeys of *The Wizard of Oz* (1939), who will provide a passage to India which, while unknown to most of *Oz*'s audiences even today, comes as no surprise to anyone familiar with Hindu religious traditions.

THE WITCH'S MONKEYS

For many of us growing up in the United States during the 1950s, '60s and '70s, the annual television airing of *The Wizard of Oz* was a national ritual event on par with Thanksgiving or the Fourth of July. Every year in the late fall, a major network (CBS from 1956 to 1967; and NBC from 1968 to 1976) would show the movie as a prime-time family feature. Every year I looked forward to it for weeks, hoping this time to be able to make it through the entire movie. The obstacle: getting past the Wicked Witch's Winged Monkeys (Figure 9). As soon as they took to the air, even before they began ripping the stuffing out of poor Scarecrow, I had to leave the room. Those monkeys chased me out of the road to Oz and pursued me into my dreams, their blue faces smiling and nodding all the way. For me, as for many others, the Winged Monkeys seemed to stand for, or rather *fly* for, a terrible and mysterious violence lurking along the edges of the right order of things and rustling amid the forest bushes at every turn.

Still, every fall I would approach the threshold of the Witch's window, the threshold of that scene in the movie once again, hoping finally to pass through it and get to Oz. When I finally did, it was a letdown. I now know that those flying monkeys were not only the most terrifying; they were also the most fascinating. They were the mystery that was not dissolved with water, the curious tug of a curtain or a reawakening in the gray Kansas morning. In retrospect I think I was coming back to *The Wizard of Oz* each year not in hope of getting past them but in hope of meeting them one more time—in hope of encountering something monstrous, something that exceeded my own sense of security within the theological and moral system in which I lived and breathed and had my being.

FIGURE 9. Commander of the Winged Monkeys in *The Wizard of Oz*, Copyright 1939 Metro-Goldwyn-Mayer.

Like other monsters, the Winged Monkeys of *The Wizard of Oz* were created by stitching together various mutually incompatible identities and othernesses into a single body. Indeed, they are complex embodiments of category-jamming: admixtures of human, land animal and bird (monkeys, with wings, in human clothing, who understand human language), thus blurring traditional categories of zoological identity, not to mention fundamental modern western distinctions between animality and humanity, wilderness and civilization, invading chaos and military order.

These monsters, moreover, have religious precedents, that is, they are also drawn from images of religious otherness. As has long been noted, they bear some resemblance to the mysterious winged, monkey-like gargoyles on the Cathedral of Notre Dame. What has been far less obvious to most western viewers, however, is the degree to which they are drawn from a figure of Hindu religious tradition, namely Hanuman, the heroic commander of the monkey army and helpmate of Rama who is celebrated in the *Ramayana* and later folklore (Figure 10).[2]

RAMA'S MONKEYS

The *Ramayana* (c. 400 BCE–300 CE) is the story of Rama's coming into the world (*Rama + yana*, "the coming of Rama"), the establishment of his dharmic rule (*ramarajya*), and his final return to heaven to resume identity as Viṣnu. Hanuman enters the story when the chaos demon Ravana kidnaps Sita, Śiva's daughter, who is married to Rama. He carries her away from the forest where he found her and holds her captive in his island fortress, threatening to kill her if she does not submit to him within a year's time. Already we can see parallels between Ravana and the Wicked Witch, and between Sita and Dorothy. But whereas in *The Wizard of Oz* the Winged Monkeys kidnap Dorothy at the Witch's bidding, this flying monkey Hanuman is the hero, saving Sita and ultimately defeating the wicked Ravana.

Hanuman, the leader of the monkey scouts who are sent to determine Sita's whereabouts, goes to her by leaping across the sea to her island prison. In one of the most popular episodes, while on the island, Ravana sets Hanuman's tail on fire (compare the Witch's threats to torch the Scarecrow in her castle) and Hanuman proceeds to torch the island with it. Upon his return, he explains to

FIGURE 10. *Hanuman*. South India, Chola period, 12th century. Bronze, H. 58.4 cm. Copyright The Cleveland Museum of Art, 2001, John L. Severance Fund, 1980.26.

Rama that the faithful Sita has only two months to live. A great battle against Ravana ensues, in which Rama and his ally Lakmana are saved from certain defeat when Hanuman brings them an entire mountain of restorative herbs.[3] They are revived, Rama slays Ravana, Sita is rescued and Rama's dharmic rule is established. Hanuman has saved the day, and the world.

Unlike the Winged Monkeys of *Oz*, then, this monkey flies, or long-jumps, for the good guys. Rather than capturing Dorothy in the forest and flying her back to the Witch's castle, he leaves his forest community and soars across the ocean to find Rama's partner Sita who is a captive in Ravana's castle. And rather than scattering Scarecrow's straw guts all over the trail through the Haunted Forest, Hanuman carries a mountain of healing herbs to the enchanted forest in order to revive Rama's vanquished army.

HORRID CHAMBERS OF IMAGERY

Hanuman is much beloved and celebrated in India. Stories about him are very popular among children and adults alike. Images of him (often colored blue and wearing clothing that indicates his position as commander of the monkey army) are among the most familiar within Hindu religious iconography, from large paintings and sculptures to children's coloring books.

Yet in many popular journals, books, and lectures of western European and American travelers to India over the past few centuries, he has been represented as a monster through the deployment of a vocabulary of horror that most of us are more accustomed to seeing in Gothic novels. In his 1897 lectures on India, for example, John L. Stoddard describes his visit to what he calls "the Monkey Temple," a temple to Hanuman, in which he and his companions, like Dorothy and her fellow travelers in the Haunted Forest, were surrounded by "a mob of long-tailed, simian deities . . . as they blinked their eyes, fought and chattered for the sweetmeats, and pulled each other's tails in a most ungodly manner."[4] Likewise, in her 1898 missionary travel journal, *Across India at the Dawn of the 20th Century,* Lucy E. Guinness is appalled by the many images of what she considers to be a monstrous god, "an inconceivably odious object . . . He is the monkey god, a shapeless scarlet idol, big or little as chance may choose, but always disgustingly ugly—a headless, limbless, formless mass, with a distant approach to the design of a sitting figure, always daubed with scarlet and regarded with reverent awe."[5]

Such horror-stricken American and European reactions to Indian religious visual culture at the dawn of the twentieth century were not limited to Hanuman, as Stoddard's general impression of the images of deities in India clearly attests:

> All of the idols on the banks of the river are hideous; some are obscene; while a few are distinguished by the expression which one is apt to assume when the photographer asks one "to look pleasant" . . . Many of those that have their origin in India are too disgusting to be illustrated, and some of the carvings on the temples of Benares are too vile to be described. Pictured and read on the other side of the globe, viewed through the long perspective of a score of centuries, discussed in a transcendental way in a "Parliament of Religions," and judged of merely by its original sacred writings, the Hindu faith appears to some a fine and wonderful religion . . . But scrutinize it practically, face to face, in India, and it becomes the most repulsive exhibition of idolatry, fanaticism, and filth that one can well imagine.[6]

Even Mark Twain, in his *Following the Equator* (1897), diverges momentarily from his usual sarcastic style of commentary on religion when he describes the visual theology of the "Hindoos":

> In fact, none of the idols in Benares are handsome or attractive. And what a swarm of them there is! The town is a vast museum of idols—and all of them crude, misshapen, and ugly. They flock through one's dreams at night, a wild mob of nightmares. When you get tired of them in the temples and take a trip on the river, you find idol giants, flashily painted, stretched out side by side on the shore.[7]

For these travelers, India's exceedingly rich and varied religious imagination was the stuff of nightmares, and the sacred city of Banaras was a religious house of horrors. Deploying a highly condensed vocabulary of monstrosity, disgust and religious horror (focused through the biblical lens of prohibitions against idolatry), Guinness writes,

> Phantasmagoria—such as it seems, a strange incredible dream—yet is it a reality. Benares! . . . O India! thy darkness is not the darkness of mere ignorance, but the darkness of lies, fantastic lies, foul lies, leprous lies, diabolical lies . . . thy gods are groveling, bestial; with swollen bellies, black faces, elephant snouts, and protruding tongues, they glower on their worshippers from filthy shrines; their name is legion, their legends infamous and monstrous . . . Who shall bring thee forth from thy dark prison-house, from thy horrid chambers of imagery . . . ?[8]

For many American and European travelers to India and elsewhere over the past several centuries (even today), encounters with religious otherness, that is, with unfamiliar religious ideas and practices, especially images of other gods, are translated for readers back home as experiences of dread horror in the face of monsters. One might suspect that the use of this language of the monstrous in such representations of encounters with unfamiliar religions is due to the pervasive influence of Gothic horror literature in the West since the beginning of the nineteenth century. One might suspect, that is, that this language in travel narratives has been borrowed from the Gothic genre. It is not so simple, however, because behind *both* modern Gothic horror and these horrified reactions of modern travelers is a great cloud of European witnesses over the past five centuries, who have demonized non-Christian, non-western religions by representing their gods as horrific monsters of biblical proportions, especially in terms of the diabolical dragon and its beasts from the Apocalypse of John.

DIABOLICAL MONSTERS

Fantastic tales of encounters with monsters while traveling in Asia go back at least as far as the late thirteenth and fourteenth centuries, with the accounts of Marco Polo, Odoric de Pordenone and

Sir John Mandeville. Their tall tales, given visual representation in the early fifteenth-century *Livre des merveilles* and numerous other popular book illustrations, conjure frightful and fascinating images of strange places populated by monsters: Marco Polo's fabulous dragons of Carajan and his legendary monsters of Merkites (Figures 11 and 12); Odoric's cycocephales on the Nicobar islands (Figure 13), and his famous corpse-strewn "perilous valley," in which there lives a winged devil-monster holding several souls captive (Figure 14), and which Mandeville would later claim was one of the mouths of Hell.[9] Often these descriptions and depictions are drawn from the imagery of the devil-dragon and beasts in the Apocalypse of John. Compare, for example, Polo's dragons with the dragon of the Apocalypse of John depicted in the Cloisters Apocalypse (pictured earlier, 5).

One of the most well-known and widely copied representations of an Indian deity as diabolically monstrous was the so-called God of Calicut described by Lodovico de Varthema. First published in Italian in 1510, over the next century his *Itinerario* was published in many different editions and was translated into every major European language.[10] Indeed, for many Europeans, Varthema's God of Calicut came to epitomize India's theological imagination and its indigenous religious practices as devotion to diabolical monstrosity. Varthema describes an image of "Deumo" (*dêvan*, godling or local deity) which he purports to have encountered in a small chapel at the home of his Indian host, the "King of Calicut."

> [H]is chapel is two paces wide in each of the four sides, and three paces high, with a wooden door covered with devils carved in relief. In the midst of this chapel there is a devil made of metal, placed in a seat also made of metal. The said devil has a crown made like that of the papal kingdom, with three crowns; and it also has four horns and four teeth, with a very large mouth, nose and most terrible eyes. The hands are made like those of a flesh-hook, and the feet like those of a cock; so that he is a fearful object to behold. All the pictures around the said chapel are those of devils, and on each side of it there is a Sathanas [Satan] seated in a seat, which seat is placed in a flame of fire, wherein are a great number of souls, of the

FIGURE 11. *Le livre des merveilles*, folio 55 verso, Marco Polo's dragons of Carajan.

FIGURE 12. *Le livre des merveilles*, folio 29 verso, Marco Polo's monsters of Merkites.

FIGURE 13. *Le livre des merveilles*, folio 106, Odoric's cycocephales on the Nicobar islands.

FIGURE 14. *Le livre des merveilles*, folio 115, Odoric's "perilous valley."

> length of half a finger and a finger of the hand. And the said Sathanas holds a soul in his mouth with the right hand, and with the other seizes a soul under the waist.[11]

Partha Mitter rightly points out that Varthema's language here draws heavily on medieval Hell and last judgment imagery. For the most part, he writes, this scene is "lifted from popular pictures of hell, where the towering figure of Satan was often shown sitting in the middle and devouring sinners while his attendant creatures tortured the damned."[12] Indeed, the woodcut illustration by the Augsburg artist Jörg Breu the Elder represents the scene described by Varthema as a kind of diabolical liturgy (Figure 15). The devil's meal of devotees is set in the context of a worship service in which a woman wafts incense toward it with a censer reminiscent of those used in the Roman Catholic Church. Breu's illustration combines common European visual signals for diabolical monstrosity with common European visual signals for Christian worship. As a result the scene becomes one of admixture, combining religious otherness (the biblical monstrous-diabolical-apocalyptic) and religious sameness (Christian worship).[13]

What might Varthema actually have been seeing? Part of the mix appears to be inspired by an image of Kali, the fierce goddess of auspicious endings, often depicted with a blood-red tongue and adorned with severed heads. But it is impossible to determine exactly what Indian religious image lay behind Varthema's description. The main reason is that what he describes is far less Indian than it is biblical. What he "saw" was his own projection of a devil monster of the Apocalypse.

Subsequent travel accounts frequently appropriated Varthema's God of Calicut, often amplifying the biblical apocalyptic imagery in the process. In his popular late sixteenth-century itinerary, for example, Jan Huygen van Linschoten's description of the "idol of Calicut" is clearly an embellishment of Varthema's scene, adding an extra face and a few other dreadful features to the monster god, expanding its tiny chapel into a full-blown church—complete with a "Sancta Sanctorium, or rather Diabolorium"—and making explicit the biblical reference to the Apocalypse of John.

FIGURE 15. Illustration of the God of Calicut by Jörg Breu the Elder in a 1515 Augsburg edition of Varthema, *Die Ritterlich un[d] lobwirdig Rayss*, i iii, John Carter Brown Library (repr. Scholars' Facsimiles & Reprints, 1992).

> At last wee came into a Village, where stoode a great Church of stone, wherein wee entered, and found nothing in it but a great [picture] that hung in the middle of the Church [with the Image of a Pagode painted therein] so mishaped and deformed, that more monsterous was never seene, for it had many horns, and long teeth that hung out of his mouth down to the knees, and beneath his Navel and belly it had an other such like face, with many hornes and tuskes. Uppon the head thereof stood a [triple Crowned] Myter, not much unlike the Popes triple crown, so that in effect it seemed to be a monster [such as are described] in the Apocalips.[14]

By the turn of the seventeenth century, then, we find a fairly standard European representation, in word and image, of Indian religion as worship of apocalyptic devil-monsters. This standard representation is based not on the wide-ranging historical and cultural particularities and rich complexities of the religious visual cultures of India, which are far from homogeneous, but on stock terms and conventional images taken from European traditions of biblical interpretation, especially from written descriptions and illustrations of the devil-dragon and its beasts in the Apocalypse of John.[15] This kind of homogenization of a wide range of cultural differences in terms of a more familiar image of monstrous otherness is a common strategy within colonial discourse. As Homi K. Bhabha points out, such a strategy "produces the colonized as a social reality which is at once an 'other' and yet entirely knowable and visible."[16] The translation of cultural, especially *religious* differences encountered by European travelers in India into biblical apocalyptic terms of monstrosity achieves precisely this end: it projects an image of *familiar otherness*, and thereby orients and stabilizes the identity of western, European, Christian, modern, civilized (non-primitive, non-ritualistic) society against that projected image—at the expense, of course, of other people's gods and their vital religious practices.

SUBLIME MONSTERS

As in other forms of colonial discourse, representations of "oriental" religions and their deities as monstrous works to *orient* western, occidental religious identity. These representations supply western culture with projections of an absolute and homogeneous otherness, an absolutely not-us, against which it can locate itself with greater stability, homogeneity and purity. At the same time, this colonial discourse identifies the colonizers with the holy armies of God and the forces of light, enlightenment and cosmic redemption, fighting a chaos battle of apocalyptic proportions. By demonizing these other religions, this discourse helps to justify colonial expansion as holy war.

Like the monsters of Gothic horror, the representation of another god as monstrous has a disciplinary effect, pulling its viewers away from it and back into the center of the order of things, encouraging them to shore up their own identity in terms of established religious norms.[17] Yet the vertiginous space of the monstrous solicits fascination as well as fear and repulsion. In eighteenth- and nineteenth-century European reactions to Indian religious iconography, for example, this desire manifests itself in a new category of aesthetic and religious experience, the sublime, especially as developed by Edmund Burke (1754) and Immanuel Kant (1790).[18] The idea of the sublime emphasizes the overwhelming sense of awe and wonder that one might experience in an encounter with something that defies comprehension. Often explicitly related to religious experience, the sublime is characterized as that which defies comprehension by reason or imagination. Shrouded in power, vastness and obscurity, the sublime solicits a non-rational combination of desire and fear.

Mitter documents the emergence of the sublime as an alternative category of aesthetic judgment to beauty in European descriptions and depictions of Indian religious iconography from the middle of the eighteenth century onward, revealing how a colonial discourse of *sublime monstrosity* takes its place alongside the earlier language of diabolic monstrosity. The tone of this emerging discourse is, moreover, unmistakably religious. One early nineteenth-century traveler, for example, describes "mythological symbols and figures" that "leave no room for doubt their owing their existence to religious zeal, the most powerful and most universal agitator of the human mind." Another recounts how the gloomy, gigantic stone figures at the temple of Elephanta impress the mind "with that kind of uncertain religious awe with which the grander works of ages of darkness are generally contemplated."[19]

In fact, this discourse of the monstrous sublime is not only an alternative category of aesthetic judgment, but also a well established biblical category of religious experience, expressed, for example, in psalms that depict God leveling mountains and snapping timbers like twigs, and in the divine voice from the whirlwind in the book of Job, praising the incomprehensible glory of Leviathan. It is, moreover, essentially this idea of the sublime as overwhelming, aweful mystery that Rudolph Otto, a post-Kantian religion scholar who traveled extensively in India and throughout Asia, would call the *mysterium tremendum*.

DISORIENTAL MONSTERS

In the twentieth century, the idea of the sublime often merges with a kind of exoticism that romanticizes earlier monstrous representations of the gods and rituals of unfamiliar, "non-western" religions.[20]

Although working largely from inherited colonialist projections of "oriental" gods and rituals as monstrous, this discourse of colonial exoticism embraces and identifies with those projections as a means of critiquing or *disorienting* established religious and cultural norms of the "West." In this discourse, then, oriental monsters are embraced as *disoriental* monsters.

This exoticizing of colonial projections of other religions as monstrous is one pole of modern primitivism. In modern primitivism, the responses of desire and fear, fascination and repulsion, are polarized into two cultural discourses: first, what Marie-Denise Shelton calls the "official" imperial discourse, which affirms modern western culture "as the perfect and ultimate state of humanity"; and second, the "poetic" discourse, which identifies with these colonized, "primitive" others as a means of condemning the modern West as "deficient and moribund."[21] The polarized discourses of "official" and "poetic" primitivism closely parallel the earlier discourses that I have described as the monstrous-diabolic and the monstrous-sublime. On the one hand, like those colonial texts that make other gods into apocalyptic devil-monsters, "official" primitivism continues to demonize unfamiliar religious deities and practices as images of western horror, thereby legitimating continued colonial expansion, which these days takes the form of post-national globalism. On the other hand, "poetic" primitivism imbues these same colonialist projections of religious otherness with a kind of monstrous sublimity that is intended to expose the West as desacralized, abstract and alienating. As in "official" primitivism, then, the gods of "primitive" or "oriental" religions are often represented as monstrous, but with a radically different aim: not to orient but to disorient.

Here we find a modern poetics of incantation, in which the image of primitive and/or oriental (these days conveniently conflated into the category of "non-western") religious monstrosity is conjured in order to crack open a calcified, depraved occident.

We see this kind of "poetic" primitivism operating in the visual arts of Picasso and Gauguin, for example. We also see it in the interwar period among thinkers like Georges Bataille, Michael Leiris, Roger Caillois and the others involved in the Collège de Sociologie and the journal *Acéphale* ("headless"). Drawing heavily from anthropological studies of non-western myths and "primitive" religious practices, they pursued a sort of Nietzschian, post-

Christian "sacred sociology" that would break open the rigidly repressive and increasingly fascistic modern West.[22] Throughout his writings, Bataille in particular sustained fervent interest in non-western religious practices, which he took to be expressions of a holy excess and effervescence, an "accursed share" of the sacred that was not reducible to use value within the order of things. In his *Theory of Religion*, Bataille describes religion as an expression of "the search for lost intimacy" which is associated with the sleep of reason and the arousing of monstrosity: "You are not any more different from me than your right leg is from your left, but what joins us is THE SLEEP OF REASON—WHICH PRODUCES MONSTERS."[23] In this passage, the sleep of reason, which signifies a lapse in the vigilant maintenance of the modern order of things, and which in Francisco Goya's famous etching signifies the awakening of terror, is here embraced as the way to a sacred intimacy. The religious search for lost intimacy is thus associated with sacred monstrosity against modern western reason and objectivity.

Similarly Antonin Artaud's exuberant *The Theater and Its Double* (1938) calls for a "return to primitive Myths" that can break through the abstracted, "calcinated" forms of occidental language and life, reawakening a "continuous creation, a wholly magical action" within which "we have sacrificed our little human individuality, like Personages out of the Past, with powers rediscovered in the Past."[24] Artaud conceives this reawakening as an embrace of vital, cosmogonic, mythic languages identified with non-western cultures, which he describes in terms that often draw together the divine, the sacred, the primitive and the monstrous as an object of nostalgia. The theater must create new, old myths, "interpreted according to the most ancient texts drawn from old Mexican, Hindu, Judaic, and Iranian cosmogonies . . . These gods or heroes, *these monsters*, these natural and cosmic forces will be interpreted according to images from the most ancient sacred texts and old cosmogonies."[25] Popularized during the first third of the twentieth century through publications like James Frazer's *The Golden Bough* (1890–1915) and through a growing mass of anthropological and mythological studies, these "most ancient sacred texts and old cosmogonies" of gods, monsters and monster gods were seen by Artaud as a way of rejuvenating and resacralizing what he believed to be an inert and ossified West.

Like others, Artaud tends to equate *ancient* religion with *primitive* religion. The logic of this equation is rooted in nineteenth-century anthropology of religion, especially that of E. B. Tylor. Noticing similarities among various myths and rituals throughout the world, Tylor posited his theory of the essential "psychic unity" of all humankind. Because of this fundamental sameness of all human minds, all human cultures must go through the same basic phases of cultural evolution. Therefore, the logic goes, similarities between two different cultures indicate that these two cultures are at the same basic evolutionary stage. Likewise, major differences between two different cultures would indicate that they are at different stages on the continuum of cultural evolution. Assuming, as Tylor and others did, that modern western culture was the most "advanced" along this developmental line, more "primitive" (that is, less modern) cultures were interpreted to be more archaic. For Artaud and others, then, it follows that we moderns can discover in these so-called primitive cultures our own origin, our own *arche*. In their myths and rituals we can discover the essential *arche*types of humanity. By the early twentieth century, much of Tylor's work had been thoroughly interrogated, complicated and often abandoned by other anthropologists and historians of religion. Nonetheless, his ideas persist in the modern association of the primitive with the archaic to this day.

In the poetic primitivism of Artaud, Bataille and others, the religious otherness that is repulsed as monstrous in earlier colonial discourse as a means of *orienting* and stabilizing modern western society is embraced as a means of *disorienting* and *resacralizing* that society, of breaking it up in order to open new possibilities. In many respects, then, "official" primitivism and "poetic" primitivism are two sides of the same colonial coin. For both sides, the gods and rituals of "primitive" cultures are often represented as monstrous threats to modern western identity. The difference is that while one side condemns and banishes this monstrous threat, the other hosts it. The monstrosity that you have rejected is the monstrosity that I embrace. What is accursed to you is sacred to me. This desire to embrace such projections of monstrous otherness is in a way apocalyptic, a solicitation of chaogony expected to usher in the end of the world as westerners have come to know it in order that something radically new might be born. It is a call for the ungrounding and unhoming of oneself, one's culture and one's world. Here the sacred is associated not with order but with chaos, not with the champion of the chaos battle who slays the monster but with the chaos monster itself.

In the course of these cultural transformations, no matter how radical, we must not forget that the image of divine monstrosity that is being embraced in these discourses is an image of the "primitive," the "oriental" and/or the "non-western" that is more a projection of one's own religious otherness than it is a reflection of another religion. It is not an embrace of that religion in its cultural and historical particularity. Rather, it is a western projection of it. Although often politically radical and transgressive, such embraces of monstrous otherness are themselves caught in the embrace of the even wider arms of a long and pervasive history of colonialism.

CHAPTER 9

The Blood Is the Life

RITUAL PURITY AND DANGER IN *DRACULA*

[Renfield] was lying on his belly on the floor licking up, like a dog, the blood which had fallen from my wounded wrist . . . "The blood is the life! the blood is the life!"

—Bram Stoker, *Dracula*[1]

Only be sure that thou eat not of the blood: for the blood is the life.

—Deuteronomy 12:23[2]

And the leper in whom the plague is, his clothes shall be rent, and his head bare, and he shall put a covering upon his upper lip, and shall cry, Unclean, unclean.

—Leviticus 13:45

[Mina Harker] sank on her knees on the floor in an agony of abasement. Pulling her beautiful hair over her face, as the leper of old his mantle, she wailed out:—

"Unclean! Unclean! Even the Almighty shuns my polluted flesh!"

—*Dracula*[3]

Bram Stoker's *Dracula* (1897) is a story of English ritual purity and danger. In this novel, it is the purity of Victorian English culture, especially its modern gentleman patriarchs and their beloved and lovely women, that is endangered by the contaminating effects of Count Dracula. Dracula is presented as a monstrous embodiment of all that modern England projects as other, not-us. His coming is represented as an invasion of unclean otherness that threatens national purity one female body at a time. This monstrous threat of contamination is conveyed in the novel through priestly biblical terms of purity and danger, and much of the story concerns the ritual means employed by the monster-slaying heroes in order to eradicate that contamination and thereby resacralize England as the sacred cosmic and political center of creation.

THE COUNT'S RELIGION

Much like the novel itself, which is pieced together as a collection of dated journal entries, transcribed audio recordings, letters and newspaper clippings from a variety of sources, Stoker's monster is pieced together from various elements of cultural otherness, a conglomeration of tabooed and *unheimlich* identities and behaviors that would have been perceived as threatening to modern Victorian English identity and national stability at the turn of the twentieth century. Dracula is a personification of an invasive cultural not-us, what Nina Auerbach calls "a compendium of fin-de-siècle phobias."[4] Indeed, that Dracula is *not good English* is signaled in the most literal way by his non-naturalized and artificial use of modern English language. Jonathan Harker's first impression when he visits Dracula at his castle in Transylvania is that he speaks "in excellent English, but with a strange intonation."[5] Dracula wants to pass as English, he confides to Jonathan, but fears that someone will hear him speak and cry out, "Ha, ha! a stranger!"[6] That Dracula's English is not good indicates the more ominous sense in which this monster, who is about to take up residency in London, is not good English.

But the heart and soul of this monstrous personification of cultural otherness, the heart and soul of Dracula, is deeply religious. That this monster has deep religious roots is indicated by his very name, which identifies him with the biblical tradition of diabolical monstrosity, especially with the great devil-dragon of the

Apocalypse of John. Count Dracula was named after the Romanian Prince Vlad of Wallachia (d. 1476), famous for impaling enemies and his own nobility on stakes around his castle. His family crest bore the Order of the Dragon, or *dracul*. His father was Vlad Dracul, or Vlad the Dragon, and he himself was called Vlad Dracula or Vlad the Son of Dracul.[7] In Romanian, moreover, the word *dracul* can mean either "the dragon" or "the devil." This association of dragon and devil probably derives from the diabolical dragon in the Apocalypse of John, who is introduced as "the great dragon [Greek *drakon*, Latin *draco*], that ancient serpent who is called the Devil and Satan" (12:9; 20:2). Thus the name of Stoker's monster identifies him not only with a legendary ruler and his reign of terror but also with a long line of diabolical dragons in English literary and religious tradition: from the dragon that is killed by St. George, the patron saint of England, back to the gold-hoarding dragon (*draca*) that kills and is killed by Beowulf, and back to the great devil-dragon of the Apocalypse who is defeated by the archangel Michael and ultimately sent to the abyss by God.

Yet Dracula is by no means reducible to the diabolical. At several points, in fact, he is described in distinctly biblical terms that suggest a certain divine semblance. When Jonathan recounts seeing Dracula crawling along the outside wall of the castle, for example, he asks in despair, "What manner of man is this?"[8] This is precisely the same question that is voiced by Jesus' disciples in Matthew 8 when he awakes from his sleep aboard their boat and calms the stormy seas. Later in the novel, Dracula, too, demonstrates his command over the elements (albeit stirring them up rather than calming them down) while sleeping aboard the ship bound for England. At another point, Mina describes his appearance in her bedroom as a "pillar of cloud," which is one of the forms God takes while guiding the people of Israel in the wilderness during their exodus from Egypt (Exodus 13:21). Mina thus envisions the coming of Dracula in a traditional biblical form of divine presence. These representations of Dracula in terms of divinity work against reducing him to a simple diabolical figure of the anti-God. He is, rather, a dangerous admixture good and evil, divine and demonic, holy and accursed. "For it is not the least of its terrors that this evil thing is rooted deep in all good; in soil barren of holy memories it cannot rest."[9]

Stoker's novel is, moreover, deeply embedded in the larger discourses of late colonialism and primitivism, and his monster is in many respects a projection of modern western representations of unfamiliar religious traditions. In fact, the novel's first four chapters are strikingly reminiscent of the late nineteenth-century travel narratives discussed in the previous chapter. In the novel, we read Jonathan's dated journal entries recounting his initial voyage into the unfamiliar, non-occidental and religiously primitive Transylvanian homeland of the Count. As the name of the region suggests (*trans* + *silva*, "across" or "beyond the wilderness"), this region is presented as an unstable and dislocating threshold space between the occidental and the oriental. In the first paragraph of his journal, Jonathan Harker writes, "The impression I had was that we were leaving the West and entering the East," crossing over by way of a bridge whose architecture he describes as "most Western."[10] The particular district in which the Count's castle is situated, moreover, is simultaneously in the easternmost region of the West and a borderland between regions: "I find that the district he named is in the extreme east of the country, just on the borders of three states, Transylvania, Moldavia, and Bukovina, in the midst of the Carpathian mountains; one of the wildest and least known portions of Europe."[11] As the story begins, Jonathan's travel journal accumulates a disorienting collection of terms connoting both easternness and betweenness. As a result, the geographical location of Dracula's home is that of otherness within sameness: the East within the West, the Orient within the Occident, accessible by a "most Western" bridge. It is neither inside nor outside. It is both inside and outside.

The religious identity of Dracula's homeland likewise represents otherness within sameness. It is a land steeped in Christian religious traditions that are represented as primitive, non-western and non-English. Jonathan locates it in a horseshoe of the mountains that is commonly known to be the center of the storm of primitive religious ideas and practices from around the world: "I read that every known superstition in the world is gathered into the horseshoe of the Carpathians, as if it were the centre of some imaginative whirlpool."[12] The geographical strangeness of Dracula's region is thus linked to religious ideas and practices that are foreign to a modern Protestant "English Churchman" like Jonathan but that are nonetheless Christian. As such, this foreign form of Christianity—including its folk traditions of vampires and the undead, of which Dracula is presented as living dead proof—is a figure of the *unheimlich* within Christianity. It is an other, non-western, primitive Christianity that threatens Christianity's place within the modern, scientific West. As Professor Van Helsing later explains, "the old centuries had, and have powers of their own which mere 'modernity' cannot kill."[13] Still later, he makes Dracula's identification with the supernatural, non-rational powers of this threateningly primitive Christianity most explicit: "The very place where he have been alive, Un-Dead for all these centuries, is full of strangeness."[14] Dracula and his homeland are thus projected as *primitive religious otherness within*, a dreadfully monstrous return of the repressed within modern English Christianity that cannot be reduced to scientific explanation.

Stoker's personification of Dracula in terms of a monstrously threatening religious otherness is not limited, however, to his identification with these projections of primitive, non-western Christianity. As Judith Halberstam has shown, Dracula is also represented, in certain respects, as a personification of anti-Semitic caricatures of European Jewish identity. These stereotypes are particularly evident in references to Dracula's relation to money (especially gold), to his parasitism, to his moral degeneracy, and to what Jonathan calls his "very marked physiognomy," including a hooked nose, arched nostrils, pointed ears and an elongated body.[15] Jonathan's reference to physiognomy and later descriptions of Dracula in terms of the pseudo-science of criminal and racial types suggest a matching of Dracula's physical appearance with anti-Semitic typologies of Jewish physical identity which were pervasive in nineteenth-century Europe and which were precursive to the pseudo-science of the Nazis. In this respect, *Dracula* may be read as a novel about the not so culturally repressed horrors of Jewish immigration into England during the 1890s, especially from Eastern Europe.

Perhaps the most explicit identification of Dracula with Judaism comes from one of the workers who haul coffins to Dracula's castle: "the place was so neglected that yer might 'ave smelled ole Jerusalem in it." Halberstam comments, "to him the smell is a Jewish smell. Like the diseases attributed to the Jews as a race, bodily odors, people assumed, just clung to them and marked them out as different and, indeed, repugnant objects of pollution."[16] Yet this is no simple association of Judaism with pollution and repugnance. Jerusalem in late nineteenth-century England was also, in a great deal of popular religious geography, represented positively as the sacred center of creation, the holy mountain, and the primary locus of divine revelation. Given this cultural background, this passage seems to be identifying the abominableness of Dracula with a place that would carry both positive and negative religious connotations for many readers. Insofar as this passage identifies Jerusalem with antiquity, moreover, it also stirs up another kind of ambivalence with regard to the archaic: the archaic as the *arche*, the sacred origin of the world and the Word; but also the archaic as the primitive, savage, against which modern European civilization defines itself. Here Jerusalem and Judaism, identified with Dracula, appear to stand for both.

By identifying Dracula with Judaism and primitive Christianity, this monster comes to represent religious otherness within sameness. Indeed, for modern Protestant European cultures, Judaism often has posed a kind of identity crisis. On the one hand, theologically, Christian identity relies on maintaining its identification with Judaism as its own religious heritage: the God of Israel is the God of the Church, the God who calls Abraham and Sarah calls Christians, and so on. On the other hand, Christianity has more often than not defined itself against Judaism, even claiming to supersede Judaism by declaring that, by rejecting the gospel, Jews forfeited their status as the chosen people, and that the new Israel is therefore the Christian church. Modern (especially Protestant) Christian discourse often regards Judaism with deep ambivalence, as both "us" and "them," self and other. Thus Jewish identity has often occupied a particular in-between space in modern European thought. As with Dracula's identification with primitive, non-western Christianity, then, this identification of Dracula with anti-Semitic stereotypes of Jewishness adds to his representation as a monstrous personification of religious otherness within sameness.[17]

Stoker's monster is also identified with a more exotic figure of so-called primitive religion, namely the ancient Greek and Roman god Dionysus, the god of madness, ecstasy, wine and blood, called "render of men" and "eater of raw flesh."[18] In the Roman Empire, the religion of Dionysus was a prominent rival to an emerging Christianity, and Christian tradition has never quite forgotten that rivalry. Indeed, Christian identity has continued to define itself against Dionysian religion, despite the fact that its rival has long since disappeared. Dracula's appearance in Stoker's England is, in some respects, an apocalyptic invasion of the Dionysian similar to Dionysus's invasion of Thebes in Euripides' *The Bacchae*. Like Dracula, Dionysus is most at home in the forests and mountains outside the city, as well as in the margins of Greek, Roman, and, later on, Christian religion. Like Dracula, Dionysus is strongly associated with animality and gender ambiguity, which in turn is associated with the transgression of established social and sexual norms. He leads hosts of society's most upstanding women to break with their patriarchal familial obligations as good wives and mothers in order to become ecstatic maenads of the wilderness, suckling animals and ripping the prince of Thebes to pieces.[19] And like Dracula, Dionysus requires the spilling of human blood. Dionysus thus provides yet another screen for projecting Dracula as an image of monstrous religious otherness.

LAWS PERTAINING TO BLOOD

Dracula's arrival in England represents a crisis of apocalyptic proportions. His invasion threatens not only the individual bodies and souls of those who come in contact with him, and not only London, which figures in the novel as a kind of new Jerusalem, the holy city of God's England, but the entire cosmos. Dracula threatens to contaminate the sacred purity of all of creation, from body to house to nation to cosmos. Yet, although the implications are broadly cosmic, the means of contamination is most personal and intimate: it travels from (monstrous male) body to (English female) body through the consumption of blood, which is conceived as the very essence of the life force and a means of immediate carnal knowledge.

Behind this idea of contamination via blood is a biblical prohibition against consuming blood, and behind that a theological understanding of blood as life. The main Scripture lesson on blood is given by Renfield, the resident "zoophagous (life-eating) maniac" in Dr. Seward's sanitarium, who has a special hankering for insects, spiders and other small lives.[20] One evening in Seward's study,

Renfield storms in and attacks him with a kitchen knife, cutting his wrist severely. Seward's blood trickles into a pool on the carpet, and Renfield, who has been knocked to the ground, begins lapping it up like a dog. Moments later, as the attendants secure him and lead him back to his cell, Seward hears him repeating "The blood is the life! the blood is the life!"[21] Later in the story, Renfield explains to Seward and the others that the line he was repeating that day is the biblical text that provides the basis for his "zoophagous" practices:

> I used to fancy that life was a positive and perpetual entity, and that by consuming a multitude of living things, no matter how low in the scale of creation, one might indefinitely prolong life. At times I held the belief so strongly that I actually tried to take human life. The doctor here will bear me out that on one occasion I tried to kill him for the purpose of strengthening my vital powers by the assimilation with my own body of his life through the medium of his blood—relying, of course, upon the Scriptural phrase, "For the blood is the life."[22]

As elsewhere, Renfield is operating within a biblical religious idiom that appears disturbingly alien to the modern, scientific mindset of Dr. Seward, who never seems to catch his references.[23] Yet Renfield's explication here only scratches the surface. We need to open up his Bible and delve a little deeper in order to tap into his vein of thought. The particular biblical passage to which Renfield refers is part of a dietary regulation prohibiting the consumption of blood: "Only be sure that thou eat not the blood: *for the blood is the life*; and thou mayest not eat of the life with the flesh" (Deuteronomy 12:23). This passage is part of a larger network of passages concerning meat-eating that identify blood with life (Hebrew *nephesh*, sometimes translated as "soul") as distinct from flesh (*baśar*). This text permits one to eat flesh but not the life, that is, the blood, along with the flesh. So also in Genesis 9:4, after the flood, Noah is instructed that they may eat animal flesh, "but the flesh with the life thereof, which is the blood thereof, shall ye not eat." Blood is life, flesh is not. While people are allowed to eat flesh, all blood, that is life, is God's and God's alone.[24] In contrast to the practices of other nations, the consumption of blood is presented in biblical dietary laws as an abomination. Not only would it render the blood-eater accursed, but it would contaminate the Holy Land itself and, by extension, the very order of creation.

So also in *Dracula*. Not only does Dracula's consumption of blood/life render himself and his victims abominable, but it endangers the entire Holy Land of England as well as the entire order of creation.

In this light, moreover, our zoophagous maniac biblical scholar Renfield occupies a particularly significant place vis-à-vis Dracula and the others. Although he is in frequent communication with Seward, Mina and Van Helsing, and although he ultimately tries to help them defeat Dracula, he is clearly identified with Dracula from the start by his biblically abominable desire to consume life-in-blood. Beyond this, he is also linked to Dracula by his identity as insane, a term that suggests psychic impurity. To be called "sane" is to be diagnosed by a culture and its psychological priesthood as psychically pure, clean, *sanitary*. To be called "insane" is to be diagnosed as psychically impure, contaminated, *unsanitary*. The insane subject is kept from contact with others in a *sanitarium*, which maintains and protects the sanitation of the society outside its walls. Dr. Seward's failure to contain him within the walls of the sanitarium, and his failure to keep him from getting through to Mina, who shows great sympathy for him, represents a threat of contamination that parallels Dracula's threat. Renfield, as psychically contaminated and communicable, is a harbinger of the Master's coming. Like John the Baptist (another socially marginal madman who eats insects and invades mainstream culture with provocative proclamations), the abominable Renfield prepares the way for the coming of the Master of contamination.

FLESH OF MY FLESH, BLOOD OF MY BLOOD

If the blood is the life, then the blood of Dracula threatens to contaminate the distinction between life and death, relocating his subjects in the between state of undeath. At the heart and soul of this novel is the ritual concern, simultaneously scientific and priestly, for proper and improper passage of blood between bodies, especially between male and female bodies. For blood is not simply life, but also masculine potency, and Dracula's blood not only threatens to contaminate the distinction between life and death; it also endangers the patriarchal order of familial relations, which are at the heart and soul of larger Victorian society (not to mention contemporary North American society).

As the blood of Dracula commingles with that of Lucy Westenra and Mina Harker, they are stolen out from under the patronage of the men who love them (Mina's husband Jonathan, Lucy's fiancé Arthur, her frustrated courtiers Dr. Seward and Quincey Morris, and their grandfather-figure Professor Van Helsing) and into the bosom of the monster. Transfer of patriarchal possession is accomplished by the transfer of blood. The most revealing scene in this regard is the so-called "primal scene" in which Seward, Van Helsing, Arthur and Quincey catch Dracula in the act of nursing Mina on his own blood while Jonathan lies sleeping on the bed next to them. In contrast to Dracula, who storms in through windows, these gentlemanly monster slayers only hesitantly break the lock and enter Mina's room, concerned as ever with the conventions of appropriate social interaction between men's and women's spaces. What they see upon entering elicits in Seward a most literal sensation of horror (Latin *horror*, "bristling"): "I felt my hair rise like bristles on the back of my neck."[25] The scene is a mix of maternal intimacy, sexual violence and adultery. Jonathan lay dazed on the bed, "his face flush, and breathing heavily as though in a stupor," while Mina knelt beside him being force-nursed from Dracula's bosom: "his right hand gripped her by the back of the neck, forcing her face down on his bosom. Her white nightdress was smeared with blood, and a thin stream trickled down the man's bare breast, which was shown by the torn-open dress. The attitude of the two had a terrible resemblance to a child forcing a kitten's nose into a saucer of milk to compel it to drink."[26] This scene is, moreover, suffused with terms of abomination, much of which echo biblical discourse: Mina's white dress stained with blood; blood consumption by both Mina and Dracula; gender ambiguity in Dracula as maternal male; suggestions of human-animal intimacy (Mina as kitten; Dracula, a few sentences later, as "wild beast").

Caught in the act, Dracula escapes in a mist. And as the stupefying blur of violence and abominable intimacy disappear like vapor along with their undead harbinger, Jonathan awakens with a shock and leaps out of bed. Hastily pulling on his clothes, he cries out indignantly, "My God, my God! has it come to this! . . . Guard her while I look for *him*!"[27]

Mina is now clearly torn between two worlds and two men: embraced by her beloved Jonathan while his comrades stand beside her, she notices that her lips, smeared with a mingling of Dracula's and her own blood, have stained Jonathan's night-robe. At this point she declares her own state of impurity: "Unclean, unclean! I must touch him [Jonathan] or kiss him no more."[28] The purity of her union to Jonathan now contaminated, she quarantines herself from him. Later, when her forehead is singed by a communion wafer that Van Helsing touches to it, she makes a similar pronouncement on her own impurity, and this time the biblical subtext is unmistakable: "She sank on her knees on the floor in an agony of abasement. Pulling her beautiful hair over her face, as the leper of old his mantle, she wailed out: — 'Unclean! Unclean! Even the Almighty shuns my polluted flesh!'"[29] Here her abominable state is clearly identified with the state of leprosy as presented in ritual purity codes of Leviticus 13, where, once diagnosed, the leper must cover her or his upper lip and call out "unclean, unclean" while in public. Not only does Mina's leper-like uncleanness signify her new physiological state, which is now intimately commingled with the blood of a monster. It also signifies her marital and theological state. Her uncleanness contaminates the sanctity of her union with Jonathan and with God. The blood of Dracula not only threatens to contaminate the distinction between life and death, relocating his subjects in the between-state of undeath; it also endangers the sanctity of marriage, framed in patriarchal terms as the right of the husband to have sole proprietary access to his wife. She and Dracula are scandalous newlyweds, as Dracula himself makes most explicit in a declaration of marriage that both draws from and twists the biblical story of the world's first marriage between Adam and his "helper" or "companion" Eve: whereas in that story Adam declares Eve to be "bone of my bone, flesh of my flesh," Dracula declares, "And you, their best beloved one, are now to me flesh of my flesh; blood of my blood; kin of my kin; my bountiful winepress for a while; and shall later on be my companion and my helper."[30] With this mangling of the first biblical declaration of marriage, Dracula's union with Mina is presented not only as a contamination of the sanctity of marriage but also an undoing of creation. Here again, the cosmic order of creation and the social order of marriage are intimately related. The contamination of one is represented as the contamination of the other. Dracula is a chaos monster who invades the divinely ordained order of the cosmos by invading the divinely ordained institution of marriage.

RITUALS OF RESACRALIZATION

Rituals often provide the means for an individual or a community to pass from one state of being to another. So it is in *Dracula*. The contamination introduced by Dracula, which fundamentally alters the state of Lucy and Mina, must be combated by the male heroes of the story with specific rituals that work to resacralize and reorient their women and their world. The purpose of these rituals is to pass the individual bodies and souls of Lucy and Mina to the right order of things and, in so doing, to eradicate the chaos monster who threatens not only them and their society but the very order of creation.

The men perform two kinds of ritual aimed at resacralizing their women and their world. One is the modern medical rite of blood transfusion, performed on Lucy, the ineffectiveness of which suggests the terrifying ineffectiveness of modern western medical science in the face of this *unheimlich* outbreak of the primitive and non-western. The other is the ritual slaying of chaos monsters, first the undead monster Lucy and finally the king of monsters Dracula. Unlike the modern medical rites practiced initially on Lucy, these rites, which are identified with primitive, non-western religion, prove effective. But both kinds of ritual, the modern and the primitive, are overseen by Van Helsing. Both professor of modern medical science and high priest of primitive occultism, he does not hesitate to wield garlic flowers, a communion wafer, a stake, or an occult missal when the ritual need arises.

TRANSFUSION

Transfusions from the gentlemen into Lucy serve as a ritual means of repossessing the woman they all love (at the beginning of the novel, Quncey Morris, Dr. Seward and Arthur Godalming were all seeking to marry her). As with Mina, the passing of blood between

Dracula and Lucy is construed as a sexual union that severs her betrothal to Arthur and her bonds with the other suitors. These blood transfusions aim to take her back. Each is represented as an intimate union, a *fusion*, of two bodies. After Lucy's first transfusion from her fiancé Arthur, a "transfer from full veins of one to the empty veins which pine for him,"[31] Lucy writes in her diary, "Somehow Arthur feels very, very close to me. I seem to feel his presence warm about me."[32] Later Arthur says "that he felt since then [the first transfusion] as if they two had been really married, and that she was his wife in the sight of God."[33] Reflecting on his own transfusion of blood to Lucy the next day, Dr. Seward, who had also sought her hand in marriage, writes, "It was with a feeling of personal pride that I could see a faint tinge of colour steal back into the pallid cheeks and lips. No man knows till he experiences it, what it is to feel his own life-blood drawn away into the veins of the woman he loves."[34] Soon after, Van Helsing and then Quincey Morris also give blood to Lucy. (Jonathan, who is married to another, does not. To do so would be adulterous.) After Morris gives blood, he wants to make sure that Arthur was the first to do so. Upon learning that he is the fourth in ten days, he remarks, "then I guess, Jack Seward, that that poor pretty creature that we all love has had put into her veins within that time the blood of four strong men."[35] Recognizing the scandalously intimate unions effected by these other transfusions, Seward makes clear that none of the men will ever tell Arthur.

These transfusions are a means of reclaiming Lucy not only from the borderland between life and death but also from her union with Dracula, which has been brought about by the intimate passing of blood between them. They are rituals of marital union that aim to divorce her from her undead partner. Yet replacement of blood does nothing to undo its contamination, and it soon becomes clear to the men that transfusions are not enough to repossess their woman and to reestablish the order of creation. These transfusions cannot repurify their blood, now intermingled with the Count's. Modern, scientific medical practice cannot filter out the archaic and primitive powers of this monstrosity. For "the old centuries had, and have powers of their own which mere 'modernity' cannot kill."[36] It gradually becomes clear that Dracula's archaic and primitive powers must be countered with archaic and primitive rites.

ONE WEDDING AND A FUNERAL

After her burial, the men discover that Lucy has herself become an undead monster, now fully wedded to Dracula. Since she is caught in a liminal state between life and death, Van Helsing explains, they must kill her once and for all in order to divorce her from Dracula and send her to heaven, where she will wait for her beloved Arthur. This killing of the monster in her is carried out under the high priest Van Helsing's direction according to a carefully prescribed ritual procedure that is presented as a combination of a mythic battle against a chaos monster, a wedding and the consummation of marriage.

The procedure takes two nights. On the first night Van Helsing seals her into her tomb by packing a putty compound made from a communion wafer into the cracks around the door, "the sacred closing of her means of entry," while the others take their places around him "in respectful silence." Thus her space, the monster space, is marked off from the rest of the world as the site for the sacred rite.[37] The next day, after other cemetery visitors have left the area, they begin the main procedure, which is described in extraordinarily minute detail, even for Stoker.[38] As they cross into the demarcated tomb area, Van Helsing further marks the ritual space by lighting it with a lamp and two candles which are set on two nearby coffins. He then removes from his bag a variety of instruments, some signaling modern industry and medicine (a soldering iron, soldering wire), others occult religion (a wooden stake with a sharp, char-hardened point, and a mallet). With these objects laid out, he gives a brief homily on the nature and history of the undead, and explains the ritual procedure by which Lucy may finally "rest as true dead." The text for this homily is not one that might be found next to the hymnal in Westminster Abbey. Rather, he explains, "it is out of the lore and experience of the ancients and of all those who have studied the powers of the Un-Dead."

Van Helsing's homily concludes with an altar call: the one who must be the central actor in this ritual, Van Helsing declares, is "him that loved her best; the hand that of all she would herself have chosen . . . Tell me if there be such a one amongst us." Arthur steps forward, of course, and Van Helsing assures him that as he carries out the task, "we, your true friends, are round you, and that we pray for you all the time."

As Van Helsing opens and reads aloud his missal of prayers for the dead, and as Seward and Quincey follow along as best they can, Arthur takes the stake and pounds it into Lucy. Likened to the story of Thor slaying the king of the frost giants with his hammer, this ritual slaughter is presented as a liturgical reenactment of a mythic battle against a chaos monster:

> The Thing in the coffin writhed; and a hideous, blood-curdling screech came from the opened red lips. The body shook and quivered and twisted in wild contortions; the sharp white teeth champed together till the lips were cut and the mouth was smeared with a crimson foam. But Arthur never faltered. He looked like a figure of Thor as his untrembling arm rose and fell . . . the sight of it gave us courage, so that our voices seemed to ring through the little vault.

As the chaos monster is killed, the pristine, sacred body of Lucy returns, "Lucy as we had seen her in life, with her face of unequalled sweetness and purity." This is a resacralized Lucy, the monster now as far removed from her as east is from west. And as a "holy calm . . . lay like sunshine" over the resacralized body, the tone quickly shifts from chaos battle to a morning wedding. Like a minister presenting the bride and groom to the congregation, Van Helsing declares to the monster killer, "And now, my child, you may kiss her." Lucy is thereby divorced from the lord of the undead and wed to Arthur. As they leave the tomb, Seward sees "gladness and mirth and peace everywhere, for we were at rest with ourselves on one account." The ritual repossession and resacralization of Lucy is complete, and once again all is right with the world.

LAST BATTLE

But to resacralize Mina—that is, to restore and repossess her from her state of abominable union with Dracula—is another matter. For this to be accomplished, the king of chaos monsters himself must be slain. Mina is torn between two lovers, married and unfailingly devoted to Jonathan, yet flesh of Dracula's flesh and psychically attuned to him and his will. For the sake of her marriage, and for the sake of the whole world, the chaos monster Dracula himself must be destroyed.

As with the ritual slaying of the undead Lucy, this final slaying of Dracula begins as the reenactment of a mythic chaos battle and ends in marital bliss. It works not only to repossess and resacralize Mina but also to reestablish and resacralize the right order of creation as well as the right order of English marriage, family and other closely related social orders. It is a chaos battle that functions on every level, from body to house to cosmos.

By the time of the final chaos battle, our heroes have hunted Dracula almost all the way back home. Mina, who recounts the battle, watches it with Van Helsing from a hollow in a rock on the road leading to Dracula's castle. The scene is pervaded by a sense of apocalyptic edginess: Van Helsing describes the area as "so wild and rocky, as though it were the end of the world,"[39] and Mina calls it "a perfect desolation" yet "wild and uncanny."[40] At twilight, that precarious and uncanny threshold between day and night, Van Helsing and Mina spy a group of horsemen racing toward the castle with a wagon carrying Dracula's coffin. In hot pursuit are Arthur, Seward, Quincey Morris and Jonathan. While the storm winds growing ever fiercer, Jonathan attacks "with a great strength that seemed incredible." He throws the coffin off the cart and onto the ground. He and Morris tear off the lid and face their adversary, whose "red eyes glared with the horrible vindictive look which I knew too well." Immediately Dracula sees the setting sun, and the look of hatred turns to triumph. "But, on the instant, came the sweep and flash of Jonathan's great knife. I shrieked as I saw it shear through the throat; whilst at the same moment Mr Morris's bowie knife plunged in the heart. It was like a miracle; but before our eyes, and almost in the drawing of a breath, the whole body crumbled into dust and passed from our sight."

Quincey Morris is fatally wounded in the fray. But before he breathes his last, he leads the men in a final prayer of praise which explicitly links the resacralization of the cosmos, indicated by the beauty of the sunset after the storm, and the resacralization of Mina, indicated by disappearance of her mark of uncleanness:

> "Oh, God!" [Morris] cried suddenly, struggling up to a sitting posture and pointing to me [Mina], "it was worth

> this to die! Look! Look!" The sun was now right down upon the mountain-top, and the red gleams fell upon my face, so that it was bathed in rosy light. With one impulse the men sank on their knees, and a deep and earnest "Amen" broke from all sides as their eyes followed the pointing of his finger as the dying man spoke:– "Now God be thanked that all has not been in vain! See! the snow is not more stainless than her forehead! The curse has passed away!"

Notice that Mina herself does not participate in this concluding prayer of thanksgiving and benediction: it is the man Morris who proclaims that her curse has been lifted, that is, that she is no longer unclean, and it is the men who together fall to their knees for a unison "Amen" as they look upon her. As in the legend of St. George, the slaying of the dragon means that the nation and the world are safe again, but the real prize is the princess.

Whereas Arthur's reunion with Lucy is signified by his kissing of the bride, this final overcoming of the chaos monster and the restoration of family happiness is signified by a man child born to Mina and Jonathan. This child is an embodiment not only of the union between husband and wife but also of their union with the other men, Seward, Van Helsing, Arthur Godalming and the late Quincey Morris. "His bundle of names links all our little band of men together," Jonathan remarks, "but we call him Quincey."[41] Here again it is *through* Mina but not with her that the men are linked together as "a little band of men." Mina is the vehicle of male bonding against the monstrous. Ironically, despite her instrumental role throughout the story, the victory over the chaos monster has led finally to the restoration and resanctification of Mina's subordinate status as second sex, an object of exchange and relation between men.

"The horror of Dracula," Anne Williams writes, "is the horror of man confronting a universe that no longer confirms or conforms to the patriarchal structure of reality."[42] Quite so. Dracula is indeed *unheimlich* in the most literal sense: he represents those things in modern English society that threaten to unhome the patriarchal household. We might add that Dracula's *religious* identity, as a personification of modern stereotypes of non-western primitivism (here including primitive Christianity), contributes to this sense of patriarchal horror. Modern science, technology and nationalism in the West are closely related to patriarchal conceptions of masculine domination and potency. Since Francis Bacon at least, modern selfhood has been conceived in masculine terms; and nature, the object that the modern self seeks to dominate and control, has been conceived as feminine.[43] Therefore, Dracula's roots in primitive religion, or "heathen theology," as Bacon called it, identified with nature and conceived throughout the novel in terms of archaic religious forces "which mere 'modernity' cannot kill," make him a threat not only to modernism in general but also to those patriarchal ideals of masculine identity that are inextricably related to modernism.

And in this light, we might even recognize, deep within Dracula's glaring red eyes, the reflected image not only of the great devil-dragon of the Apocalypse, but also of the ancient monstrous-feminine Tiamat, whose chaotic waters are both source of and threat to the cosmic and social order of things established by her divine sons. And with one impulse the men sink on their knees, and a deep and earnest "Father in heaven help us" breaks from all sides.

CHAPTER 10

SCREENING MONSTERS

MOVIE TIME, SACRED TIME

We gather together, seated in pew-like rows, necks craned, silently facing the screen of light and revelation (the source of which, we almost forget, is behind a curtain in the back). We share a common meal uniquely blessed for movie time: hyper-yellow popcorn, Good 'n' Plenty, Junior Mints, which are passed down the row in special, movie-house-only vessels and portions. We follow a carefully patterned and widely familiar liturgical sequence which moves us from the profane space and time of cars, parking lots, malls and food courts into the sacred space and time of the movie event and then back out. Passing through the narthex of concessions and bathrooms, we meet the well-dressed usher at the entrance, near the ticket-font. As we settle into our seats and quiet ourselves, we attend to announcements of forthcoming events, followed by a reminder to be still and keep silence. At the center of it all is the Feature Presentation, usually of a certain length, with certain narrative expectations. Afterward, accompanied by rolling credits, closing songs and raised lights, we quietly file out (except for a few more fervent devotees who tarry a bit longer to read and meditate). Movie time can be a kind of sacred time.

Film artists often describe their films in terms of religious ritual and religious experience. Pioneering filmmaker Maya Deren, for example, describes her film work as ritual because, "anthropologically speaking, a ritual is a form which depersonalizes . . . and, in so doing, fuses all individual elements into a transcendent tribal power towards the achievement of some extraordinary grace . . . and, above all, for some inversion towards life."[1] For Deren, rituals have the power to break individuals out of themselves as discreet subjective units and put them into intimate communion with others. She sees ritual in film as a primary means of transcending individual consciousness and opening onto a sacred realm of intimacy and interconnection.

In a similar vein but with far greater zeal, Stan Brakhage describes the relationship between film artists and film lovers as a community of spiritual seekers, "an ideal of anarchic religion where all are priests both giving and receiving, or rather witch doctors, or better witches, or . . . O, for the unnamable." In contrast to the "unbelievers who attend the carpeted temples where coffee and paintings are served . . . the devout, who break popcorn together in your humblest double-feature services, know that you are still being born."[2] Brakhage is a religious reformer, calling for a cinematic priesthood of all believers, those devotees who understand that movie going, as much as movie making, is not about detached spectatorship but ritual participation, a collective work of divination.

Jean Epstein goes so far as to proclaim that the cinema is "polytheistic and theogonic. Those lives it creates, by summoning objects out of the shadows of indifference into the light of dramatic concern, have little in common with human life." For Epstein, the cinema event, in which various film technologies, filmmakers and viewers converge within the space and time of the theater, is not only cosmogonic, "world-generative," but theogonic, "god-generative." "Alien to human sensibilities" and more akin to "the ominous, tabooed objects of certain primitive religions," the mysterious lives we watch on the screen "can inspire respect, fear and horror, those three most sacred sentiments."[3]

MONSTROUS REVELATIONS (*NOSFERATU* AND *SHADOW OF THE VAMPIRE*)

Mysterious lives . . . "alien to human sensibilities" . . . inspiring "respect, fear and horror, those three most sacred sentiments." Sounds like the recipe for a monster movie. Recalling the basic meaning of *monstrum* as a showing or portent from a god or gods, monsters have often been presented on screen as revelations of dreadful and fascinating religious otherness, a "wholly other" envoy of the sacred.

So it is with F. W. Murnau's *Nosferatu, eine Symphonie des Grauens* ("a symphony of horror"; 1922), the first and by many accounts best film to be based on Bram Stoker's *Dracula*. *Nosferatu* is a theogony as *monstrogony*: its monster, Count Orlok (Max Schreck, the Dracula character), is a revelation of the other within, an icon of desire laced with repugnance, an apocalyptic epiphany of the monstrosity latent within self, society and world.

Orlok is an image of diabolical monstrosity. He is a walking embodiment of plague and death, "from the seed of Belial," doomed to live unredeemed "on the cursed earth from the graveyards of the Black Death." First appearing as an abominable, carrion-eating hyena, his primary form is that of a human rodent with rat teeth, pointed ears, and ever-growing fingernails dangling from arms that he holds in front of himself like paws. When his coffins are opened by the crew of the Demeter (the name of a Greek goddess of crops and fertility), plague-carrying rats pour forth from the dirt therein. Indeed, Orlok kills far more with plague than he does with fangs. His coming to Bremen, like Dracula's coming to London, threatens to contaminate "our" fertile land and society and selves.

Yet Orlok is also an image of fascinating and terrifying religious mystery. In contrast to the other characters, he invariably appears, disappears and reappears in the center of the screen, often in Gothic archways which frame him as though he were a religious icon (Figure 16). And only he and the mad Knok are able to understand the mysterious hieroglyphic text of the letter that leads to Orlok's move to Bremen (Figure 17; "hieroglyph" means, most literally, sacred [*hieros*] writing or carving [*glyphé*]).[4] In the supernaturally shifting image of Orlok, the filmmakers weave together a socially impossible tangle of awesome and awful divinity. Orlok is presented as a hierophany of dreadful and fascinating religious otherness, a "wholly other" envoy of the sacred.

The ambiguity of the monster as demonic-divine is accentuated by his relation to Ellen Hutter (Greta Schroeder-Matray; the Mina Harker character) whose expressions of devotion to her husband Thomas (Gustav von Wangenheim) sometimes appear as expressions of devotion to Orlok instead. In one scene, for example, we see her sitting in her bedroom chair reading *The Book of Vampires*. There she learns that the only way to destroy a vampire is for "a woman of pure heart" to give herself to him all night so that he will forget to leave before sunrise. She is clearly thinking about Orlok and what she must do about him. The next scene in which she appears shows her in the same chair, this time not reading about vampires but needlepointing a pillow case on which we read "Ich liebe dich," "I love you." (Figure 18). The scene closes with her looking off in the direction of the window (through which Orlok's house is visible) and sighing. In fact, the two scenes match quite precisely in shot sequence: each involves a shot facing her on the chair, followed by a shot focused on the text (*The Book of Vampires* and the text on the pillow, respectively), and concluding with a shot facing her once again as she looks toward the window. One assumes that the pillow-talk and the night of self-surrender with Orlok are for her true love Thomas, but this assumption about the object of her desire sits uneasily with what the camera allows us to see. This ambiguity is heightened in the final scene: as Orlok kneels at her bedside, the shading and point of view makes it difficult to determine whether he is feeding on her, kissing her or whispering in her ear (Figure 19).

Screenwriter Henrik Galeen worked from Stoker's novel in a very loose manner, dropping most of the characters, changing all the places and names, and adding a number of innovations to popular vampire lore in the process—most notably their susceptibility to the dangers of sun exposure. In fact, the only text that the film does take directly from Stoker is the strange biblical pronouncement that "The blood is the life! the blood is the life!," which is given by Knok (Alexander Granach; the Renfield character) from his cell in the insane asylum.

The fact that the only text Galeen retains from Stoker is a cryptic biblical passage reflecting an archaic, even "primitive" religious

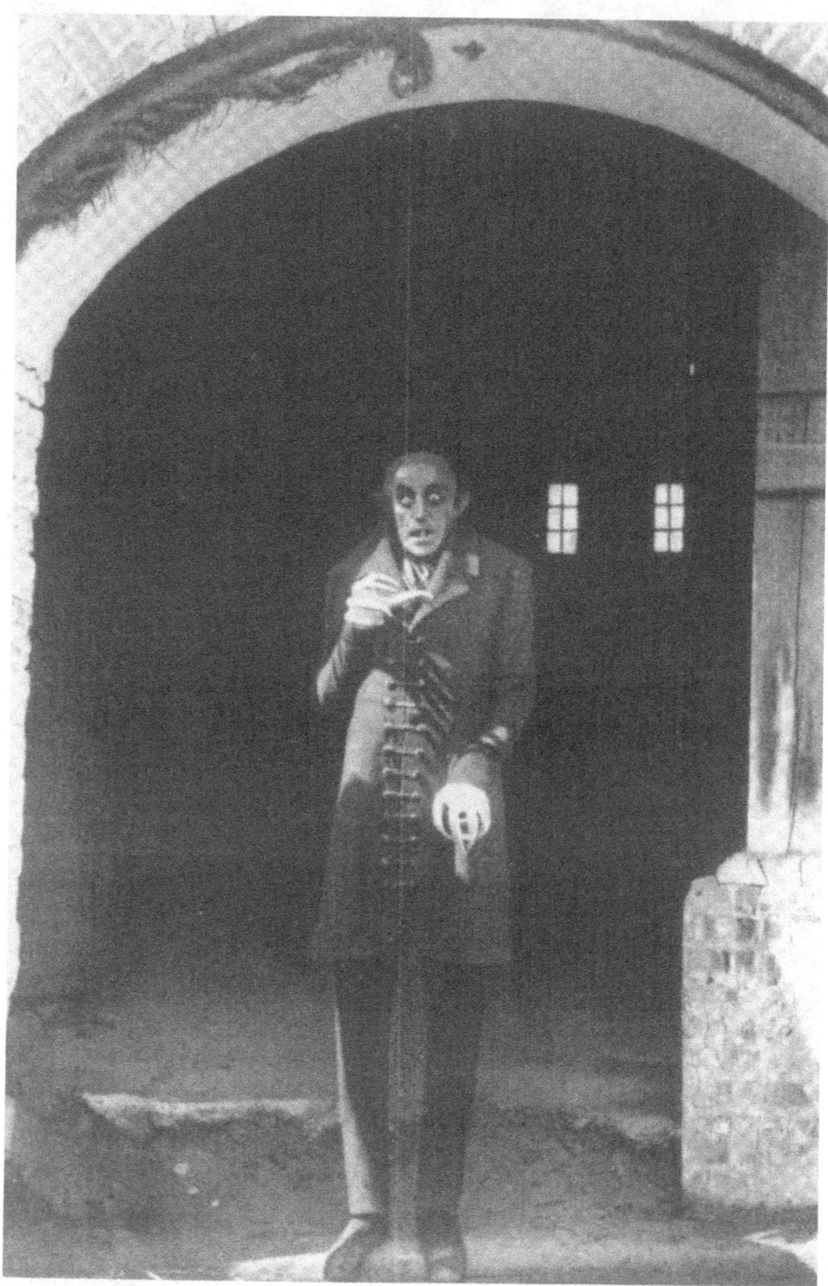

FIGURE 16. Orlok in archway, *Nosferatu*, 1922 Prana-Film G.M.B.H.

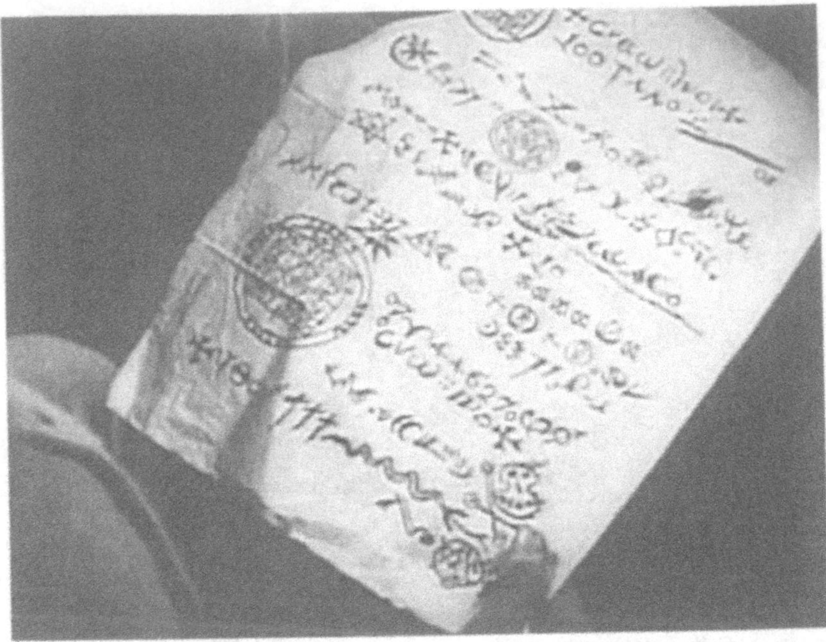

FIGURE 17. Hieroglyphs in *Nosferatu*, 1922 Prana-Film G.M.B.H.

conception of life-blood may indicate some of the religious interests of Galeen, who also co-directed *Der Golem* in 1914 and co-wrote the second *Der Golem: Wie er in die Welt kam* ("how he came into the world") in 1920.[5] Both films concern pre-Frankenstein Jewish legends about a homunculus that is brought to life through rites associated with the reading of an esoteric Hebrew text called the *Sefer Yetsirah*, which is an important early text for the Jewish mystical tradition of Kabbalah.[6] What do the biblical passage, the vampire legends and the Golem legends have in common? They all represent a paradoxical religious *otherness within*; that is, they represent religious ideas and practices *within* Christianity and Judaism that are particularly out of place in relation to late nineteenth-century modernism. Like Stoker's Count Dracula, then, part of what Galeen calls the "ambiguous thickness" of his Golem and Count Orlok is drawn from forms of religious otherness that are latent (occult, "hidden") within more or less familiar, mainstream European Christianity and Judaism. Here, however, these elements are solicited in the interest of producing an experience of

FIGURE 18. "I love you," *Nosferatu*, 1922 Prana-Film G.M.B.H.

FIGURE 19. Orlok and Ellen, *Nosferatu*, 1922 Prana-Film G.M.B.H.

religious fascination and desire as much as repulsion and fear. Indeed, they are images of the *self* as monstrous.[7]

Nosferatu's producers, Albin Grau and Enrico Dieckman of the Berlin-based Prana-Film company, were themselves explicitly interested in making the monster movie into an alternative venue for religious reflection. Their announcements declared that this film was to be the first in a series of films and other artistic works that would offer "much reflection on the occult aspects of life."[8] (Due to bad budgeting and legal troubles with widow Florence Stoker, it ended up being their first and last production.) The company name, Prana, is itself a Sanskrit word meaning "breathing forth," which refers in early Vedic texts both to the life spirit that infuses the entire cosmos and to the life spirit that animates the human body, and which is an important term in both Buddhist and Hindu tradition.[9] Their company logo, moreover, which appears on posters and other announcements for *Nosferatu*, is an image of the now well-known *t'ai chi* disk, which visually represents the ancient Chinese concept of yin and yang as complementary principles of cosmic harmony and the interrelatedness of all things. And Grau, who did the initial design sketches and the posters for *Nosferatu* as well as the occult-inspired hieroglyphic texts mentioned earlier, was especially inclined toward mystical religious ideas and practices. His eclectic orientalist and occult interests suggest an affinity with turn-of-the-century theosophy, a popular movement of comparative religion that was rooted primarily in western mysticism and sought to discover a mystical unity within the diversity of the world's religions.[10]

Like other works identified with the German Expressionist art movement of the interwar period (sometimes called "apocalyptic adolescents"), *Nosferatu* reflects the belief that cinema, like ancient myth, possesses cosmogonic and theogonic potential. It gives form to new worlds in which, "at any one moment, Mind, Spirit, Vision and Ghosts seem to gush forth."[11] And it gives form to a new god conceived within the hidden recesses of mind. Its vampire is an icon of monstrous divinity.

Continuing to blur monstrosity and divinity, E. Elias Merhige's *Shadow of the Vampire* (2000) re-imagines the making of *Nosferatu*, suggesting that Max Schreck (Willem Dafoe) is not an actor who plays a vampire but a vampire who plays an actor. Drawing from a variety of ancient mythologies and mystical religious practices, *Shadow of the Vampire* presents Schreck/Orlok as, among other things, a monstrous epiphany of the sun-god. At one point Murnau (John Malkovich) calls Schreck "Moonchaser. Blasphemer. Monkey. Vase of pre-history . . . finally to Earth, finally born." In an interview Merhige comments, "If you look at early Gnostic, Assyrian and Greek mythologies, those are all names for the sun," which he connects "to the Gnostic sense that there is this 'invisible' sun that animates everything, that penetrates both the night and the day."[12] Indeed, akin to Grau and others involved in making *Nosferatu*, Merhige himself has described filmmaking as a "cosmological ritual" and "shamanic experience," conjuring new worlds of monster gods. *Shadow of the Vampire* is just such a world, and its vampire is just such a monster god.

STAGE RITE (*DRACULA*)

From the experimental films of Maya Deren to the blockbusters of Hollywood, film opens up possibilities for the ritual transformation of time and space. On the most basic level, this is evident within particular scenes. Through lighting, film exposure, tinting, camera speed, the placement of objects in a scene, choreography, camera angle, framing, editing, iconography, sound and other filming strategies, a common meal around a long dinner table is transformed into a Passover Seder or the Last Supper. A dip in the river becomes a baptism. A mosh pit full of drunken college students rocking back and forth before a musical performer becomes a Bacchanal of maenads worshiping the masked Dionysus. And in the famous first night scene in Tod Browning's *Dracula* (1931), a monster attacking his victim becomes a wedding ceremony.

Having fainted at the sight of a bat at the window, the visitor from London, in this story Renfield (Dwight Frye) rather than Harker, swoons and falls to the floor.[13] He is on his back in the right-center of the screen, in front of a wall of windows and at the foot of two steps that stretch like church altar steps across the screen. From a side door in the lower left-hand corner, just offscreen, Dracula's three women attendants process toward him in equal step, wearing matching white flowing gowns, their hands folded as though they are bridesmaids carrying bouquets in a wedding processional. As they approach him, Dracula (Bela Lugosi) enters through the main window door in the center like a groom, wearing, of course, his trademark tuxedo. He dismisses the three women with the sweep of a hand, and they, in careful step and without tripping on the long trains of their dresses, slowly recess to the left corner of the screen and out of sight (Figure 20). As the camera closes in, Dracula kneels before Renfield as though to kiss his bride, and then the camera cuts to black. The next scene is the honeymoon cruise to London, on which Renfield already begins showing signs of jealousy over the attention Dracula is giving to others.

Whether or not you think "the book was better than the movie," even a quick skim of Stoker's novel makes clear that Browning's *Dracula*, which was based on the theatrical adaptation (also starring Bela Lugosi), does not even try to be faithful to the text. In Stoker's novel, for example, Dracula uses both Renfield and Jonathan in order to get to London and establish good contacts, but he far prefers the blood of women. He victimizes men not by taking their blood but by taking their women. Relatedly, in the first night scene in Stoker's novel, erotic energy centers on the three women who visit Jonathan in the night, in whom Jonathan sees "a deliberate voluptuousness which was both thrilling and repulsive."[14] Dracula catches them just before they descend on Jonathan, and drives them away, thus blocking desire: "How dare you touch him, any of you? How dare you cast eyes on him when I had forbidden it? Back, I tell you all! This man belongs to me!" When they complain that he does not know how to love as they do, he responds, "Yes, I too can love; you yourselves can tell it from the past . . . now I promise you that when I am done with him, you shall kiss him at your will."[15] In these last lines there are strong homoerotic overtones, and these overtones were drawn out further in Stoker's theatrical adaptation, in which Dracula takes his fainted visitor into his arms and disappears into the shadows. But within the larger plot it is clear that Dracula wants Jonathan not as flesh-of-his-flesh, blood-of-his-blood bride/victim, but as the means to landing himself in London where he will be a rival suitor for Jonathan's wife Mina. In Browning's film, on the other hand, Dracula's guest (here Renfield instead of Jonathan) is the first passive object of both the women's and Dracula's desire.

FIGURE 20. *Dracula*, Copyright 1931, 1999 Universal Studios.

More often than not, Browning's film *de-ritualizes* Stoker's most ritualistic scenes. In the film there is no scene involving the ritual killing of Lucy in the tomb, for example, and Dracula himself is killed offstage with whatever stuff just happens to be lying around his basement. (Van Helsing says to Jonathan, "Get me a piece of stone—anything," and then breaks off a board from the coffin lid to serve as the stake.) In this first-night bedroom scene, however, Browning uses lighting, choreography and set design to project Dracula's attack on Renfield as a kind of wedding ceremony and sacrificial rite, thereby teasing out a homoerotic element more or less latent in Stoker's work (more so in his novel, less so in his theatrical adaptation).[16]

EXORCISM (*METROPOLIS*)

German filmmaker Fred Keleman (*Fate*, 1994) suggests that cinematic horror is about naming otherness so as to control and ultimately exorcize it. He makes this suggestion by way of popular speculation about the primitive origins of religion in the desire to objectify otherness by depicting it as an image on a wall:

> . . . in the ancient caves of Lascaux, France, for example, the first reason for mankind to make pictures was to "bannen" [ban, banish, exorcize], to fix it, to bring out, to capture the demons, because when you name them, they'll lose their power. That was the first reason people started to paint. . . . I think that is a lot like film, because cinema is like a modern cave, people come together—that's why the darkness is so important—and you have the screen like a wall in the old caves. And the aim is to put a spell on the demons. To exorcise, if you want.[17]

What horror films do, for Keleman, is conjure, then trap, then name our demons and monsters within the frame of projection. A new pictographic language projected on white screens in theaters rather than stone walls in caves, film is endowed with the magical power of reducing the unknowable and unimaginable to a captured image.

Fritz Lang's classic science-fiction film *Metropolis* (1926) may be viewed as a conjuring and banning, an exorcism, in this sense: in it the monstrous is conjured and captured on screen in order that it may be eradicated from the fantasies and nightmares of its viewers. In fact, *Metropolis* conjures a pair of closely related monsters, representing what the film suggests are two terrifying political extremes that must be exorcized from society: unregulated industrial capitalism and worker revolution. In this way the film serves as a kind of a cinematic Gospel for a chillingly conservative public rite whose function is to establish a sacred order and homogeneity by banning social chaos.

Both monsters are projected as images of religious otherness. First, unhindered industry is projected as a cult of human sacrifice to the industrial machine. When Freder (Gustav Fröhlich), son of Jon Frederson, the Master of Metropolis (Alfred Abel), first descends to the underground world of labor which fuels the city that rises from the ground above it, he finds himself facing a giant, steam-spewing industrial machine—the "central power house"—with a large stairway in the center (Figure 21). On its face are niches in which workers rock back and forth in regular, pendulum-like movements that make them appear to be parts of the machine.[18] Although the film is silent, Lang's use of light-dark contrasts and regular explosions from steam valves gives the impression of an overwhelming cacophony of industrial noise. Thus the image elicits incongruous feelings of both vast structural symmetry and chaotic distortion. It is an image of the industrial sublime: a monstrously overwhelming motor of productive efficiency which fills the screen and subsumes all particular human forms and movements into its deafening, fearful symmetry.

As Freder cowers before his father's machine in fear and trembling, a worker in one of the niches fails to open a pressure valve, and there is an explosion, causing many to fall from the face of the machine to their deaths. As other men blankly march over to remove the bodies, the camera reverses to face Freder, who cries out in horror, "MOLOCH!" The next shot reverses to Freder's point of view again, in which the machine has been transformed into the gaping face of a monster god of human sacrifice (Figures 21 and 22). Ascending the tongue-like staircase are men, costumed in 1920s generic "savage" wear (skirts, no shirts), forcing bound victims into its fiery gullet. Following them are rows of workers in uniform, hunched over, marching at a slow, even pace into the mouth of this insatiable monster god.

Lang has cast his industrial monster in terms of an amalgamation of ancient biblical and contemporary primitivist figures. On the one hand, the monster's name, Moloch (a.k.a. Molech), is biblical. It refers to a non-Israelite god associated with prohibited rituals of child sacrifice (e.g., "causing one's son or daughter to pass over by fire to Molech"; 2 Kings 23:10). Within biblical tradition, Moloch is a name for religious otherness, and Lang assumes that the film's viewers will be familiar with it. On the other hand, the costumes, choreography and iconography of the scene are based on modern western stereotypes of non-western, "savage" religious rites of blood sacrifice. By combining the name of a biblically tabooed god with terrifying stereotypes of modernity's primitive religious other, this image of the industrial sublime is transformed into a cthonic monster god of the underworld who must be fed human lives in order to protect the Metropolis above ground from chaos and calamity.

FIGURE 21. Central power house, *Metropolis*, 1926 Ufa.

FIGURE 22. MOLOCH!, *Metropolis*, 1926 Ufa.

Sometimes it takes a monster to kill a monster, and so it is in this film. The Moloch machine is destroyed by another monster machine, this one embodying revolution (Brigitte Helm). Freder's father hires the mad inventor Rotwang (Rudolf Kleine-Rogge), whose small thatched hut amid the skyscrapers of Metropolis immediately identifies him with pre-modern Gothic, to create a robot that will replace the story's saintly heroine Maria, Freder's new soul-mate, who preaches that there must be a mediator between "the brain that plans and the hands that build." Freder's father, here presented as Pharaoh against the Moses-like liberator Maria, commands the robotic replica of Maria to undo her teaching and to sow discord and criminal behavior among the workers.

This revolutionary monster is projected as a figure of Dionysus, an ecstatic embodiment of dread and desire, death and eros.[19] Like Dionysus, the robotic Maria incites her mesmerized devotees to ecstatic revelry and violence that transgresses social norms and is ultimately self-destructive. Incited by her entrancing sermon, the women and men rise up en masse and destroy the central power house machine. As they dance before its smoking ruins, the flood waters rise in the underground worker's city to destroy their children. Returning to the Metropolis above ground, the robotic Maria continues inciting her bacchic revelry among the elite, who dance around her bearing lanterns on sticks that are reminiscent of the Dionysian thyrsi, the ivy spears that were carried by the Bacchic maenads during their ecstatic ritual dances.

Soon both monsters have been destroyed in the flames that they themselves have stirred up: with the flip of a switch by the robotic Maria, the Moloch machine explodes under its own pressure and is consumed by its own fire. Soon after that she herself is burned by her own mad maenads as a scapegoat for the death of their children (ever ignorant and prone to mass frenzy, they do not know that the children have been saved by the real Maria). By the end, then, the monsters are all gone. To borrow ritual terminology from Victor Turner, the time of monsters, the liminal, in-between time of anti-community, has been resolved, de-monstrated. Signifying that the world is now safe again, the final scene is of a reconciliation on the cathedral steps between labor ("the hands that build"), represented by the labor foreman, and capital ("the brain that plans"), represented by Jon Frederson.

Thus *Metropolis* conjures for its congregation of viewers a pair of closely related monsters, unhindered industry and revolution, in order to exorcize them both from the metropolitan scene outside the theater. Within the ritual time and space of the movie, opened and closed with holy Scripture from Lang's co-writer and spouse Thea von Harbou ("the mediator between brain and muscle must be the heart"), these political monsters are faced and overcome, and reconciliation is realized.[20]

We must not forget that the film's monster of revolution, like its monster of industry, is created by the master of capital, not by the masses of labor. The audacious suggestion here is that even the threat of revolution comes from the mind of capital, not labor. Indeed, the suggestion is that revolution poses no real threat to capital but only to the workers themselves. (Frederson wants them to rebel because he is sure that their rebellion will only harm themselves.) By conjuring and banning this monster the film, we may well suspect, seeks to ban another, largely repressed, yet unnamed and far more terrifying monster: an underground revolution that directs its subversive force not inward but outward onto its Metropolitan lords—not only a rage against the machine but also a rage against its creator and overseer.

And although he can be a bit of a Pharaoh at times, the Master of Metropolis is never represented as a monster. The politically tame and taming message of the film for fellow masters of Metropolis is that they should show a little more compassion for their slave laborers, which, of course, like young and noble Freder, they would do if given the opportunity.

Nosferatu pries at a crack in the world that opens onto an abyss of chaos. When we peer in we are confronted with a monstrous image of the demonic-divine that cannot ultimately be eradicated from self, society or world. *Metropolis*, by radical contrast, ultimately sacralizes social order and sameness against the least trace of chaos or otherness. Its gospel assurance is that there are no such things as monsters in the Metropolis, only malfunctioning machines in need of a careful tune-up.

In the end, the film's sentimental moral that the heart must mediate between hand and brain is by no means universal, ahistorical or beyond vested interests in class, despite von Harbou's utopian claim to the contrary ("This film is not of today or of the future. It tells of no place. It serves no tendency, party or class"). In fact, the time and place of this film is interwar Germany, in the chilling "stabilized period" six years before the rise of Nazism, when mass rage would be increasingly refracted through the distorting lenses of anti-Semitism, homophobia and other monstrous self-projections, and when millions of people would be forced into uniforms and carried into the fiery mouths of new machine-like furnaces of mass death.[21]

By conjuring the monster of industry as a machine with no maker (pay no attention to the man behind the curtain) and the monster of revolution as a machine of self-destruction, and by representing workers as docile, easily riled masses with very little discernment of the reality of their surroundings (strong hands, weak brains), the film works to render real subterranean revolutionary rage impotent. In this way, the film ultimately affirms the subordination of all individual wills to the absolute authority of a metropolitan regime.

"Whenever Hitler harangued the people," Siegfried Kracauer writes, "he surveyed not so much hundreds of thousands of listeners as an enormous ornament consisting of hundreds of thousands of particles."[22] Social chaos is ultimately choreographed out, formed into a neat, ornamental whole in which no individual piece is out of place. This is precisely the scene of the happy ending on the cathedral steps, the union of the hands and brains into one single metropolitan, indeed cosmopolitan Body Politic. In this light, the precursor for this final vision of Metropolis is none other than Hobbes' Leviathan, in which all individual wills are sewn into the body of this one "Mortall God," whose benevolent smile is as haunting and unsettling as the happy ending of *Metropolis*.

CHAPTER 11

ECOMONSTER

I AM BECOME DEATH

On July 16, 1945, moments after the detonation of the first atomic bomb in the Jornada del Muerto ("Journey of Death") desert of New Mexico, when the director of the Manhattan Project, J. Robert Oppenheimer, sought words to express his own sense of awe and fascination at the destructive power he and his colleagues had unleashed, he drew language from a familiar passage in the Hindu religious tradition: "I am become Death, the shatterer of worlds." Oppenheimer was paraphrasing a passage from chapter 11 of the *Bhagavadgita*, in which Krishna reveals himself to Arjun as a wonderful and terrifying figure of cosmic beginnings and endings, creation and destruction, brighter than a thousand suns. Other eyewitnesses also drew from traditional religious language in order to describe their experience, often employing a biblical apocalyptic mixture of cosmic destruction and new creation. Recalling biblical passages in which mountains and hills rejoice at the glory of God (e.g., Psalm 65:12; Psalm 98:8; and Isaiah 49:13), *New York Times* writer William L. Laurence described the explosion as a sublime revelation of divine power that was both awesome and awful: "The hills said 'yes' and the mountains chimed 'yes' . . .

It was like the grand finale of a mighty symphony of elements, fascinating and terrifying, uplifting and crushing, ominous and devastating, full of great promise and great forebodings."[1] Put in biblical terms as both cosmogony and apocalypse, Laurence describes the explosion as an awakening of an otherworldly, subterranean primordial chaos that signals both the end of the world and the first moment of creation:

> And just at that instance there rose from the bowels of the earth a light not of this world, the light of many suns in one . . . an elemental force freed from its bonds after being chained for billions of years . . . It was as if the earth had opened and the sky had split. One felt as though he had been present at the moment of the Creation when the Lord said: Let There be Light . . . The Big Boom came about 100 seconds after the Great Flash—the first cry of the newborn world.

Another eye-witness, George B. Kistiakowski, told Laurence that it was "the nearest thing to Doomsday that one could possibly imagine . . . I am sure . . . that at the end of the world . . . the last man will see what we saw!"[2] Likewise General Thomas Farrell's account from the July 16 War Department press release describes his experience in explicitly religious terms of horror, describing an "awesome roar which warned of doomsday and made us feel that we puny things were blasphemous to dare tamper with the forces heretofore reserved to the Almighty."[3]

Like Victor Frankenstein, who also identified himself with the biblical God of creation, these eyewitnesses express both giddiness and dread after tampering "with the forces heretofore reserved to the Almighty," forces that they identify not only with the divine power of creation but also and especially with the divine power of chaos and destruction. And in these accounts, as in Shelley's novel and Whale's films, the terrible implication is that the hubris of humankind bent on messing with creation has awakened an ecological catastrophe of apocalyptic proportions.

Indeed, along with the fires of the Holocaust, the blinding flash of the atomic bomb marked the twilight of modernism, especially of its confidence in human progress through the unhindered march of science and technology. In the same moment that laid modernism to rest, it awakened a new breed of monster, the ecomonster.

ECOHORROR ON SCREEN

In movie theaters from New York to Tokyo, ecohorror gives popular cultural expression to the ecological nightmare that has pursued us since the dawning of the atomic era. The undisputed king of ecohorror monsters is Inoshiro Honda's *Gojira* (1954) and its Japanese-American version *Godzilla, King of the Monsters* (1956; Terry Morse). Like its many relatives in the film industry, Godzilla is an old mythological chaos god in newly irradiated skin, a primordial chaos monster known from the ancient legends of native islanders who nearly destroys Tokyo after being accidentally resurrected by nuclear explosions. Godzilla and its many cousins personify ecological horror in two ways. First, in tandem with the moral urgency and apocalyptic fear of a new age of ecology, these monsters stand for deep anxieties about the effects of modern science and technology on complex ecological systems that we do not fully understand.[4] Whether the result of nuclear explosions or genetic alterations, ecomonsters stand for what happens to our environment when we try to play God with it. In this sense, ecohorror movies present a moral lesson that is impossible to miss and as old as the oldest monster tale: pull back into your proper place, let God be God and creature be creature, or you will pay for your hubris. None of this would be happening, none of these monsters would be stomping your cars, if you would refrain from pressing limits. In this respect, the ecomonster represents a divine message or portent, a *monstrum* in the most literal sense, warning us to retreat into the established order of things. This assumes, of course, as does the environmental movement that runs in tandem with it, that the onslaught of ecological chaos is entirely the responsibility of humankind and not inherent in ecology itself.

On another level, however, and despite the baggy rubber suits and flimsy model sets, these monstrous figures of nature going awry also represent something more dreadful and largely repressed in contemporary environmental thought. As a return of the ecologically repressed, ecomonsters are personifications of an ecological chaos that is and always has been in the world, however latent.

They are not created but awakened. Here in the twilight of modernity, it appears that ecological order lasts only as long as the chaos monsters sleep.

It is therefore not surprising that the monsters of ecohorror often bear strong family resemblances to primordial chaos gods and monsters of various religious traditions, including those of biblical literature. Likewise, the typical plot of the rise and fall of the chaos monster in ecohorror movies is a twentieth-century version, made for popular consumption, of the ancient chaos battle motif. In these movies the specter of ecological chaos reenters the world, usually in the form of an ancient mythological chaos monster, and is ultimately overcome. In this way, the ecohorror movie serves as a kind of public rite within the popular culture of horror. Like the dramatic retelling of Marduk's victory over Tiamat and the subsequent establishment of a divinely ordained cosmic and political order in the Babylonian new year's festival, the time and space of the ecohorror movie event provide a structured context in which latent fears about ecological chaos can be faced and exorcized. In this sense, the ecohorror movie is a cosmogonic religious event which recreates and resacralizes world order against the monstrous threat of primordial chaos. Thus the monster movie offers a ritual context in which to encounter and overcome monstrous otherness, assured by a well-established mythic structure that, although there will be some collateral casualties along the way, in the end the monster will be vanquished and the world will be safe once more, at least for the time being.

DEMYTHOLOGIZING THE MONSTER

Often what imbues an ecomonster with a sense of mysterious otherness is its identification with ancient religious mythology. In some cases, the identification is only implied, as in *Leviathan* (1989), where the film title and the fact that the story takes place at the bottom of the ocean are the only obvious links between the film's monster and the Leviathan of biblical tradition. In many other cases, however, the identification is made explicit by one or more of the characters in the film. Often, the identification of the monstrous with the mythological is first made by not-so-modern, not-so-cosmopolitan townsfolk, and only later acknowledged by men (nearly always men) of science, suggesting that such "primitive" folk are more mythologically inclined and that, as such, they may be able to give a name to that which modern consciousness has largely repressed. In *Godzilla*, for example, it is the natives of a small island who first give Godzilla its name, thereby identifying it with their own counter-modern, primitive legends and rituals concerning a primordial chaos god whose threat is appeased by the annual sacrifice of a young girl. Only later is this identification affirmed by the sage scientist Dr. Yamane (Takashi Shimura) who, like van Helsing in *Dracula*, is a crossover figure, in touch with both modern science and the primitive religion.

So also in Eugene Lourie's *The Giant Behemoth* (1958), in which a chaos monster is roused from its slumber in the deep by offshore atomic bomb testing.[5] In this movie the monster is identified, albeit confusedly, with a mythological figure from biblical tradition. As the monster's first victim, a local fisherman named Thomas Trevethan, breathes his last, he declares, "From the sea . . . burning like fire . . . Behemoth!" Did he mean Leviathan? Apparently Thomas knows the book of Job well enough to identify this monster with one of the two described there, but not well enough to avoid confusing the marshy landlubber Behemoth in Job 40 with the sea monster Leviathan in Job 41. This (mis)naming is soon reinforced by the preacher in his graveside homily for Thomas:

> "Man that is born of woman is of few days and full of trouble. He cometh forth like a flower and is cut down" (Job, chapter 14, the first verse). And if any man could know the sufferings of Job, it was Thomas Trevethan. Job, in his suffering, turned to God for an answer. "Then answered the Lord unto Job and said, 'Behold thou the Behemoth, which I made with thee. He moveth his tail like a cedar. Out of his mouth go burning lamps. And spouts of fire leap out from the Behemoth. He maketh the oceans to boil like a pot. His breath kindles coals and a flame goeth out of his mouth.'"

Leaving aside whether this is an adequate theological explanation for either Job's or Thomas' suffering, the preacher here provides confused scriptural backing for Thomas' confusion of Behemoth with Leviathan. In the book of Job, only the first two sentences quoted here (from "Behold" to "cedar") refer to Behemoth (Job 40:13a and 40:17a); the remaining lines refer not to Behemoth but to the sea monster Leviathan, whose description follows that of Behemoth (41:19–21; "from the Behemoth" is not in the biblical text). Nonetheless, here as elsewhere we find the local folk first identifying the monster in traditional religious terms as an ancient chaos monster.

Eventually, however, the American hero Steve Karnes and his colleagues in science are able to demythologize it, and this signals its doom. They determine that it is a 200–foot "electric" (like an eel) "paleosaurus" which, after swallowing a few too many radioactive particles, has acquired the power to "project the radiation" at its victims. This explanation, by which they come to know the formerly unknowable monster, provides the means to destroy it: they will pierce it with a radium-tipped torpedo that will push its radiation levels over the top, leaving it to "burn itself out." This is precisely what Karnes does, and the chaos monster is vanquished.

As in *Dracula*, then, the battle is not simply man against monster, but science against primitive mythology. The chaos monster is initially identified as a mysterious figure of ancient religious traditions largely foreign to the modern world. It is overcome by being scientifically *explained away* as much as by being *blown away*. The means of destroying the monster can be developed only after it has been reduced to modern scientific terms. This is one reason why the big-budget American *Godzilla* of 1999 was not in the least bit scary: its monstrosity was scientifically defined and explained almost before it had a chance to make landfall.

The mysterious and threatening otherness of the monster within the modern world is signaled by its identification with ancient, counter-modern mythology (in the case of *The Giant Behemoth*, biblical mythology). By the same token, as soon as it has been explained and thereby objectified by modern scientists in modern scientific terms, it is dead monster meat. Karnes' scientific explanation de-monstrocizes the monster. Its threatening monstrosity, signaled by its identification with ancient, counter-modern religious mythology, is reduced to a zoological novelty. When the modern lord of cosmic order demythologizes the monster he transforms it from a subject of religious awe to an object of scientific knowledge. "The ocean is my province, gentlemen," Karnes declares. Like some modern-day Marduk battling Tiamat, or Baal battling Yamm, the man of science proves himself a worthy cosmic champion against the chaos monster.

SHOOTING THE MONSTER

The victory over the monster by way of scientific objectification is expressed *visually* in the ecohorror movie by the gradual revelation of the monster on screen. The mysterious and threatening otherness of the chaos monster is maintained by resisting clear and steady visualization. By the same token, its inevitable appearance on screen is linked to its ultimate objectification and destruction. In the beginning, we only see traces of the monstrous other in its effects: boils on the skin, a charred corpse, wreckage. Then we catch partial glimpses: a shadow, a rustling in the woods, a glowing eye, a tail slithering back into the sea or around the corner.[6] Yet the monster inevitably crosses over into the visible world, and once it does its days are numbered. Once caught on camera, it will not be long before it will be caught in the crosshairs and shot to pieces. The full-frame camera shot is fatal for the monster, reducing it to nothing more than big game.

This progression toward full visualization, which runs in tandem with its full scientific explanation, is carried out in *The Giant Behemoth* and many other monster movies primarily through the use of two kinds of filming strategies: *the solitary reaction shot* and *the shot/reverse shot formation*. To be more precise, the gradual visualization and objectification of the monster begins with a single solitary reaction shot in the first encounter, leaving the monster completely unseen, and then progresses through a series of shot/reverse shot formations toward its final full revelation and demolition.

The solitary reaction shot gives a close-up view of the face of someone reacting to something, but does not provide a subsequent point-of-view shot to show us what the person is reacting to. In monster movies, the solitary reaction shot holds on the horrified face of the victim without allowing the viewer to see what the victim sees. Thus, although the monster is revealed to the victim at this very moment, we do not see it. In fact, our point of view is more closely aligned with that of the monster than it is with that of the victim. At the same time, the monster remains, for us but not for the victim, beyond visualization. In *The Giant Behemoth*, the monster's attack on the first victim, Thomas Trevethan, utilizes this classic shot. Thomas is kneeling at the water's edge gutting a fish when a siren-like whining starts to overtake the orchestral soundtrack. As the sound gains volume, he slowly looks up and his face contorts in a terrified, frozen scream while radiant light engulfs the screen. Thomas sees the monster but we do not. It is present without being presentable, unimaginably "there." Indeed, as boil-ridden Thomas himself attests to his daughter and her friend immediately before dying, he himself did not see the monster so much as its radiant emanation: "From the sea . . . burning like fire . . . Behemoth!"

Following this initial solitary reaction shot, the progressive visualization of the Behemoth is accomplished through a series of shot/reverse shot formations. In the shot/reverse shot formation, the camera cuts from an initial shot to a reverse shot (turned approximately 180 degrees), so that we are given the point of view of the character(s) in the initial shot. In monster movies, this formation typically opens with a shot of the face of someone reacting to the monster, and then reverses to show the monster, or part of it, as that character sees it. The effect of this shot formation is to align our point of view with that of the character in the first shot, thereby encouraging us to identify with that character's subject position and her/his reaction to whatever s/he sees. This is the key shot formation for cinematic "suture," by which the subjectivity of the viewer is identified with (sutured to) a particular subject position within a particular scene.[7] In *The Giant Behemoth*, a series of cinematic sutures takes us from identifying with the hunted victims of a seeing but not fully seen monstrous other to identifying with the victorious hunter as he (along with the camera) targets a fully visible, easily objectifiable, over-radiated and overrated electric eel.

There are several significant shot/reverse shot formations in the course of the film, each of which adds at least a third shot, reversing back to the initial camera position. Interestingly, each of these shot formations is related in some sense to hunting and/or shooting a weapon. In the first, just after Karnes has determined to "track down this thing, find out what it is, and then destroy it," we see him in a fishing schooner searching for the monster through binoculars.

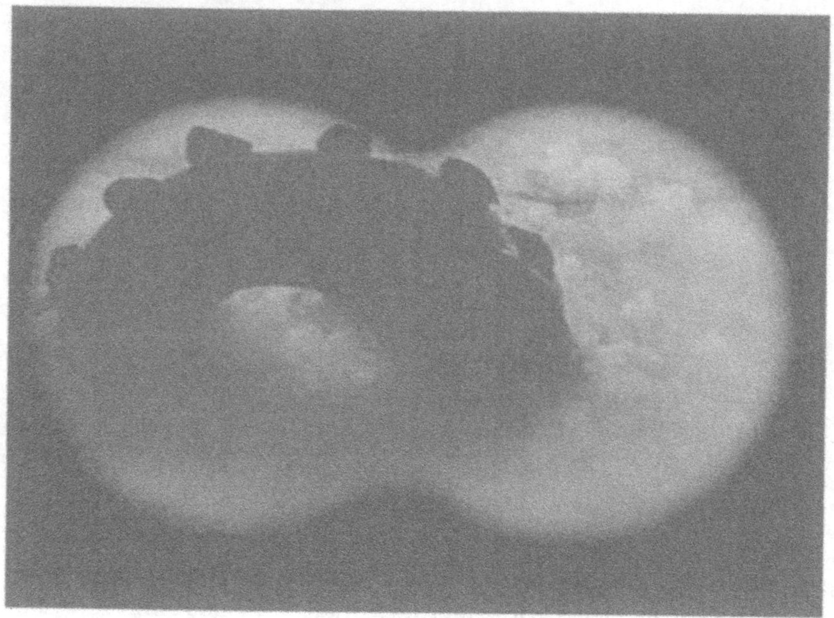

FIGURE 23. Partial shot of the monster, *The Giant Behemoth*, Copyright 1958 Allied Artists.

A modern-day Ahab from California, he is hot on the trail of the monstrous Leviathan. Just after we hear that the Coast Guard is trying to locate a large steamship that has disappeared on its way to Hull, the Geiger counter on the wall begins clicking. As Karnes stares through the binoculars in edgy fascination, the camera gives the reverse shot, framed in binocular-vision, of the monster's scaly neck and part of its head as it slips back into the churning sea (Figure 23), and then reverses back to Karnes' face as he puts down the binoculars. "That's it," he tells the skipper with a fearlessly determined face, and the chase begins. It is soon over, however, as the monster quickly leaves them behind. Thus this first shot/reverse shot formation identifies the viewer with Karnes, the hunter, and yet resists fully visualizing the object of the hunt. Indeed, insofar as this shot formation is immediately preceded by news that a steamship in the same waters has recently been hunted down and destroyed by the monster, this scene plays in the tension between identification with the monster-hunter (Karnes) and the monster-hunted (other victims at sea).

The second shot/reverse shot formation takes place when a boy and his father go outside to see why the family dog is barking. The father grabs the shotgun on his way out, and the boy unchains the dog. It looks like a father-son hunting trip. The dog goes around a corner, we hear a yelp, and then silence. As the boy and his father go after the dog, they both look up in terror. The father aims his gun and fires, and then the camera reverses to catch radiating light and part of Behemoth's hide. He has it in his gun sight, yet he, and we, cannot really see it; we are looking down the barrel at an impossible target. The camera then reverses to show the squinting father being swallowed up by light. So also the son, leaving him charred like the victim of a nuclear explosion. As with Karnes on the schooner, then, this scene begins with an image of the monster hunters; but whereas last time the monster escaped its hunters, here the hunters suddenly become the hunted. The effect of the suture here, then, is to identify us with the hunting subject turned hunted object, face to face with something that is at most only partially imaginable. We had it in our sights for a second but we never really saw it.

Soon after, the monster emerges from the threshold of the visible world, captured on camera as it stomps through the London streets Godzilla-style, smashing cars, chasing down herds of commuters and toasting them in their tracks. Anticipating just such a confrontation, military forces are on hand, and the chaos battle moves rapidly toward its conclusion. As is typical in monster movies, the full appearance of the monster here leads to an immediate increase in collateral damage and casualties, from isolated attacks to a full-blown monster mash. Yet it will also lead rapidly to the monster's demise. Its full appearance, from head to tail, signals not only the peak of its power but also its inevitable disempowerment. Now that the monster has been fully captured on screen (and fully explained, demythologized, by Karnes and his scientific colleagues), its demise is not far off. Though dangerous game, it is game nonetheless.

The last shot/reverse shot formation takes place in the climactic scene of the undersea chaos battle, in which Karnes chases down and destroys the monster by firing a radium-tipped torpedo into its body, thus giving it a taste of its own medicine. First, as the monster swims into the crosshairs, we see Karnes excitedly call out to

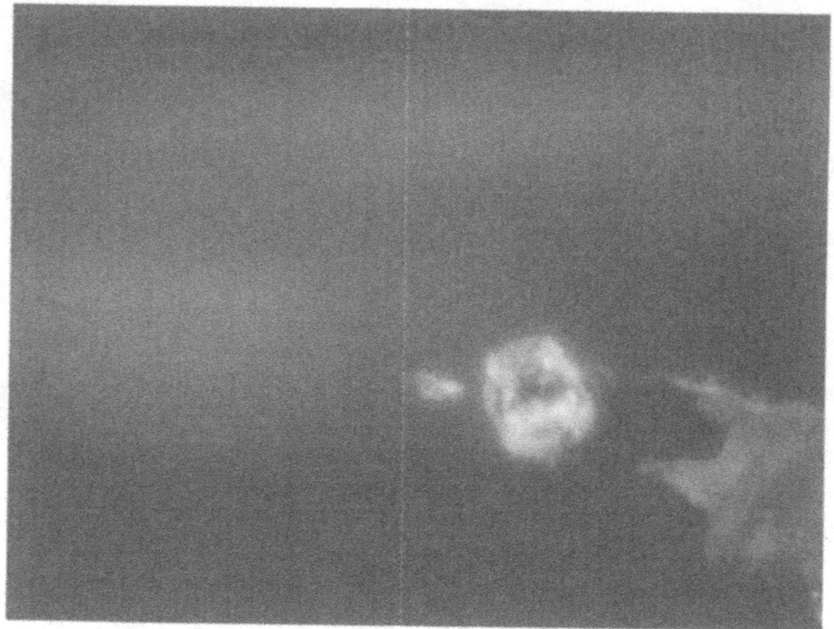

FIGURE 24. Full shot, *The Giant Behemoth*, Copyright 1958 Allied Artists.

his submate, "Fire!" The lever is pulled, and the camera reverses to the monster, who turns to face the speeding missile and catches it straight in the mouth (Figure 24). As the torpedo blows it apart, the camera reverses to the triumphant face of Karnes.

Such is the common end for the chaos monster, in ancient chaos battles and in ecohorror alike. It is expelled from the cosmos with its tail between its legs, gutted like a fish or blown to bits. Indeed, by the time of the final battle, the sense of horror that was experienced previously in relation to the monster has often been replaced by the adrenaline rush of a street fight, even as the hero of the chaos battle takes on a certain demonstrocizing bravado: "I got you! You son of a bitch." (*Alien*) . . . "Say aah, mother fucker!" (*Leviathan*) . . . "Smile, you son of a bitch!" (*Jaws*).

Isabel Cristina Pinedo identifies the two most important appearances of the monster as its initial birth, transformation, or entrance, and its destruction—that is, its first and last appearances in the film.[8] In fact, these two appearances are inextricably related. The monster's first full appearance marks the inevitability of its last.

The camera shot is fatal. The camera eye de-monstrates the monstrous and targets it for annihilation. For the monster, looks kill. For the viewer, seeing is disbelieving.

In the monster movie, then, the monster's uncanny resistance to explanation (often associated with pre- or counter-modern primitive religious mythology) is expressed on screen as visual obscurity: out of focus, overexposed or double-exposed, partial. Likewise, its intellectual objectification (associated with its demythologization), which leads inevitably to its downfall, is expressed on screen through the sharp focus and objective clarity of the full-view shot. In the same way that explaining the monster away leads inevitably to blowing it away, shooting it on film leads inevitably to shooting it with a torpedo.

THESE ARE OURSELVES

The ritual space and time of the monster movie as chaos battle provides a more or less safe context in which to face and overcome latent anxieties about the chaos rumbling just beneath the surface of the modern world ecology. More or less safe, because narrative expectation assures us that by the end of the drama the monster will have been faced and overcome. In another sense, however, there is always the lurking awareness that the world can never be rid of its monsters. As with Leviathan, Tiamat and other chaos monsters from ancient religious traditions, the monsters of modern horror, once conjured, always seem to survive the end designated for them within the narrative. They resist oblivion. No matter how many times we blow them up, gut them, send them back to the grave or jettison them back into deep space, they keep creeping back into our world and under our skin. The world cannot be de-monstrated.

Perhaps neither can we. In a sense, the final shot that blows away the monster also shoots us in the foot. For the process of objectifying and destroying the monster reveals ourselves as monstrous. After the opening credits in *The Giant Behemoth*, for example, the first images are of nuclear bomb tests, followed by images of faceless figures in leaded suits with Geiger counters, wandering through the ruins of an explosion. These images, we soon realize, are from a film that Karnes himself is showing to a group of scientists. He comments: "And afterwards [after the bombing], these mysterious figures, faces masked with lead, these are ourselves, men, the kings of the earth, trying to measure the extent of the destruction they themselves have created." Here in the movie's opening lecture, "we" (men of modern science) are mysterious, masked monster-gods who have "created" in turn an even more monstrous catastrophe, which will lead, Karnes prophesies, to a "radioactive conglomerate" resulting from a "biological chain reaction, a geometrical progression of deadly menace." "For all we know," he says, "what we have started may have already matured, and who can tell when this, this whatever it is, will rise to the surface and strike back at us." The sense is that "we" modern scientists are monsters engendering monsters. The chaos monster that will soon rise to the surface mirrors our very own monstrosity. In fact, as noted earlier, the radioactive chaos monster is ultimately destroyed by a torpedo that Karnes and his colleagues, working in a dark and mysterious laboratory, wearing the same outfits as those in Karnes' film ("mysterious figures, faces masked with lead"), have tipped with radium. The implication is not only that fire is fought with fire, but that monsters are destroyed by monsters. In this sense, the monster projected onto the silver screen may be the projection of a latent chaos that is not only in our world but also in ourselves. These are ourselves.

CHAPTER 12

Our Monsters, Ourselves

ISLAND OF THE MISFIT BOYS

Hate you father, for you have sinned
Why did you, Lord, let this life begin? . . .
Mother, Father, you answer me
Your soul-less son, your thing that should not be
A brilliant demon, a monster god
You gave me life but took the soul away
With these final words I pull the switch
We turn to dust (dust to dust)

—Misfits, "Dust to Dust" (*Famous Monsters*)

"So, what's your favorite 'Fits song?" asks the Ticketmaster operator, breaking from his sales script. "I don't really know," I said. "I guess I like '20 Eyes in My Head' and a couple of songs on the new album." I am not a fan, or "Fiend" as they say, of the Misfits, a pioneering punk band whose songs are all about B-movie monsters. Much of their early material from the '70s and early '80s, written by former member Glenn Danzig, seemed to me the product of young white male angst, sometimes infused with sexual violence. But this was not so much the case with their latest album, *Famous*

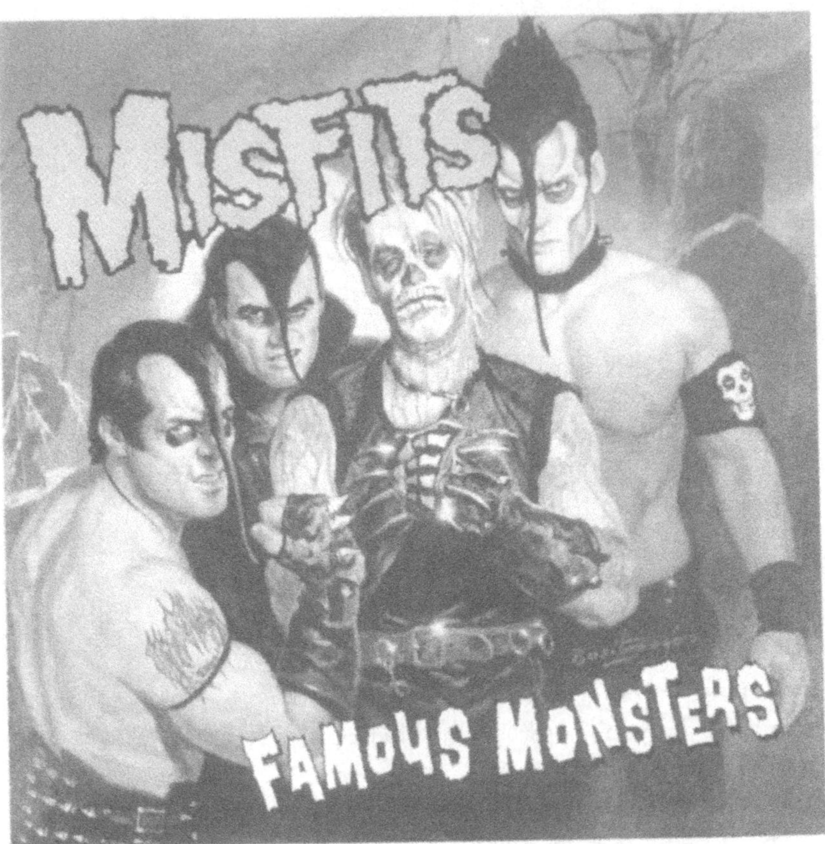

FIGURE 25. Cover art for Misfits, *Famous Monsters* (Roadrunner Records, 1999), by Basil Gogos. Pictured from left to right: Jerry Only, Dr. Chud, Michael Graves, Doyle Wolfgang von Frankenstein.

Monsters (1999), and I had heard that if I was interested in ritual performance in the popular culture of horror, the opening to their live show was not to be missed.

It turns out that my Ticketmaster ticket was a pass from the commercial mainstream to a countercultural eddy where playing monster did not just happen on screen but was a way of life. The Fiends, mostly male and ranging in age from 21 to 50, come dressed in black with faces and arms painted like skeletons. As the show opens, the Crimson Ghost, a kind of grim reaper wearing a silky red cape, comes onto the stage area rolling a six-foot-high 1950s-style television. It is family time for the Fiends. The Crimson Ghost turns the television on, and we watch a long series of clips from B-monster movies, mostly depicting the moment of the monster's revelation. When the show ends, the television is rolled away, and the Misfits themselves take the stage, replacing the TV movie monsters with live monsters. They look like monsters, and the lyrics to their songs are all about identifying with the monsters of the popular culture of horror, as in "Dust to Dust," which is reminiscent of the final scene of self-destruction in *The Bride of Frankenstein*. Indeed, the band members themselves are famous monsters, especially bassist Jerry Only and his brother, guitarist Doyle Wolfgang von Frankenstein (Figure 25). They even have their own action figures. Throughout the show, moreover, the line between performer and audience blurred. At several points Fiends in the mosh pit, some dressed more outrageously than the Misfits themselves, were lifted on stage where they sang the lyrics to the band's high-speed punk songs without missing a beat. All were one in their embrace of monstrosity.

Often within the story worlds of horror movies and literature we find that monster creators and monster killers inadvertently end up being more monstrous than the monsters they create and kill. The fact that Frankenstein's unnamed monster is so often called Frankenstein is telling. But within the popular culture of horror, in performances like those of the Misfits, we often find people identifying with these monsters in the most *advertent* ways. Our monsters become us.

BELA'S HIDEOUS PROGENY

In her 1831 introduction to *Frankenstein* for the Standard Novels series, Mary Shelley sent her book off with a mother's blessing, claiming it as the offspring of her own monstrous imagination: "I bid my hideous progeny go forth and prosper."[1] With this maternal blessing and claim, Shelley echoes a long tradition of interpreting "monstrous births" as manifestations of dangerous maternal fantasies or desires.[2] Many critics had attacked the novel as precisely that. Here Shelley does not defend her monster as a misunderstood beauty, but identifies with it as such, claiming it as her own, holding it close to her bosom before sending it out to face the cruel gaze of a public skilled at dragon slaying, witch burning and exorcism.

In Whale's *The Bride of Frankenstein*, a similar identification of Shelley with her monstrous progeny is cast into the frame of the movie itself: the same actor, Elsa Lanchester, appears both in the opening scene as Mary Shelley narrating her story to Percy Shelley and Lord Byron, and in the final scene as the monstrous bride herself (Figures 26 and 27). The not so subtle suggestion is that Shelley is her own monster, and her own monster's bride.

To the best of my knowledge, Bram Stoker never took his vampire to his bosom or claimed him as his own, flesh of his flesh and blood of his blood. Perhaps that is why his monster seeks family elsewhere. Indeed, although he found little kinship among the mothers and fathers of England at the end of the nineteenth century, he has certainly borne his own monstrous progeny in the more recent popular culture of horror, beginning with Bela Lugosi, whose crowning achievement as an actor was his role as the Count in Tod Browning's *Dracula* (1931). Lugosi remains Dracula's undisputed heir. Today one can hardly read Stoker's novel without imagining its vampire wearing Lugosi's black cape, pancake makeup and red lipstick. In fact, when Lugosi died in August of 1956, he was buried, at the request of his family, in his Dracula makeup and costume. If Stoker's Dracula has a family plot, it is with Lugosi.

Within Goth culture, Dracula has many grandchildren by the quintessential *monstre sacré*, Lugosi, who was memorialized in the song "Bela Lugosi's Dead" by the seminal Goth band Bauhaus:

The bats have left the bell tower,
The victims have been bled,
Red velvet lines the black box,
Bela Lugosi's dead

Undead, undead, undead.

The virginal brides
File past his tomb,
Strewn with time's dead flowers,
Bereft, in deathly bloom.
Alone, in a darkened room,
The Count,
Bela Lugosi's dead

Undead, undead, undead.[5]

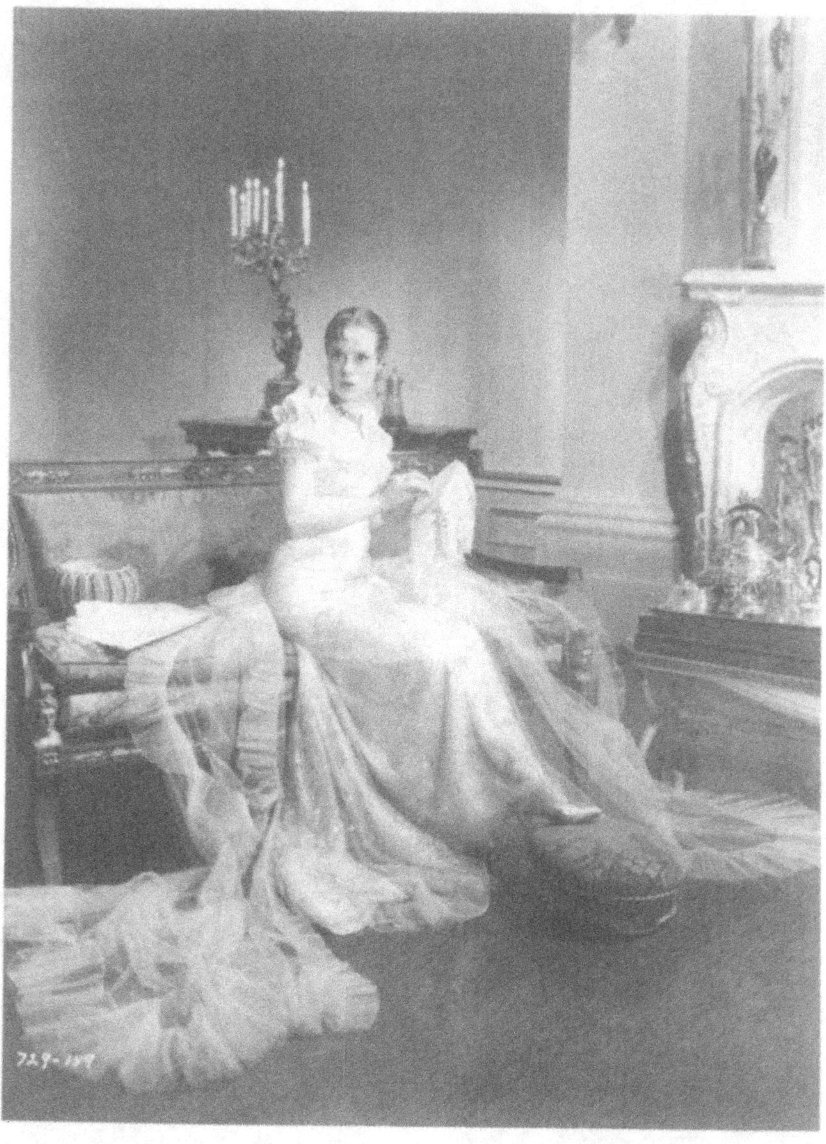

FIGURE 26. Elsa Lanchester as Mary Shelley, *The Bride of Frankenstein*, Copyright 1935 Universal Studios.

FIGURE 27. Elsa Lanchester as the monster bride, *The Bride of Frankenstein*, Copyright 1935 Universal Studios.

As Lugosi's Hollywood movie set turns into a funeral home, the pronouncement of his death is echoed by a confessional counter-pronouncement, "undead undead undead." Almost twenty-five years after his death in relative obscurity, the Bauhaus song canonized him. Lugosi as Dracula has been reincarnated within Goth horror culture as undead patron saint and, of course, fashion authority on how to perform monstrosity, that is, how to play monster.

Among Goths, the monstrous forms that the builders of mainstream culture rejected have become the cornerstones of a counterculture that mirrors that same mainstream culture's repressed monstrosity—a counterculture infused with a mix of monstrosity and pre-modern Christian religious iconography and architecture. Although increasingly diverse and difficult to define (especially as Goth spills over into industrial, death rock, ambient, etc.), these two elements remain its most distinctive features. In some cities, Goth nightclubs are even housed in the downtown church buildings of "white-flight" congregations that fled to the suburbs. Within this iconographic and architectural context, which is a kind of sacred space, musical performances like Bauhaus and fashion performances by those in congregation function as rites that lay claim to their inheritance as the true hideous progeny of "classic" cinematic and literary monstrosity.

The broad popularity of monsters like Lugosi's Dracula is important to such rites of self-definition, insofar as it makes them widely recognizable signifiers of abomination and taboo. The embrace of classic monstrosity feeds on the general public's "unclean" parts. Much like the poetic primitivism of intellectuals like Bataille and Artaud in the interwar years, the Goth counterculture of the late twentieth and early twenty-first century bears itself and nourishes itself on mainstream culture's most well-known projections of monstrosity.

CTHULHU MYTHOS

Goths may love their Bela. But there is no more devoted group of monster enthusiasts than those who have consecrated themselves to the late horror writer Howard Phillips Lovecraft (1890–1937). In the years since his untimely death, Lovecraft has been sainted by countless disciples worldwide who long for the return of the monster gods of his "Cthulhu Mythos."

The "Cthulhu Mythos" refers to an artificial mythology developed by Lovecraft during his last decade and a half of writing for pulp horror zines like *Weird Tales* and *Astounding Stories*, beginning with "The Call of Cthulhu" (1928) and "The Dunwich Horror" (1929), and including "The Haunter of the Dark" (1936), "At the Mountains of Madness" (1936), and "The Shadow Out of Time" (1936), among several others.[4] In each of these tales, Lovecraft provides fragments of a fragmented mythosphere, a storied world that he pieces together, according to his own testimony in letters, from childhood memories, from dreams and from various bits of mythology drawn from a wide range of ancient and contemporary sources.

Lovecraft's aim in developing this mythosphere in his stories is best understood in terms of his own theory of the purpose of supernatural horror, namely, to elicit *cosmic fear*. In his 1927 essay, *Supernatural Horror in Literature*, which was first published in a small-run amateur zine called *The Recluse*, Lovecraft argued that the truly horrifying tale (as opposed to what he called "literature of mere physical fear and the mundanely gruesome") awakens an awareness of the limits of the known and knowable world, "a profound sense of dread, and of contact with unknown spheres and powers; a subtle attitude of awed listening, as if for the beating of black wings or the scratching of outside shapes and entities on the known universe's utmost rim." Horror, for Lovecraft, is an awed and awful listening for the radically other, for that which is unimaginably there "in the defeat of those fixed laws of Nature which are our only safeguard against the assaults of chaos."[5] Lovecraft attributes a certain unimaginable agency to this radically anti-cosmic, chaotic otherness that threatens us in horror: scratching, beating, assaulting, but always from beyond, never fully within the cosmic sphere. In the sleep of reason, as one's fragile faith in a knowable, reasonable, all-embracing cosmic order falls away, monsters of supernatural horror awaken.

Lovecraft considered cosmic fear to be coeval with religious experience, but he believed that modern religion (especially mainstream American Protestantism) had attuned itself exclusively to the more beneficent dimensions of cosmic mystery, identifying them with a cosmically beneficent God, and had left the "darker and more maleficent side of cosmic mystery" to the popular culture of horror, which for him includes literature as well as folklore. Within the dualized, sterilized mainstream of modern theology and religious practice, this "darker side," this cosmic maleficence is not only ignored but divorced from the beneficent aspects of the unknown, setting up a clean opposition of moral and spiritual good versus evil.

"The Call of Cthulhu" is the best known of Lovecraft's Cthulhu Mythos tales. The story is presented as an open letter found among the papers of the late Francis Wayland Thurston, and begins with his inheritance of the estate of his great-uncle George Gammell Angell, Professor Emeritus of Semitic Languages at Brown University. Thus the reader, inheriting Thurston's papers after *his* death, is in the same position he was in at the beginning of the story, inheriting Angell's papers after his death. And in both cases death turns out to be the result of the revelation of a world on the brink of a monstrous chaogony.

Among his great-uncle's papers, Thurston discovers a small locked box containing news clippings, cryptic notes, and a strange clay bas-relief, all bound together with a document titled "Cthulhu Cult." The clippings center on a series of "outré mental illnesses and outbreaks of group folly or mania in the spring of 1925,"[6] and the bas-relief includes ancient text of unknown provenance along with an image of an unimaginable monster: "a sort of monster, or symbol representing a monster, of a form which only a diseased fancy could conceive. If I say that my somewhat extravagant imagination yielded simultaneous pictures of an octopus, a dragon and a human caricature, I shall not be unfaithful to the spirit of the thing."[7] It turns out that the bas-relief was made by a young art student based on dreams, and that his dreams and subsequent madness coincided with the other spring 1925 outbreaks which were the focus of the clippings. As Thurston's research continues, he soon discovers a broad and disparate collection of secret religious groups located throughout the world, each of which is, like the monstrosity on the bas-relief, an admixture of unfamiliar elements from various religions, from Louisiana Vodou sacrifice to proto-Sumerian hermetics to Bacchanal incantations. All of these groups are seeking through their rites "to shadow forth the prophecy" of the chaophany of the Old Ones and their great priest Cthulhu.

Lovecraft's "The Dunwich Horror" provides another window onto this abyssal mythos. In this story, Dr. Henry Armitage, a linguistics scholar and librarian from Lovecraft's fabled Miskatonic University, finds himself involved in a case of immaculate conception in which a young woman named Lavinia Whateley has given birth to twin chaos monsters: one named Wilbur, who was full-grown by the age of four and a half, who had a gift for reading hieroglyphic incantations of unknown provenance, and was in the habit of performing strange mountaintop rites that caused the earth to rumble and crack; and another whom we do not meet until it makes its monstrous epiphany at the end of the story. The librarian scholar first meets Wilbur when he tries to gain access to an infamous text called the *Necronomicon,* Olaus Wormius' Latin translation of the mad Abdul Alhazred's *Al Azif.* As Dr. Armitage sight-reads over Wilbur's shoulder in the library, we learn of the "Old Ones," who were before humankind and who will be yet again. These monster gods are paradoxically in the world but not of it:

> Not in the spaces we know, but *between* them. They walk serene and primal, undimensioned and to us unseen . . . they walk unseen and foul in lonely places where the Words have been spoken and the Rites howled through at their Seasons. The wind gibbers with Their voices, and the earth mutters with Their consciousness. They bend the forest and crush the city, yet may not the forest or city behold the hand that smites . . . Their hand is at your throats, yet ye see Them not; and Their habitation is even one with your guarded threshold."[8]

Reminiscent of theological language about the paradoxical immanence and transcendance of God, the sense here is that these otherworldly chaos gods are intimately near and yet wholly other. The cosmic horror lies in the anticipation that this paradox will be resolved not in a triumphant chaos battle but in the annihilation of human subjectivity.

The Old Ones cannot be seen, the text explains, "*saving only in the features of those They have begotten on mankind,* and of those are there many sorts, differing in likeness from man's eidolon to that shape without sight or substance which is *Them.*"[9] Upon reading this, Dr. Armitage turns to Wilbur, who suddenly appears as the very embodiment of this paradox, part human and part abyss: "the bent, goatish giant before him seemed like the spawn of another planet or dimension; like something only partly of mankind, and linked to black gulfs of essence and entity that stretch like titan phantasms beyond all spheres of force and matter, space and time."[10] Armitage soon realizes that Wilbur, old Whateley, and whatever is being fed bull-offerings in their attic (Wilbur's twin brother) are preparing the way for the inbreaking of an extraordial pantheon that will lay waste the earth and humankind.

Simultaneously Dionysian and Leviathan, Lovecraft's monstrous pantheon endangers both the cosmic and social-political order of things. On the one hand, like Leviathan and other chaos monsters from the ancient Near Eastern religious traditions, Lovecraft's chaos gods lurk along the edges of the known as primordial threats to cosmic order. They are the divine harbingers not of cosmogony but chaogony. On the other hand, and at the same time, like Dionysus, whose followers transgress normative sexual politics as well as basic distinctions between human and animal, civil and wild, Lovecraft's monster gods are known by the transgressive behavior of their Bacchic devotees: human and animal sacrifices, secret mountaintop rites, erotic-ecstatic flopping hordes of "mindless and amorphous dancers," "braying" and "bellowing" like wild animals, threatening legal authority and causing reputable scholars to go off the deep end (so help me God). The chaotic, havoc-reeking hierophanies of these monstrous deities are invariably linked to socially and politically abhorrent groups of hierophants.

Not only are these monstrous epiphanies represented as threats to the cosmological and socio-political order of things; they are also physiologically abominations: their presence in this world is sensed primarily by the smell of rot and filth, which elicits a sense of ineffability and otherworldliness: "a touch of ineffable foetor,"[11] reminiscent of "alien things that festered in earth's nether abysses."[12] When they do manifest themselves, moreover, they are extreme examples of impurity and abomination as defined by Mary Douglas: impossible combinations of species (an octopus plus dragon plus human caricature, for example), whose stinking, puss-filled insides are continually overflowing their bodily boundaries. "Of genuine blood there was none; only the foetid greenish yellow ichor which trickled along the painted floor beyond the radius of the stickiness, and left a curious discoloration behind it."[13] "There was a bursting of an exploding bladder, a slushy nastiness as of a cloven sunfish, a stench of a thousand opened graves."[14] These monstrous epiphanies are both scatological and eschatological, signifying the end of the world as we know it in a sea of rot, puss and urine.

It is clear from his voluminous correspondence (he wrote thousands of letters), as well as from a careful reading of any of his Cthulhu Mythos stories, that Lovecraft himself did not believe in these or any other gods. At the same time, as Edward J. Ingebretsen makes clear, Lovecraft's writings are steeped in an American theological discourse of terror inherited from Jonathan Edwards, Cotton Mather, Nathaniel Hawthorne and others. Indeed, Lovecraft is a theologian without God. "It is a sign of Lovecraft's intellectual complexity that the God denied so thoroughly by his materialism returns so insistently in the arcane horrors of his fiction."

> Lovecraft's tales are a representative guide to the American theological imagination in all its bristly contrariness. Post-Puritan moralist, Lovecraft writes in the traditional cadences of religious discourse: salvation and damnation; grace and sin; surface and interiority; faith and unbelief. His is the widening abyss beneath the sheen of appearances, the great fragility of things as they seem.[15]

For Lovecraft, the language of theology and cosmology open toward a revelation of chaogony. The chaos monster gods of the Cthulhu Mythos, drawn from numerous theological and mythological discourses, are personifications of cosmic fear lurking just beneath the pathetically thin anthropocentric cosmological veneers we have painted over unplumbed abysses of unknowing. Lovecraft's mythology is a monstrosity in and of itself, stitched together from mutually incompatible religious discourses and ritual practices. It seeks to bring about a failure of imagination and reason by jamming together theological and mythological categories. Each of Lovecraft's mythos stories leads to a revelation of the fragility of this veneer, a revelation that takes the form of a rupture.

LOVECRAFT'S HIDEOUS PROGENY

Since Lovecraft's early death from intestinal cancer in 1937, his writings, especially those identified with the Cthulhu Mythos, have become mainstays within the popular culture of horror. Look through the horror section in almost any major bookstore, and you are likely to find as many works by and about Lovecraft as you will Clive Barker and Stephen King combined. From pulp zines to comics to bestselling novels to concordances, there have been thousands of Cthulhian works published since Lovecraft's death, including those by well-known writers like Fred Chappell, Robert Bloch, Poppy Brite and Stephen King.

There are also dozens of Cthulhu-inspired films, including Roger Corman's *The Haunted Palace* (1963; based on "The Case of Charles Dexter Ward"), Daniel Haller's *Die, Monster, Die!* with Boris Karloff (1965, a.k.a. *Monster of Terror*; based on "The Colour out of Space") and *The Dunwich Horror* with Sandra Dee (1970), Vernon Sewell's *Curse of the Crimson Altar* with Boris Karloff, Christopher Lee and Barbara Steele (1968, a.k.a. *The Crimson Cult*; based on "Dreams in the Witch House"), Stuart Gordon's *Re-Animator* and *Bride of Re-Animator* (1985 and 1990; based on "Herbert West—Reanimator"), Howard Hawks' and Christian Nyby's *The Thing from Another World* (1951) and John Carpenter's remake, *The Thing* (1982; both reminiscent of "At the Mountains of Madness"), to name just a few. There are numerous other films, moreover, whose monsters bear strong resemblance to his Cthulhu Mythos monstrosities, such as the one created by Lovecraft enthusiast H. R. Giger in the *Alien* films.

The Cthulhu Mythos has likewise found its way into a great deal of popular and countercultural music, including early Black Sabbath, Blue Oyster Cult, Iron Maiden and Metallica, as well as an international collection of lesser-known industrial, Goth and unclassifiable groups with strong "cult" followings, such as Gwar, Deicide, Blood Ritual, Cassandra Complex, Endura, Fields of Nephilim and The Darkest of the Hillside Thickets. There are also many bands named either after Lovecraft himself (such as the 1960s and '70s American band Lovecraft/H. P Lovecraft and an Argentine band named Lovecraft) or after an element from his mythos (e.g., the Spanish hardcore band Ktulu, the German metal band Necronomicon, and the Canadian spiritual death metal band NecronomicoN).[16]

FROM SCHOLARS TO THE CAMPUS CRUSADE FOR CTHULHU

Since his untimely death, Lovecraft has achieved sainthood in the works of his own progeny within the American popular culture of horror, and his Cthulhu Mythos stories have gained something of a canonical status as scripture. Stephen King speaks for many of Lovecraft's devotees when he confesses,

> Lovecraft opened the way for me, as he had done for others before me . . . The reader would do well to remember that it is his shadow, so long and so gaunt, and his eyes, so dark and puritanical, which overlie almost all of the important horror fiction that has come since.[17]

In this eulogistic expression of debt and gratitude, King dwells on the image of Lovecraft's face with the religious devotion of one standing before the icon of his saintly benefactor.

The process of canonizing Lovecraft began shortly after his death, when his writings were saved from pulp oblivion by his friends August Derleth and Donald Wandrei, who founded Arkham House (Arkham was the name of Lovecraft's own Yoknapatawpha) in order to publish Lovecraft's works. Not only did these and other friends and admirers canonize his writings for posterity, but some also began to canonize particular interpretations of his mythos. Glossaries were published along with attempts at systematization, often supplementing apparent gaps in the mythos and emending its apparent incongruities—assuming, of course, that Lovecraft meant the various epiphanies of Cthulhu and its cohorts in various stories to fit together into a larger mythological whole. Even more influential on the emerging canon of Lovecraftian interpretation were the writings of one of Arkham House's founding editors, August Derleth. Derleth wrote his own Cthulhu Mythos stories, as well as "posthumous collaborations" using Lovecraft's own notebook jottings. He also wrote editorial prefaces to each Arkham House collection of Lovecraft's works, in which he presented a particular apocalyptic construal of Lovecraft's mythos. According to Derleth, Lovecraft intended to present a scene of cosmic battle between good and evil, in which the Elder Gods are the good gods who will save humanity and the world by destroying the Old Ones who threaten total destruction.

In contemporary Lovecraftian hagiography, Derleth is sometimes remembered disdainfully as his well-meaning but misguided disciple who institutionalized certain misunderstandings of Lovecraft's life and work, which many contemporary canonical scholars of Lovecraft feel they are still struggling to correct. What Bonaventure was to Saint Francis, it appears, Derleth was to Saint Lovecraft. Derleth turned Lovecraft's abysmal openings onto cosmic fear and theological madness into cathedral windows that look onto an apocalyptic horizon of cosmic battle between good and evil in which goodness is sure to triumph on our behalf. Indeed, there is a second generation of more scholastic criticism of the Lovecraft canon that is working with great diligence and devotion to get back to the true Lovecraft. As one learned Lovecraftian writes,

> Recent Lovecraft scholars, armed with a surer feel for Lovecraft's art, have set about scraping away Derleth's overlay and, with difficulty, sometimes tedious to bystanders, have begun to lay bare the original vista painted so subtly by Lovecraft himself. That vista, Lovecraft knew, would be a difficult one for most to view unflinchingly. Derleth flinched when he saw it and sought to soften the blow for subsequent viewers. Dare we contemplate the vision embodied in Lovecraft's 'artificial mythology' as he intended it?[18]

These recent Lovecraft scholars see themselves as a generation of reformers whose aim is to peel back the layers of the traditioning process to reveal the work of the master and thereby establish him firmly within the canons of American literature. They take great pains to emphasize that what distinguishes them from earlier Lovecraft aficionados is their *scholarly* character and methodology. At the same time, as the passage above makes clear, their work is a labor of love and devotion to the master's original intentions. They represent a movement of canonical scholarship on Lovecraft, securing the Lovecraft corpus and its proper interpretation for future generations.

But not all those dedicated to Lovecraft and the Cthulhu Mythos play so seriously. There is Oderus Urungus, for example, the lead singer for the monstrous performance art band Gwar, who wears as part of his costume an appendage called "The Cuttlefish of Cthulhu". And there are the various college chapters of the international Campus Crusade for Cthulhu, a play on the Christian evangelical Campus Crusade for Christ. Its main internet site opens with this invitation to join the ranks of Cthulhian maenads:

> Bored by an ordinary, nothing life? Searching for excitement, power? Seeking a higher cause, one worthy of your very life? The Campus Crusade for Cthulhu offers all this, AND MORE! How does Tall, Green, and Slimy sound to you? Pretty scary. But you can handle it. You will have to learn how to. You will learn to yearn for the soft squeezing caress of undulating tentacles. Or you will be eternally sorry that you did not.[19]

This site also includes hymns to Cthulhu sung to the tune of traditional church camp songs like "Old Time Religion" and "Lord of the Dance," a special section on the Cthulhu Scouts of America, and evangelical posters proclaiming "Cthulhu is coming! Are you ready for the New Time?" (Figure 28).

Another is the Chaos Cult of Cthulhu 33, whose "Manifesto" announces that it "has decided to appear before the eyes of humanity as a Cult, incorporating all existing lore, traveling the paths untrodden, illuminating and thus eliminating the passing stranger. Hearken: The Chaos Cult of Cthulhu has risen . . . The dead should prove their death, and implode with a snigger. The living should join the Cult and explode with glee." Throughout their materials one encounters a ludic, willfully absurd yet highly literate admixture of the Cthulhian lingo with more traditional religious elements (for example, mystical recipes for Kaballah Rabiata and Ganesh en Pied).

On these websites, as with bands like Gwar, the performance of monstrosity becomes a kind of self-subverting, socially transgressive play whose superficiality and cheekiness masks a deeper sense of irony.

FIGURE 28. "Cthulhu is Coming! Are You Ready for the New Time?" Campus Crusade for Cthulhu website (by Joe Bethancourt, White Tree Productions). Used by permission of Joe Bethancourt.

HOMESICKNESS

In his assessment of the popular explosion of occultism and secret societies in Europe and America in the 1970s, especially within "youth culture," Mircea Eliade concluded that, beneath the obvious dissatisfaction with mainstream western Christianity and a corresponding romanticization and exoticization of the "oriental," "primitive" and "archaic" expressed by such movements, there lies a naively optimistic hope for *renovatio*.[20] That is, a hope for a resacralization of humanity and the cosmos through a return to or remembering of mythic (pre-Christian) origins which are revealed in ancient and venerable secrets passed down in the form of clandestine texts and ritual practices. Consistent with Eliade's interpretation of myth and ritual in religion, the ritual remembering and reenactment of myth within these occult movements is understood to be a means of marking present time and space as sacred. These movements, like their eighteenth- and nineteenth-century theosophic predecessors, give expression to a profound sense of nostalgia for lost origins, a homesickness rooted in the common experience of feeling not-at-home in the modern West.

This diagnosis of homesickness may be apt with regard to the semi-hermetic societies of Cthulhu Mythos devotees in the Derleth circle: as they fill out and reorient Lovecraft's fragments in order to create a full blown mythology, from cosmogony to apocalypse, they sacralize our present situation as being on our way home. Far from pushing readers to the edge of an abyss of cosmic terror, as Lovecraft tried to do, they seek to create a mythology that locates the current human situation somewhere on the salvific road between remembrance of cosmic origins and hopeful expectation of apocalyptic renewal.

Eliade's diagnosis of homesickness also makes some sense with regard to the many Lovecraft devotees who play monster with a straight face, arguing vehemently about the correct way to pronounce the name Cthulhu and its ritual incantations, or searching for the original archaic *Necronomicon* as for lost treasure (despite the fact that Lovecraft himself made clear in letters that he just made it up along with its author, Abdul Alhazred). This may also be a fair diagnosis of those Goths whose performance of Draculian monstrosity sometimes goes beyond black capes and pancake makeup to include sleeping and eating patterns. Such performances of monstrosity express both senses of homesickness: on the one hand, aching for home, and, on the other hand, being utterly sick of this home. My identification with monstrosity signifies that this world is not my home. That which is dreadful and monstrous to you is beloved and sacred to me. Come Lord Cthulhu! In such serious performances, often devastatingly bereft of irony, mainstream culture's projection of monstrous otherness represents a longed-for wholly other world. One comes to personify the *unheimlich* as an expression of one's own experience of feeling not-at-home.

Lovecraft's own use of mythology, however, could not be further from this kind of nostalgic religious longing. Although he created his Cthulhu Mythos from a wide range of "archaic" and "primitive" religious myths and rituals—from Sumerian to Egyptian to Puritan to Vodou—his mythos leads not to an ultimate sense of home but to an ultimate experience of being unhomed, ungrounded. For Lovecraft, nostalgia is only a symptom of the terrifying existential reality of human life, which is incurable.

Neither is homesickness an apt diagnosis for those who pronounce Cthulhu's incantations or imitate Lugosi's accent with tongue in cheek. This kind of ritual recuperation of the monstrous endlessly subverts any sense of nostalgia for home or origin. Shot through with heterodox amalgamations of religious language and imagery, such monster play operates as a critique of more culturally mainstream religious institutions, ideas and practices. Like the ludic masquerades of the traditional Jewish Purim play, or the transgressive, decreative performances of ritual clowning within Pueblo and other Southwestern Native American communities, this kind of ritual monstering involves a "disconfirmation of familiar forms" and puts the performer and the spectator in a liminal space "between inside and outside, self and other, creation and destruction, order and chaos."[21]

There are many instances in which novels and movies within the popular culture of horror provide the central plot for a kind of social drama of monster killing. Much like the ancient reenactments of Marduk's victory over Tiamat or Re's victory over Apophis, the ritual public sharing of the monster tale often provides a more or less safe, predictable and structured context in which deep and often repressed fears, uncertainties and insecurities about

FIGURE 29. *The Bride of Frankenstein*, Copyright 1935 Universal Studios.

the accepted order of things are projected in the form of monstrous otherness and then, in the last battle, are dramatically overcome.

But in instances of playing monster, in which monstrosity is embraced, even taken on as a form of one's own identity, something radically different is at work. Such monstrous performance art works against the general tendency to use monsters to mark the distance between normative and non-normative identity, pushing us to get to know our monsters face to face—and perhaps, like the blind man in *The Bride of Frankenstein* (Figure 29), to share a good smoke and some new music. Gwar, for example.

CONCLUSION

HERE BE MONSTERS

This book began with Frankenstein's monster, so it seems appropriate to end with him too.

We tend to forget that unlike James Whale's two-part film version of the Frankenstein story, which begins in the graveyard and ends in the laboratory, Shelley's novel begins and ends at sea, on a voyage that is quickly slipping off the edge of the map of the known world. While on "pathless seas" heading toward the North Pole, explorer Robert Walton discovers Victor Frankenstein paddling along by himself in a dinghy, and brings him aboard his ship. Walton, still enchanted with his own romantic search for uncharted territory, is immediately drawn to Frankenstein, who is at the very end of his own tale. Sensing a kindred spirit, Walton shares with Frankenstein his deep desire to push past the edge of the map, to venture beyond the boundaries of the known world. But as he speaks a "dark gloom" spreads over Frankenstein's face. "Unhappy man! Do you share my madness? Have you drunk also of the intoxicating draught? Hear me,—let me reveal my tale, and you will dash the cup from your lips!"[1] Frankenstein immediately recognizes the essential similarity between Walton's adventure beyond accepted cosmological boundaries and his own adventure beyond accepted biological boundaries. Although their adventures involve the transgression of different kinds of boundaries, both are venturing off the established charts of the known and into radically unfamiliar territory. The main difference between them is that whereas Walton is at the beginning of his adventure, about to cross the uncrossable boundary, Frankenstein is at the bitter end, having already crossed over and deeply regretting it. And that has made all the difference. What follows, then, in the bulk of the novel, is Walton's recounting of Frankenstein's own monster tale, which he tells to the young adventurer in a desperate effort to discourage him from pushing any further off the map, to scare him back home. Then, as Frankenstein's tale ends and he dies, Walton meets the monster, who comes aboard to present his own version of the story. Walton hears the monster tale and then ultimately meets the monster himself while in this uncharted territory.

Maps plot the lay of the land, making it known and knowable. In the process they also mark off what is unknown along their edges and within their deepest seas. On ancient maps, the *terra incognita*, or "unknown territory," was sometimes marked by images of fantastical monsters accompanied by textual warnings, the most famous being *hic sunt dracones*, "here be dragons."[2] These monstrous figures indicate regions of dangerous uncertainty. They show where the limits of knowing are. They dwell on the threshold between the known and the unknown, this world and its otherworldly beyond. These monsters are interstitial figures, markers of the inside/outside.

Shelley's novel is something of a literary cartography in this sense, complete with a foreboding monster paddling along its edges. In fact, just as *Frankenstein* is a story within a story, it is also a map within a map. First, Walton's story in the frame narrative is a literary cartography: far out from the center of the map, where home and loved ones are, he meets the monster and hears the monster story in the unknown, unmapped border regions of the north seas. Second, Frankenstein's own monster tale, which he recounts to Walton, is also a map in narrative form, plotting out Frankenstein's movement from the known geographical and cultural landscapes of his childhood—in the center of the map and in the center of Europe—into the unknown border regions where be monsters, and where he himself is ultimately revealed as monstrous. In Shelley's novel, the monster tale and the monster himself, both of which Walton meets in the unmapped, unknown border regions of the north seas, are portents and warnings against Walton's desire to venture beyond the edge of the map.

WARNING

Like the monsters on ancient maps, the monsters within biblical religious traditions and the monsters within the popular culture of horror—as well as its various countercultures—stand on and for the threshold between world and abyss. They are personifications of that which is in the world but not of it, appearing on the ambiguous edges of the conceptual landscape, where the right order of things touches on a wholly other chaos, where inside and outside, self and other intertwine. Whether demonized or deified or something in between, monsters bring on a limit experience that is akin in many respects to religious experience, an experience of being on the edge of certainty and security, drawn toward and repulsed by a *monstrum tremendum*. The monstrous is an embodiment of overwhelming and chaotic excess, a too-muchness that brings on a vertigo-like sense of fear and desire: standing on the threshold of an unfathomable abyss, I am aware of myself simultaneously pulling back and pulling over. In this teetering, an irreducible ambivalence is revealed within me. The monstrous can elicit an urge to pull back from the edge of order at which it appears and, at the same time, an urge to cross over, to transgress, to lose ground.

The politically and religiously conservative function of the monstrous is to encourage one to pull back from the edge. The monster is a warning or portent, *demonstrating* what to avoid, and *remonstrating* with anyone who would challenge established social and symbolic boundaries. They literally scare the hell out of us. Let sleeping leviathans lie, as they say.

Without denying that this is often the conservative aim of monstrous horror, and without denying that this is also often its achieved effect, it cannot be denied that horror swings us both ways, soliciting both conservative and radical impulses. Although the aim is often to warn readers and viewers to pull back from the margins and into the cultural center, to send us home with our tails between our legs, our desire for the monstrous other often undermines this purpose. It draws us away from home and over the edge.

Perhaps this is because the monster is never entirely outside or other, can never be a purely negative image of us and our world. Perhaps part of what makes monsters horrifically *unheimlich* is that we see ourselves in them. Monsters blur lines between inside and outside, this worldly and otherworldly, self and other. My sense of vertiginous horror in the face of the monstrous emerges from the feeling that it is both within me and beyond me. It reveals an abominable, monstrous otherness within, without reducing that otherness to sameness, without making it entirely familiar. It tells me that I cannot be de-monstrated.

Monstrum: a portent or warning. The monster's warning is distressingly double. On the one hand, as a disciplinary figure, it warns against tampering with the order of things, urging us to pull back from the threshold of the known at which it appears, into the social and symbolic center, examining ourselves for any traces of its touch, reinvigorating a vigilant reason, letting sleeping leviathans lie. On the other hand, as a sign of unaccountable and unimaginable excess, it warns against the limitedness of our well-constructed cosmologies and against simplistic but widespread understandings of religion as morality or ideological system. The monster lulls reason into a night of unknowing in which sleeping leviathans do not lie.

NOTES

INTRODUCTION

1. Friedrich Nietzsche, *Beyond Good and Evil: Prelude to a Philosophy of the Future*, trans. Walter Kaufman (New York: Random House, 1966) section 146.

2. Mary Wollstonecraft Shelley, *Frankenstein or The Modern Prometheus*, ed. M. K. Joseph (Oxford: Oxford University Press, 1969) 1.

3. Sigmund Freud, "The Uncanny," *The Standard Edition of the Complete Psychological Works of Sigmund Freud*, XVII (1917–1919), trans. James Strachey *et al* (London: Hogarth Press, 1955) 222, 226.

4. Herbert Marcuse, *Eros and Civilization: A Philosophical Inquiry into Freud* (Boston: Beacon, 1955) 72.

5. On early conceptions of the idea of "monstrous births" (*teras* in Greek, *monstrum* in Latin), see Marie-Hélène Huet, *Monstrous Imagination* (London: Harvard University Press, 1993), whose larger focus is on the closely related history of the idea that "monstrous births" were divine revelations of the mother's imagination, especially of her unfulfilled desires (esp. 1–10, 61–78). This led to ideas about art as the offspring of an artist's monstrous imagination.

See also chapter 12, below, on Shelley's description of her novel as "hideous progeny."

6. Rudolph Otto, *The Idea of the Holy: An Inquiry into the Non-Rational Factor in the Idea of the Divine and Its Relation to the Rational,* trans. John W. Harvey (2d ed.; New York: Oxford University Press, 1950) 28. See the discussion of Otto and the book of Job in chapter 4, below. Otto's essay has had tremendous influence in studies of horror as religious experience. See, e.g., S.L. Varnado, *Haunted Presence: The Numinous in Gothic Fiction* (Tuscaloosa: University of Alabama Press, 1987). See also the critical discussion of this trend in Noël Carroll, *The Philosophy of Horror or Paradoxes of the Heart* (New York and London: Routledge, 1990) 165–67.

7. Otto 40.

8. Freud 241. There are many recent studies of modern horror as the return of the repressed, including, most recently, Valdine Clemens, *The Return of the Repressed: Gothic Horror from* The Castle of Otranto *to* Alien (New York: SUNY Press, 1999); see also Eve Kosofsky Sedgwick, *The Coherence of Gothic Conventions* (New York and London: Methuen, 1986). In film studies, particular attention has been paid to horror as the return of repressed sexuality that threatens established social norms of heterosexuality, monogamy and family. Robin Wood ("An Introduction to the American Horror Film," *Planks of Reason: Essays on the Horror Film,* ed. Barry Keith Grant [Metuchen: Scarecrow Press, 1984] 177) summarizes the sociological implications: " . . . that in a society built on monogamy and family there will be enormous surplus of sexual energy that will have to be repressed; and that what is repressed must always strive to return." See also Wood, "Return of the Repressed," *Film Comment* 14 (July-August 1978). A particularly influential psychoanalytic study of the horror of abjection is Julia Kristeva, *Powers of Horror: An Essay on Abjection,* trans. Leon S. Roudiez (New York: Columbia University Press, 1982).

9. Mircea Eliade, *The Sacred and the Profane: The Nature of Religion,* trans. Willard R. Trask (New York: Harcourt Brace & Company, 1959).

10. Eliade 20.

11. Eliade 29–30.

12. Eliade 48.

CHAPTER 1, CHAOS GODS

1. For a critical analysis of the history of modern theories of "myth" and "mythology," see Bruce Lincoln, *Theorizing Myth: Narrative, Ideology, and Scholarship* (Chicago: University of Chicago Press, 1999). Lincoln's theory of myth as "ideology in narrative form" (147–49) is suggestive, even while it invites further theorizing of the term "ideology."

2. Leonard H. Lesko, "Ancient Egyptian Cosmogonies and Cosmology," *Religion in Ancient Egypt: Gods, Myths, and Personal Practice*, ed. Byron E. Shafer (Ithaca: Cornell University Press, 1991) 92; Richard A. Parker and Leonard H. Lesko, "The Khonsu Cosmogony," *Pyramid Studies and Other Essays Presented to I.E.S. Edwards*, ed. John Baines *et al* (London: Egypt Exploration Society, 1988) 168–75. For a broad comparative study of this and related motifs as they relate to the legacy of western apocalypticism, see Norman Cohn, *Cosmos, Chaos and the World to Come: The Ancient Roots of Apocalyptic Faith* (New Haven: Yale University Press, 1993).

3. E.g., Ilya Prigogine and Isabell Stengers, *Order out of Chaos* (Toronto: Bantam, 1984); M. Mitchell Waldrop, *Complexity: The Emerging Science at the Edge of Order and Chaos* (New York: Simon & Schuster, 1992); and John Briggs and F. David Peat, *Turbulent Mirror: An Illustrated Guide to Chaos Theory and the Science of Wholeness* (San Francisco: HarperCollins, 1990), which draws explicitly from ancient Near Eastern and Chinese cosmogonic narratives.

4. Although the earliest surviving Akkadian cuneiform tablets date to the beginning of the first millennium BCE, the *Enuma Elish* (whose title comes from the story's first two words, which mean "when above") was composed much earlier, probably between the nineteenth century, when King Hammurabi (1848–1806 BCE) established Marduk as the king of Babylonian deities, and the twelfth century BCE, when King Nebuchadnezzar I (1125–1104 BCE) restored Marduk as a central figure. Translations are from Stephanie Dalley, *Myths from Mesopotamia* (Oxford: Oxford University Press, 1989) 232–77, supplemented on occasion by my own exegesis of the Akkadian text. Parallels between this text and biblical accounts of creation and apocalypse have been studied

extensively since Hermann Gunkel, *Schöpfung und Chaos in Urzeit und Endzeit: Eine religionsgeschichtliche Untersuchung über Gen 1 und Ap Joh 12* (Göttingen: Vandenhoeck & Ruprecht, 1895).

5. Gwendolyn Leick, *Sex and Eroticism in Mesopotamian Literature* (London and New York: Routledge, 1994) 13–14.

6. Tablet IV; in Dalley 253–54.

7. A. Sachs, trans., "Temple Program for the New Year's Festivals at Babylon," *Ancient Near Eastern Texts Related to the Old Testament,* ed. James B. Pritchard (3d ed.; Princeton: Princeton University Press, 1969) 331–334, includes instructions for reading the *Enuma Elish* to the god Bel in the afternoon of the fourth day of the month of Nisan.

8. Barbara Creed, *The Monstrous-Feminine: Film, Feminism, Psychoanalysis* (New York: Routledge, 1993).

9. Tablet I; Dalley 236.

10. Tablet VII; Dalley 273.

11. E.g., *Rig Veda* 10.50; 10.55; 10.89. By the creative force of Indra, the chaos monster Vṛtra is remade into a divine figure of *both* cosmic and social law and order. See Calvert Watkins, *How to Kill a Dragon: Aspects of Indo-European Poetics* (Oxford: Oxford University Press, 1995) 446. The hymns of the *Rig Veda* were probably first collected and written down early in the first millenium BCE, but were no doubt circulated orally for centuries before.

12. Excerpts concerning Apophis are translated and discussed by John A. Wilson, "Egyptian Myths, Tales, and Mortuary Texts," *Ancient Near Eastern Texts Relating to the Old Testament,* ed. James B. Pritchard (Third edition with supplement; Princeton: Princeton University Press, 1969), 11–12; cf. 6–7. One of the texts concerning the overthrow of Apophis includes ritual instructions that make clear how such monsters can stand simultaneously for cosmic, political, and personal threat: as the story of Re's overthrow of Apophis, is recited at dawn and dusk, an image of Apophis is drawn on a green sheet of papyrus, which is put in a fire box bearing Apophis name and then burned and stamped out; in addition, the names of Pharaoh's enemies and their families are to be put in wax and burned in the fire box along with Apophis (Wilson 7).

13. Collectively known as the Baal-Anat Cycle, the six tablets that contain this story series date to the fourteenth century BCE,

several centuries before most scholars would date the earliest biblical texts. The tablets are damaged to such an extent that it is not entirely clear whether they should be read as a single coherent narrative or as a collection of related stories. A new edition of the transliterated Ugaritic text along with new translations of these major texts and other important fragments is in Simon B. Parker, *Ugaritic Narrative Poetry*, trans. Mark S. Smith, Simon B. Parker, Edward L. Greenstein, Theodore J. Lewis and David Marcus (Atlanta: Society of Biblical Literature, 1997), abbreviated *UNP*. Unless otherwise noted, the discussion here is based on these transliterations and translations. Other editions include M. Dietrich, O. Loretz and J. Sanmartín, *The Cuneiform Alphabetic Texts from Ugarit, Ras Ibn Hani and Other Places* (Münster: Ugarit-Verlag, 1995), abbreviated *CAT*; and A. Herdner, *Corpus des tablettes en cunéiformes alphabétiques découvertes à Ras Shamra-Ugarit de 1929 à 1939* (Paris: Imprimerie Nationale, 1963), abbreviated *CTA*.

14. J. C. L. Gibson, "The Theology of the Ugaritic Baal Cycle," *Orientalia* 53 (1984) 202–19.

15. Athirat is sometimes called "Athirat of the Sea," or "of Yamm" (*aṯrt ym*), as in the sixth tablet, *UNP* 12 (*CAT* 1.6) I, 43–47 and 53. The context is Anat's announcement to El and Athirat that Baal (who ascended after killing Yamm) is dead, which Anat assumes will be cause for rejoicing by Athirat and her sons.

16. Smith, trans., *UNP* 8 (*CAT* 1.2) IV, 11–33; the challenge from Yamm is related in *UNP* 8 II (*CAT* 1.2 I).

17. Smith, trans., *UNP* 9 (*CAT* 1.3) III, 36–42. It is not entirely clear how to understand the relationship between the name Yamm and the other names or epithets mentioned in this and other passages, especially Tunnan (= Hebrew *tannin*, "sea monster"), the Twisty Serpent, the Potentate with the Seven Heads, and Litan (related to the Hebrew name Leviathan; also mentioned in Mot's taunt). Although it is possible that they are distinct monstrous opponents to Anat and Baal, recent research on this text and a related fragment suggests that they may be parallel references to the same figure, who is variously called Yamm, Tunnan and Litan. Wayne T. Pitard, "The Binding of Yamm: A New Edition of the Ugaritic Text KTU 1.83," *Journal of Near Eastern Studies* 57 (1998) 261–80, argues convincingly that Yamm/River [Nahar] in lines 4–7 and 8–10 of this fragment are parallel to Tunnan in lines 8–10.

Then, returning to Anat's speech in *CAT* 1.3 III, 38–46 (*UNP* 9), quoted above, he argues for a line division that would identify Tunnan as a parallel to Yamm/River in a tricolon. In fact, these same monstrous names will reappear in similarly serpentine tangles of identity confusion in the Hebrew Bible, on which see the next chapter.

18. Smith, trans., *UNP* 11 (*CAT* 1.5) I, 1–8, repeated 27–35.

19. Smith, trans., *UNP* 12 (*CAT* 1.6) II, 30–35.

20. Smith, trans., *UNP* 9 (*CAT* 1.3) II, 9–15.

21. Neil H. Walls, *The Goddess Anat in Ugaritic Myth* (Atlanta: Scholars Press, 1992) 220. Walls makes clear that Anat "consistently acts on her own desires and is submissive to no one in the extant literature" (107). Although she appears to be committed to Baal and his initiatives in tablets 4–6 of the Baal-Anat Cycle, for example, she works against Baal in the story of Aqhat.

22. Gibson 218–19.

CHAPTER 2, THE BIBLE AND HORROR

1. The relationships between these terms are discussed at length in Mary K. Wakeman, *God's Battle with the Monster: A Study in Biblical Imagery* (Leiden: Brill, 1973) 56–105. Following Wakeman's general conclusions, I treat *tannin* not as a proper noun but as a generic term for chaos monsters associated with the sea ("sea monsters"). Leviathan and Rahab (which does not appear in any of the extant Ugaritic texts; on which see below) are proper names that function in similar ways in different contexts (but never appear together). The Hebrew *yam* is particularly slippery, insofar as it is both a proper noun (Yam), representing a monstrous personification of the sea, and a generic noun ("sea," especially when it appears with a definite article, i.e., *hayyam*, "the sea"). On the relationship between the Hebrew name Leviathan and the Ugaritic name Litan, see J.A. Emerton, "Leviathan and ltn: The Vocalization of the Ugaritic Word for the Dragon," *Vetus Testamentum* 32 (1982) 327–31.

2. Unless otherwise indicated, all translations of biblical passages are my own. LORD is used in place of the divine name Yhwh.

3. Another hymn in praise of creation that clearly locates figures known elsewhere as chaos monsters within the divinely

ordained ecology is Psalm 148. Here the psalmist summons "all sea monsters" (*tanninim*) and all of "the deep" (or "abyss," *tehom*) to praise God who is their creator and sustainer.

4. The Hebrew here is uncertain, depending on the meaning of *ṣiyim*, which can be taken as plural of "ship" (*ṣiy*; cf. Numbers 24:24), "desert-dweller" (also *ṣiy*), or "drought" / "desert" (*ṣiyyah*). If we go with the first, then the phrase translates most literally as "for people for ships," suggesting it as food for seafaring people, perhaps even whalers. If we go with the second or the third, then it might be translated as "for desert-dwellers [animals or people]," "for the people in the desert," or "for the people for drought."

5. Walter Brueggemann, *Israel's Praise: Doxology against Idolatry and Ideology* (Philadelphia: Fortress Press, 1988); and *The Message of the Psalms: A Theological Commentary* (Minneapolis: Augsburg, 1984).

6. John Day, *God's Conflict with the Dragon and the Sea: Echoes of a Canaanite Myth in the Old Testament* (Cambridge: Cambridge University Press, 1985) 88–140, presents this "historicization" of the chaos battle motif primarily as a development in the chaos battle motif, in which the historical-political plane replaces the cosmic plane: "That this could be done is indicative of the fact that the powers of chaos, though subdued at the creation, were still liable to manifest themselves in the present on the historical plane" (88). My reading diverges insofar as I see the cosmic and political planes as integrated from the start within the conceptual landscape of the Hebrew Bible as manifest in the chaos battle motif. As in similar Egyptian, Vedic and Babylonian stories discussed in chapter 1, the monster's threat always traverses the cosmic, the political and the personal.

7. Other texts that refer to Egypt as the defeated Rahab or the primordial chaos waters include Psalm 87:4, in which Rahab is a name for Egypt listed as one of the nations "who acknowledge me [God]"; Psalm 77:17–21, in which the cosmogonic chaos battle of God versus the raging chaos waters is linked to the Exodus ("the waters saw you and convulsed . . . your way was through the sea [*bayyam*] . . . you led your people like a flock under the care of Moses and Aaron"); and Isaiah 30:7, a text dated after the fall of the northern kingdom of Israel to Assyria (c. 721 BCE) and before Assyria's attack on Jerusalem (701 BCE), in which the prophet

scolds the southern kingdom of Judah for considering assistance from Egypt, recalling God's "silencing" or "thwarting" (emending *hem shabet* to *hammoshbat*) of Egypt in and after the exodus as a victory over the monstrous Rahab, who is now "worthless and empty" (Day 89, Wakeman 58, Gunkel 39).

Cristiano Grottanelli, *Kings and Prophets: Monarchic Power, Inspired Leadership, and Sacred Text in Biblical Narrative* (Oxford: Oxford University Press, 1999) 47–72, identifies four biblical stories in which a defeated enemy king or deity is identified with a defeated chaos monster without ever being explicitly called Rahab, Leviathan, Yam, *tannin* or the like: Moses' destruction of the golden calf in Exodus 32; Ehud's slaying of King Eglon of Moab in Judges 3; Saul's/Israel's victory over Nahash (*naḥash*, "serpent") and the Ammonites in 1 Samuel 11; and Samuel's slaying of King Agag of Amalek in 1 Samuel 15.

8. In addition to Leviathan (Ugaritic Litan) and *tannin* (Ugaritic Tunnan), compare Isaiah's "fleeing serpent" and "twisting serpent" (*nḥš brḥ* and *'qltwn*) with the "fleeing serpent" and "twisty serpent" (*bṭn brḥ* and *'qltn*) associated with Tunnan, Litan and Yamm in the Baal-Anat Cycle.

9. In this context, it is worth noting that "river" (*nahar*) is consistently used as an epithet for Prince Yamm (*ṯapat nahar*, "Judge River") in the Baal-Anat Cycle (e.g., *UNP* 8 [*CAT* 1.2]; and in *UNP* 9 [*CAT* 1.3] III, 39, Anat calls him "River, the Great God" [*nhr.il.rbm*], which is close to Isaiah's "the mighty and great waters of the River" [*hannahar . . . weharabbim*]). Given the use of Ugaritic parallels elsewhere in Isaiah (esp. 27:1), it is not unreasonable to ask whether the use of *nahar* in this passage is meant to recall Yamm's epithet in the Baal-Anat Cycle.

CHAPTER 3, THE SLEEP OF WISDOM

1. E. M. Cioran, *On the Heights of Despair*, trans. Ilinca Zarifopol-Johnston (Chicago: University of Chicago Press, 1992) 55. Many years later, in an interview with Zarifopol-Johnston, he said that he no longer wrote because "I don't want to slander the universe anymore; I've done it long enough, don't you think so?" (xiv).

2. Cioran 109.

3. Elaine Scarry, *The Body in Pain: The Making and Unmaking of the World* (New York and Oxford: Oxford University Press, 1985) esp. 4–5, 161–63, 172. Scarry focuses on the relation between pain's unmaking of the world and its unmaking of language.

4. Cioran 12.

5. Cioran 5.

6. On the relation between wisdom and creation in the Hebrew Bible, see esp. Roland E. Murphy, "Wisdom and Creation," *Journal of Biblical Literature* 104 (1985) 3–11. Whether one agrees or disagrees with the argument that wisdom influences Deuteronomy (so Moshe Weinfeld, *Deuteronomy and the Deuteronomic School* [Oxford: Oxford University Press, 1972]), it is clear that there are strong relations between Deuteronomic and wisdom traditions.

7. Tod Linafelt, "The Undecidability of *brk* in the Prologue to Job," *Biblical Interpretation* 4 (1996), describes Job as a fault line that runs to the very character of God. Also Carol A. Newsom, *Job, The New Interpreters Bible IV* (Nashville: Abingdon, 1996) 358–61.

8. Emmanuel Levinas, "Suffering and Death" (excerpt from *Time and the Other* [1946–47]), trans. R. A. Cohen, *The Levinas Reader*, ed. Sean Hand (Oxford: Blackwell, 1989) 40.

9. This interpretation of the creation of the first human as having two faces is based in part on the fact that in the Hebrew text of Genesis 2:7 the verb *yaṣar* occurs with two initial yods rather than one. Thus it is read as an indication of a double creation, forming a human that is two-in-one.

10. Emmanuel Levinas, "And God Created Woman," *Nine Talmudic Readings*, trans. A. Aronowicz (Bloomington: Indiana University Press, 1990) 167; italics mine. The passage from the Babylonian Talmud is Tractate Berakhot 61a.

11. The idea of Satan as an embodiment of absolute evil or anti-god is not present in the Hebrew Bible, but rather develops during the intertestamental period. 1 Chronicles 21:1 is the only Hebrew Bible text in which the noun *śatan* (without the definite article) could be taken as a proper name. In that text, however, it may just as well be translated "an accuser" or "inciter." A summary discussion of the various meanings and transformations of this figure in Judaism and Christianity may be found in Victor P. Hamilton,

"Satan," *Anchor Bible Dictionary*, 5, ed. David Noel Freedman et al (New York: Doubleday, 1992) 985–89.

12. Mary Douglas, "The Abominations of Leviticus," *Purity and Danger: An Analysis of Concepts of Pollution and Taboo* (London: Routledge & Kegan Paul, 1966). For uses of *'ofel* ("gloom") in the sense of calamity or cosmic breakdown, see, e.g., Job 23:17; 30:26; Amos 5:20; cf. similar uses of the feminine noun form in Isaiah 8:22; 58:10 and 59:9. For uses of *ga'al* as "defile" or "pollute," see Isaiah 59:3; 63:3; Lamentations 4:14; Zephaniah 3:1; Malachi 1:7; Ezra 2:62 and Nehemiah 7:64.

13. Reading *yom* ("day") as *yam*, following Gunkel 59–62 and others. On the problems with this reading, see Newsom 368.

14. Cioran 5, 12.

15. Cioran 90.

16. Cioran 90.

CHAPTER 4, FROM THE WHIRLWIND

1. Note the remarkable similarities between the imagery employed in this passage and that found in the *Enuma Elish*, when Marduk set half of Tiamat's body "to roof the sky" and "drew a bolt across and made a guard to hold it," arranging "her waters . . . so they could not escape," and grouping her spittle into little clouds (see IV and V in Dalley 255–57, discussed in chapter 1).

2. Most English translations follow the chapter and verse numbering of the Greek Septuagint and Latin Vulgate of the Old Testament, which sometimes differs from that of the Hebrew text and the Tanakh translation. Wherever they diverge, as in Job 40–41, I use the Hebrew text versification and indicate the alternative chapter and verse numbers in parentheses.

3. Samuel E. Balentine, "'What Are Human Beings, that You Make So Much of Them?' Divine Disclosure from the Whirlwind: 'Look at Behemoth'," *God in the Fray*, ed. Tod Linafelt and Timothy K. Beal (Philadelphia: Fortress Press, 1998) 269; also Johannes Hempel, "The Contents of the Literature," *Record and Revelation*, ed. H.W. Robinson (Oxford: Clarendon Press, 1938) 73. Balentine provocatively argues that God presents Behemoth and Leviathan, "who are celebrated as near equals to God," not in order to subju-

gate Job, as is commonly believed, but to challenge him to be like them.

4. Many translations, following the Septuagint, emend the first-person pronouns in this passage to third-person, so that the text reads, "who then can stand before *it* [or *him*]?," and change the last line from "it [or he] is mine" (*lî hû'*) to an interrogative "who?" (*mî hû'*). E.g., Marvin H. Pope, *Job: Introduction, Translation, and Notes* (Anchor Bible 15; New York: Doubleday, 1965) 335–38.

5. Carroll 194–95.

6. Some modern versions take it as a form of the verb *mashal* ("rule" or "dominate"), thus "there is no one on earth who can dominate it." If read thus, Leviathan is being described not as beyond capture by language or analogy, but as beyond domination by any other earthly creature (including humans, whom God commands to subdue and dominate the rest of creation in Genesis 1:27–28).

7. Otto 28.

8. Otto 31.

9. Otto 40.

10. Otto 79.

11. Otto 79.

12. Otto 80.

13. Stephen King, *Danse Macabre* (New York: Everest, 1981) 22; in Roger C. Schlobin, "Prototypic Horror: The Genre of the Book of Job," *Semeia* 60 (1992) 28.

14. Schlobin 28.

15. Nietzsche, section 146. This is the second part of his warning, quoted in the introduction, that "whoever fights monsters should see to it that in the process he does not become a monster."

CHAPTER 5, DINNER AND A SHOW

1. Except where noted, translations of passages from the Babylonian Talmud and Midrash Rabbah are from the Soncino editions (*The Babylonian Talmud, Seder Nezikin, vol. II, Baba Bathra*, trans. Isidore Epstein et al [London: Soncino, 1935]; *Midrash Rabbah Leviticus*, trans. J. Israelstam and Judah J. Slotki [New York: Soncino, 1983]).

2. The Soncino edition translates the Aramaic *tannina'* as "snake." In keeping with my earlier translations of the biblical Hebrew *tannin,* I translate it here and throughout the discussion as "sea monster."

3. Soncino translation has "slant serpent" and "tortuous serpent" for these two phrases from Isaiah 27:1. On these phrases in biblical and Ugaritic texts, see chapters 1 and 2.

4. The phrase "Behemoth on a thousand hills" is from Psalm 50:10. Most modern translations read *behemot* in this psalm as the plural form of *behemah* (thus "beasts" or "cattle on a thousand hills"). The rabbis in Talmud and Midrash (see below), however, took it as the proper name Behemoth, as in Job 40. For several interpretations of "upon a thousand hills" (does Behemoth feed from a thousand hills? does it actually span a thousand hills?), see Midrash Leviticus Rabbah XXII.

5. I have replaced the Soncino translations of these two lines from Job 40:16 with my own, so that their biblical source is clearer in English. The Hebrew here is identical to that of the Masoretic Hebrew text of Job 40:16.

6. An early (second century CE) pseudepigraphal text, 2 Baruch 29:1–5, anticipates that Leviathan and Behemoth are being preserved for a future banquet. In the final days, "Behemoth will reveal itself from its place, and Leviathan will come from the sea, the two great monsters which I created on the fifth day of creation and which I shall have kept until that time. And they will be nourishment for all who are left" ("2 Baruch," trans. A.F.J. Klijn, *The Old Testament Pseudepigrapha,* I, ed. James H. Charlesworth [Garden City and New York: Doubleday, 1983] 630). Cf. the first century BCE text 1 Enoch 60:7–10, which refers to the female Leviathan and the male Behemoth as a pair who must be separated (see also 4 Ezra 6:49–52).

7. Modern translations of this verse (Job 40:30 [or 41:6]) make no sense as a basis for bar Bar Hana's claim here. The Masoretic text, for example, reads "Shall traders traffic in him? Will he be divided up among merchants?" Bar Bar Hana, however, is reading the *yikru* (from *krh*) as an imperfect verb meaning "they will banquet" (not as an inferred rhetorical question), thereby producing the statement "traders will make a banquet of

him," instead of the question, "will traders traffic in him?" Likewise the second line of the verse is read as "they will divide [not 'will they divide?'] him up among the *kena'anim*," which they take to mean "scholars" rather than "merchants." Thus the statement "they will divide him up among the *kena'anim* [i.e., the righteous scholars]."

8. This translation is based on the discussion of *ḥiddush torah* in Marcus Jastrow, *Dictionary of the Targumim, Talmud Babli, Yerushalmi and Midrashic Literature* (New York: Judaica, 1982) 427. The Soncino translation is: "The Holy One, blessed be he, said: *Instruction shall go forth from Me* (Isa. LI, 4), i.e. an exceptional temporary ruling will go forth from me." In fact, the passage in the Masoretic text of Isaiah has neither *ḥiddush torah* nor *torah ḥadashah* but simply *torah*, that is, "Torah will go forth from me." It is not clear whether the Midrash is working from a different version of Isaiah 51:4 or is simply misquoting it. Given that this discussion concerns Leviathan, moreover, it is probably no coincidence that Abin ben Kahana quotes from Isaiah 51, for it is in this same chapter that Isaiah calls on God to awaken, as in previous generations, when God "hacked Rahab to pieces" and "pierced the sea monster" (Isaiah 51:9–10). As discussed in chapter 2, this text remembers both God's cosmogonic defeat of the primordial chaos monster and God's creation of Israel by defeating its monstrous oppressor Egypt/Rahab. Although neither Behemoth nor Leviathan are personifications of Rome, that empire's atrocities against Jerusalem and the Jewish people do loom large in the background of this text.

9. See also Leviticus 17:15; 22:8; Exodus 22:30 (or 22:31).

10. A similar line of thought concerning the eating of Leviathan, Behemoth and other monstrous figures (e.g., the Ziz) is found in Leviticus Rabbah XXII.10: "As recompense for the prohibition of certain fish you will eat Leviathan, a clean fish; . . . as recompense for the prohibition of certain cattle (*behemoth*) you shall eat Behemoth on a thousand mountains." That Behemoth is on a thousand mountains, it is asserted, means that it eats the herbs of a thousand mountains, suggesting that its meat will be particularly tasty.

11. Chapter 10 of *Pirke de Rabbi Eleazer (The Chapters of Rabbi Eliezer the Great according to the manuscript belonging to Abraham Epstein*

of Vienna), trans. G. Friedlander (New York: Bloch Publishing Company, 1981). See the excellent interpretation by Yvonne Sherwood, *A Biblical Text and its Afterlives: The Survival of Jonah in Western Culture* (Cambridge: Cambridge University Press, 2000) 108–16.

12. Sherwood 109.

CHAPTER 6, TO THE DEVIL

1. Except where noted, translations are from the New Revised Standard Version. My own comments on and occasional translations of the Greek text are based on the twenty-sixth edition of the *Nestle-Aland Novum Testamentum Graece* (Stuttgart: Deutsche Bibelgesellschaft, 1979).

2. The literary history of the Apocalypse of John is not clear. It is likely that some form of it, though not necessarily the final form, was in circulation by the end of the Roman Emperor Domitian's reign (by around 95 CE). It is also possible that its composition began during the reign of Nero in the late 60s and continued decades or more after Domitian. Its status within the Christian canon of the New Testament was disputed in some circles as late as the fourth century. Authorship, composition date and canonical status are discussed in Adela Yarbro Collins, "The Book of Revelation," *Anchor Bible Dictionary* 5:698–99; and esp. *Crisis and Catharsis: The Power of the Apocalypse* (Philadelphia: Fortress Press, 1984) 54–83; and Elisabeth Schüssler-Fiorenza, *The Book of Revelation* (Philadelphia: Fortress Press, 1985).

3. Tina Pippin, *Apocalyptic Bodies: The Biblical End of the World in Text and Image* (London and New York: Routledge, 1999) 112.

4. This image of the risen Jesus in Apocalypse 1:12–16 also draws imagery from Daniel's vision of God as "the Ancient of Days" with clothing as white as wool, hair as white as snow and surrounded by fire (Daniel 7:9–10).

5. This image of the woman clothed in the sun, about to give birth, also echoes the story of Leto known in Greek and Roman traditions. Leto is hidden on the island of Delos along with her newborn son, who is threatened by a dragon named Python. See Adela Yarbro Collins, *The Combat Myth in the Book of Revelation* (Missoula:

Scholars Press, 1976) 57–85. On the use of symbolism in the Apocalypse see David L. Barr, "The Apocalypse as a Symbolic Transformation of the World: A Literary Analysis," *Interpretation* 38 (1984) 39–50.

6. Clive Barker, "On Censorship," *Clive Barker's Shadows in Eden*, ed. Stephen Jones (Lancaster: Underwood-Miller, 1991) 402; in Ingebretsen xi.

7. As Pippin has made particularly clear, not only does the Apocalypse of John continue to have tremendous influence on the late twentieth- and early twenty-first-century popular culture of horror, it is inextricably *part of* that culture. Most striking in this respect is the central role that this text has within certain subcultures of Christian fundamentalism. Pippin's account of a class visit to "Tribulation Trail," offered by a suburban Atlanta church as an alternative to Halloween haunted houses, is a remarkable example (Pippin 78–99).

8. Watkins, *How to Kill a Dragon*, provides valuable etymological background to the dragon-serpent slaying formula in Indo-European traditions. The Greek word *ophis*, "serpent," is etymologically related the Vedic *áhi-*, a term associated with the chaos demon Vṛtra and the primordial Serpent of the Deep, *Ahi Budhnyà* (Watkins 460–63; cf. 360–64, 370).

9. Verse 13 of the Psalm refers to "the heads of the dragons," whereas verse 14 refers to "the heads of the dragon." The dragon of the Apocalypse has seven heads, just like Litan (=Hebrew Leviathan), "the Potentate with the Seven Heads" in the Baal-Anat Cycle, discussed in chapter 1.

10. The Hebrew proper name Leviathan is also translated into Greek as *drakon* in Psalm 104 (LXX 103) and Job 41. But it is translated as *mega ketos*, "great whale" or "sea monster," in Job 3:8. Hebrew Yam/*yam* is consistently depersonified as *thallasa*, "sea," losing its monstrous connotations. Rahab is translated in various ways (most notably as *ketos* in Job 9:13 and 26:12, thus identifying it with Job's monster [*mega ketos*, Heb. Leviathan] in 3:8, and distinguishing all these references from God's dragon [*drakon*, Heb. Leviathan] in Job 41). Rahab is not used in the LXX as a proper name.

11. Lines 2200–2846; Seamus Heaney, *Beowulf: A New Verse Translation*, Bilingual Edition (New York: Farrar, Straus and Giroux, 2000) 149–91.

12. J. R. R. Tolkein, "*Beowulf*: Its Monsters and Its Critics," *Proceedings of the British Academy* 22 (1936) 245–95; and Fred C. Robinson, *Beowulf and the Appositive Style* (Knoxville: University of Tennessee Press, 1985).

13. The Latin Vulgate Bible, which soon gains ascendancy in western Christendom, also calls it a dragon ("*draco magnus rufus* [great red dragon] . . . *ille serpens antiquus qui vocatur Diabolus et Satanas* [that ancient serpent who is called Devil and Satan]"; 12:3, 9).

14. Robinson 10 and 31; and Ruth Mellinkoff, "Cain's Monstrous Progeny in Beowulf," *Anglo-Saxon England* 8 (1979) 143–62; and 9 (1980) 183–97.

CHAPTER 7, NEW MONSTERS IN OLD SKINS

1. Stephen Toulmin, *Cosmopolis: The Hidden Agenda of Modernity* (Chicago: University of Chicago Press, 1990) 98; also 107–115 on the "intellectual scaffolding" of this cosmopolis.

2. Toulmin 71.

3. Thomas Hobbes, *Leviathan*, ed. Richard Tuck (Cambridge Texts in the History of Political Thought; Cambridge: Cambridge University Press, 1996) 9. All quotations are from this edition of Hobbes' text, which is based on the copy in the Cambridge University Library (*Syn*.3.65.I).

4. Hobbes 9–10.

5. Hobbes 120.

6. Hobbes did not do the engraving for the frontispiece image, but he certainly influenced its design. An earlier drawing for the vellum edition that Hobbes had commissioned for Charles II (see below) was probably drawn by Wenceslas Hollar. A revised version of that drawing was then used as the basis for the engraving on the printed book. See Keith Brown, "The Artist of the Leviathan Title-page," *British Library Journal* 4 (1978) 24–36; and Tuck, "Introduction" lii.

7. Recounted in Edward Hyde, Earl of Clarendon, "A Survey of Mr Hobbes *His* Leviathan" (1670), *Leviathan: Contemporary Responses to the Political Theory of Thomas Hobbes*, ed. G. A. J. Rogers (Bristol: Thoemmes Press, 1995) 180–85. According to Tuck, "A note on the text" lii–lvi, Hobbes probably had intended to dedicate

the book to Charles II (the Godolphin dedication was added late in the print process).

8. Gerald Reedy, *The Bible and Reason: Anglicans and Scripture in Late Seventeenth-Century England* (Philadelphia: University of Pennsylvania Press, 1985); also Christopher Hill, *The English Bible and the Seventeenth-Century Revolution* (New York: Penguin, 1993) 425–28.

9. Hobbes 3.

10. The Latin text printed here differs from the established text of the Latin Vulgate for Job 41:24. In the Vulgate, "potestas" appears after "terram" and before "quae." Hobbes' title-page quotation, which has "potestas" before "Super Terram," may have been drawn from a different copy of the Latin text, or, more likely, is a misquote.

11. Hobbes 220–21. Hobbes' versification follows that of Christian Bibles, which correspond to the Vulgate. Hobbes' English translation here is not from the King James Version (1611), but appears to be his own.

12. Hobbes 247.

13. George Lawson, "An Examination of the Political Part of Mr. Hobbs His *Leviathan*," in Rogers 19, 90, 91.

14. John Bramhall, "The Catching of Leviathan, or the Great Whale," in Rogers 151. Alluding to the rabbinic tradition, discussed earlier, in which Leviathan is to be killed and eaten by the righteous in a final banquet, Bramhall concludes his critique of Hobbes with the suggestion (179) that if he were given the chance to implement his political theory, "his supposed subjects might tear their *mortal God* in pieces with their teeth, and entomb his Sovereignty in their bowels." Hobbes' *Leviathan* was often criticized by contemporaries as a work of political theory whose weakness was the author's own lack of experience and his inclination toward speculation. This is evident in Bramhall's critique, as well as in the well-known commentary of Edward Hyde, Earl of Clarendon, "A Survey of Mr Hobbes *His* Leviathan," in Rogers 115–300.

15. Although the sequel to Clive Barker's *Hellraiser* (1987), *Hellbound: Hellraiser II* (1988) was directed by Tony Randel and written by Peter Atkins.

16. Tuck, "Introduction" xliii.

CHAPTER 8, OTHER GODS

1. Judith Halberstam, *Skin Shows: Gothic Horror and the Technology of Monsters* (Durham: Duke University Press, 1995) 1–27 on the technology of monster making.

2. In the *Ramayana* narrative itself, Hanuman is not a deity but a legendary helper of Rama. (In some popular images of Hanuman, Rama and Sita are pictured on his chest, indicating his devotion to them.) Although he is not a deity in the *Ramayana*, in contemporary Hindu practice he is a very popular figure and sometimes even serves as a Vaiṣṇava image. In these cases, "deity is focused through a beloved animal representation, often a cult object in its own right" (Julius Lipner, *Hindus: Their Religious Beliefs and Practices* [London and New York: Routledge, 1994] 283).

3. He had been sent to the mountain in order to get a particular healing herb, but when he was unable to find the particular herb he brought back the whole mountain. This demonstrates his great strength and devotion, if not intellect or discernment.

4. *John L. Stoddard's Lectures, IV* (Boston: Balch Brothers, 1897) 89. On Banaras, compare M.A. Sherring's reactions to "the worship of uncouth idols, of monsters, of the linga and other indecent figures, and of a multitude of grotesque, ill-shapen, and hideous objects" in *The Sacred City of the Hindus* (London: Trubner & Co., 1868) 37; cited in Diana Eck, *Darśan: Seeing the Divine Image in India*, 3rd ed. (New York: Columbia University Press, 1998) 17–18. For examples of similar reactions from earlier western travelers, see William Foster, ed., *Early Travels in India 1583–1619* (London: Oxford University Press, 1921).

5. Lucy E. Guinness, *Across India at the Dawn of the 20th Century* (New York: Fleming H. Revell Company, 1898) 75–76.

6. *Stoddard's Lectures* 83–84.

7. Mark Twain, *Following the Equator: A Journey Around the World* (Hartford: The American Publishing Company,1897) 504.

8. Guinness 199–200.

9. These and others are discussed at length in Partha Mitter, *Much Maligned Monsters: A History of European Reactions to Indian Art* (2d edition; Chicago: University of Chicago Press, 1992). The subsequent discussion of early European reactions to Indian religious

iconography, especially on the legacy of Varthema, is greatly indebted to Mitter's research.

10. *The Itinerary of Lodovico de Varthema of Bologna from 1502–1508*, trans. John Winter Jones, ed. N. M. Penzer (London: The Argonaut Press, 1928). Varthema's *Itinerario* was first translated into Latin in 1511, and Richard Eden's 1577 English translation, *The Navigation and Voyages of Lewis Wetomannus*, was based on the Latin rather than the Italian. The German edition is *Die Ritterlich un[d] lobwirdig Rayss* (Augsburg, 1515; repr. of the edition in John Carter Brown Library by Scholar's Facsimiles and Reprints, 1992). Calicut appears to have been located on India's southwest coast, south of Mangalor and Cannanor and north of Ponnani and Cochin.

11. *Itinerary* 55–56.

12. Mitter 17–18.

13. Given the historical context (the manuscript in which it appears is dated 1515, just two years before the Protestant reformer Martin Luther presented his ninety-five theses against Pope Leo X's use of indulgences), it is just possible that the Augsburg artist Breu, who would later identify explicitly with the Reformation, intended to put an anti-papal spin on the scene. On Breu's religious and political history, Pia F. Cuneo, *Art and Politics in Early Modern Germany: Jörg Breu the Elder and the Fashioning of Political Identity ca. 1475–1536* (Leiden: Brill, 1998) 15–81.

14. *The Voyage of John Huyghen van Linschoten to the East Indies: from the Old English Translation of 1598*, volume I, trans. Arthur Coke Burnell (London: Hakluyt Society, 1885) 296–97. Burnell indicates that the Dutch text describes the teeth hanging over the chin rather than down to the knees.

15. European representations of human sacrifice and of Indian gods devouring people may also allude to another biblical figure of religious otherness, namely Molech, a god identified with human sacrifice in several passages of the Hebrew Bible. Molech (sometimes spelled Moloch) is a rival deity mentioned at several points in biblical literature, especially in prohibitions against child sacrifice (2 Kings 23:10; Leviticus 18:21 and 20:2–5; 1 Kings 11:7; Jeremiah 32:35; Acts 7:43). Discussed in George C. Heider, *The Cult of Molech: A Reassessment* (Sheffield: Sheffield Academic Press,

1985); and John Day, *Molech: A God of Human Sacrifice in the Old Testament* (Cambridge: Cambridge University Press, 1990); summarized in Heider, "Molech," *Anchor Bible Dictionary*, ed. David Noel Freedman (New York: Doubleday, 1992) 895–98. Another figure of religious otherness that is sometimes projected onto unfamiliar religious practices (and that may be part of the projection in these texts) is Dionysus, the Greek god identified with social transgression, madness, ecstasy, flesh, wine and human sacrifice, called "render of men" and "eater of raw flesh" (Walter F. Otto, *Dionysus: Myth and Cult*, trans. Robert B. Palmer [Bloomington: Indiana University Press, 1965]113). In the Roman Empire, the religion of Dionysus was a prominent rival to an emerging Christianity. There is evidence that Christianity was still struggling to define itself against the Dionysian religion as late as 692 CE, when the Trullian Synod of Constantinople warned against Dionysian dancing, transvestism and liturgical masks. See Albert Heinrichs, "Loss of Self, Suffering, Violence: The Modern View of Dionysus from Nietzsche to Girard," *Harvard Studies in Classical Philology* 88 (1984) 212–13.

16. Homi K. Bhabha, *The Location of Culture* (London and New York: Routledge, 1994) 70–71.

17. On the monster as "disciplinary sign," see Halberstam, esp. 72.

18. Edmund Burke, *A Philosophical Inquiry into Our Ideas of the Sublime and Beautiful*, ed. Adam Phillips (Oxford: Oxford University Press, 1998); Immanuel Kant, "Analytic of the Sublime," *Critique of Judgment*, ed. J.C. Meredith (Oxford: Oxford University Press, 1987). The primary precursor to the eighteenth-century discussion of the sublime was the Greek essay *On the Sublime* (*peri huphous*) traditionally attributed to Longinus but of unknown authorship. Interestingly, that essay refers to Euripides' *The Bacchae* and Dionysian religion as examples of the sublime's ability to carry one away with emotion (*On the Sublime: The Greek Text Edited after the Paris Manuscript*, ed. and trans. W. Rhys Roberts [Cambridge: Cambridge University Press, 1899] 89).

19. "Description of the Caves or Excavations on the Mountain . . . eastward of the Town of Ellora," *Asiatic Researches* VI (1801) 382–83; William Erskine, "Account of the Cave-Temple

of Elephanta," *Transactions of the Literary Society of Bombay* (1819) I, 198. These and many other examples are given in Mitter 120–70.

20. This exoticism may be latent even in such negative accounts as those of the mission-oriented Lucy E. Guinness, quoted earlier. On closer reading, what appears initially to be pure disgust in response to the "phantasmagoria" and "horrid chambers of imagery" of India may in fact be something far more ambivalent. At one point, frustrated with her inability to describe her experience, she focuses on her dressmaker as an object of desire pulled out of the profusion: "I lay hold of him as the last and therefore uppermost object in this world of novel, startling objects and sensations—lay hold of him as something to capture for you, out of the sea of strange impressions that makes me almost despair of ever telling you one-thousandth part of what we see and feel. Can you see and feel it with me? Can you fancy yourself snatched away from foggy little England . . . ?" (58–59). Here, as in other texts from the same period, a poetics of disgust and demonization is intertwined with a poetics of fascination and desire.

21. Marie-Denise Shelton, "Primitive Self: Colonial Impulses in Michel Leiris's 'L'Afrique fantôme'," *Prehistories of the Future: The Primitivist Project and the Culture of Modernism*, Elazar Barkan and Ronald Bush, eds. (Stanford: Stanford University Press, 1995) 327.

22. Bruce Lincoln points out an important genealogical connection between the Collège de Sociologie and Georges Dumézil (1898–1986), a scholar of mythology whose early works were especially inclined to the same kind of poetic primitivism, and who had a tremendous influence on both Claude Lévi-Strauss and Mircea Eliade. Roger Callois was Dumézil's first doctoral student (Lincoln, *Theorizing Myth*, 143).

23. Georges Bataille, *Theory of Religion*, trans. Robert Hurley (New York: Zone Books, 1989) 112; *Théorie de la religion* (Paris: Éditions Gallimard, 1973). Though not published until 1973, it was written in 1948.

24. Antonin Artaud, *The Theater and Its Double*, trans. Mary Caroline Richards (New York: Grove Press, 1958) 103, 116.

25. Artaud 123; italics added.

CHAPTER 9, THE BLOOD IS THE LIFE

1. Bram Stoker, *Dracula* (Oxford: Oxford University Press, 1996) XI. Given the many editions of this novel, all references will be to chapter numbers.

2. All biblical references in this chapter are from the King James Version.

3. Stoker XXII.

4. Nina Auerbach, *Our Vampires, Ourselves* (Chicago: University of Chicago Press, 1995) 7.

5. Stoker II.

6. Stoker II.

7. R. McNally and R. R. Florescu, *In Search of Dracula: The History of Dracula and Vampires* (Boston: Houghton Mifflin, 1972); and Lloyd Worley, "Impaling, Dracula, and the Bible," *The Monstrous and the Unspeakable,* ed. George Aichele and Tina Pippin (Sheffield Academic Press, 1997) 173–75.

8. Stoker III.

9. Stoker XXVIII.

10. Stoker I.

11. Stoker I. On folk legends and ritual practices related to vampires and the undead, see Paul Barber, *Vampires, Burial, and Death* (New Haven: Yale University Press, 1990).

12. Stoker I.

13. Stoker III.

14. Stoker XXIV.

15. Halberstam 86–99.

16. Halberstam 96.

17. Howard Eilberg-Schwartz, *The Savage in Judaism: An Anthropology of Israelite Religion and Ancient Judaism* (Bloomington: Indiana University Press, 1990) 1–86, shows how this "Jewish problem" (a problem, that is, for modern western Christian identity) plays out in the nineteenth-century anthropological discourses on "primitive" religions. On the one hand, great effort was exerted to avoid identifying Judaism with the "primitive," because maintaining a privileged status for Judaism as the locus of God's special revelation was linked to maintaining the same status for its heir, Christianity. To study Judaism in light of the "primitive" might open the door to studying Christianity in the same light. On the

other hand, bolstered by anti-Semitic discourses in criminology and other burgeoning nineteenth-century quasi-sciences, and tying into earlier European rumors of bloody Jewish religious practices, Judaism was often identified with the religions of other so-called "savages."

18. Walter Otto, *Dionysus* 113. See also the note in chapter 8.

19. On associations of the name Dio-nysos with nursing and with the *nysai* (nurses) who attend to him as a child and as his devotees, see Walter Otto, *Dionysus* 60–62.

20. Stoker VI.

21. Stoker XI.

22. Stoker XXVIII.

23. Elsewhere in conversation with Seward, Renfield makes another obscure biblical reference, comparing himself to Enoch, mentioned briefly in a genealogy in Genesis 5:21–24. "And why Enoch?" Seward asks. Renfield answers "because he walked with God" (XX, 296). Seward says that he "could not see the analogy." But Renfield did not include the full verse, "And Enoch walked with God: and he was not; for God took him" (5:24), which has sometimes been taken to suggest that Enoch never died. Thus Renfield may be indicating his own hope for immortality, reflected likewise in his incessant desire to consume the life force of other creatures.

24. Indeed, some passages indicate that God alone consumes the blood of sacrificed animals (Psalm 50:13; Isaiah 1:11; Ezekiel 44:7). Leviticus 17:10–11 suggests that the reason God takes the blood is for the purpose of atonement, or covering, of human sin. Other biblical prohibitions against blood-eating include Leviticus 3:17, 5:9, 7:26–27 and 19:26–27.

25. Stoker XXI.

26. Stoker XXI.

27. Stoker XXI.

28. Stoker XXI.

29. Stoker XXII.

30. Stoker XXI.

31. Stoker X.

32. Stoker X.

33. Stoker XIII.

34. Stoker X.

35. Stoker XII.

36. Stoker III.

37. Stoker XVI.

38. Stoker XVI.

39. Stoker XXVII.

40. Stoker XXVII. Unless otherwise noted, all subsequent quotations are from the scene of the battle.

41. Stoker XXVII. The fact that they call their son Quincey for short highlights how the process of the monster hunt has led to a reconciliation of England to its rebellious progeny in the United States of America. With the sacrificial death of the Texan Quincey Morris in the battle to save London from Dracula and restore Mina's purity, England and America are effectively unified *against* those threatening borderlands and foreign religiosities of Eastern Europe and beyond.

42. Anne Williams, *Art of Darkness: A Poetics of Gothic* (Chicago: University of Chicago Press, 1995) 134.

43. E.g., Evelyn Fox Keller, *Reflections on Gender and Science* (New Haven: Yale University Press, 1996); Carolyn Merchant, *The Death of Nature: Women, Ecology and the Scientific Revolution* (San Francisco: Harper & Row, 1980).

CHAPTER 10, SCREENING MONSTERS

1. Maya Deren, program notes for *Ritual in Transfigured Time*, reprinted in *Film Culture* 39 (1965) 6. See also Rudolph Arnheim, "To Maya Deren," *Film Culture* 24 (1962).

2. Stan Brakhage, *Metaphors on Vision*, in *Film Theory and Criticism*, ed. Gerald Mast, Marshall Cohen and Leo Braudy (4th ed.; Oxford: Oxford University Press, 1992) 72–73.

3. Jean Epstein, "*Bonjour cinéma* and Other Writings," trans. Tom Milne, *Afterimage* 10 (1981) 22; in Rachel O. Moore, *Savage Theory: Cinema as Modern Magic* (Durham: Duke University Press, 2000) 22. Similarly Charles Boultenhouse, "The Camera as a God," *Film Culture* 29 (1963), declares that good film-making "is engaged (consciously or unconsciously) in preserving and perfecting the demon in the camera; the very best film-maker is he who is engaged in transforming the demon into the god."

Moore shows how early film artists like Epstein often envisioned film as a kind of magic that mixes modern western technology and the non-western "primitive" religion. Reminiscent of Artaud's writing on the theater, and like other neo-primitive artistic and intellectual movements, filmmakers and theorists often embrace exoticized stereotypes of non-western savage otherness as a means of resacralizing what is perceived as a desacralized, degenerated industrial modern West. Thus the cinematic event is envisioned as a return of modernity's repressed, a "modern primitive" religious ritual.

4. A discussion of the letter vis-à-vis occult mysticism of the period is found in Silvain Exertier, "La lettre oubliée de Nosferatu," *Positif*, March 1980, 47–51. On the history of mystical ideas about the beginnings of language, especially as it relates to Egyptian hieroglyphs, see Erik Iverson, *The Myth of Egypt and Its Hieroglyphs in European Tradition* (Princeton: Princeton University Press, 1993).

5. Galeen wrote and co-directed the first *Der Golem* with Paul Wegener; the second was directed by Paul Wegener and Carl Boese.

6. See Moshe Idel, *Golem: Jewish Magical and Mystical Traditions on the Artificial Anthropoid* (New York: SUNY Press, 1990). *Nosferatu* may also be seen as part of a back-and-forth conversation between Galeen and Freud. On the one hand, Rank and Freud developed the idea of doubling in relation to the 1913 film *Der Student von Prague* (*The Student of Prague*), for which Galeen had served as assistant director to Stellan Rye. On the other hand, Galeen studied Freud's writings and was clearly influenced by them in his writing of *Nosferatu*; moreover, in 1926, Galeen directed the highly acclaimed remake of *Der Student von Prague*, which he wrote in collaboration with the original film's author, Hanns Heinz Ewers. Given Galeen's other interests in, for example, the legend of the Golem, his work may represent an early cinematic convergence of religion—especially late nineteenth- and early twentieth-century occultism—and Freudian thought.

7. Siegfried Kracauer, *From Caligari to Hitler: A Psychological History of the German Film* (Princeton: Princeton University Press, 1947) 31–33, offers early interpretations of the monster in the 1915 *Der Golem* and the 1916 *Homunculus* as reflections of German self-understanding.

8. The announcement is quoted in M. Bouvier and J.-L. Leutrat, *Nosferatu* (Cahiers du Cinema; Gallimard, 1981) 230. The full story of the legal ordeal with Florence Stoker is recounted by David J. Skal, "The English Widow and the German Count," *Hollywood Gothic* (New York: W. W. Norton, 1990) 43–63. For a thorough account of the rise and fall of Prana-Film, see Bouvier and Leutrat 230–36.

9. The Vedic concept of *prana* is similar in some respects to the Hebrew *ruaḥ*, "breath" or "spirit," which hovers over the deep before the creation of the world in Genesis 1:1, and which God breathes into the first earth creature in order to bring it to life in Genesis 2:7.

10. A central text of this movement in the late nineteenth and early twentieth centuries was Helena Petrovna Blavatsky's two-volume work, *The Secret Doctrine: The Synthesis of Science, Religion, and Philosophy* (London: The Theosophical Publishing Company, 1888). Prana was also a central term and concept in Blavatsky's work (e.g., vol. I, 95, 153, 157, 224, 526).

11. Lotte H. Eisner, *The Haunted Screen: Expressionism in the German Cinema and the Influence of Max Reinhardt*, trans. Roger Greaves (Berkeley: University of California Press, 1973) 15.

12. Chuck Stephens and E. Elias Merhige, "Sunrise, Sunset," *Filmmaker* 9, 1 (2000) 58–61, 101–104.

13. Renfield will subsequently go mad and find himself in Seward's sanitarium. Incidentally, Dwight Frye, who plays Renfield here, was cast as the mad lab assistant Fritz in James Whale's *Frankenstein* (1931).

14. Stoker III.

15. Stoker III.

16. Note that in both the approved script and the Spanish version of the film, the three women (rather than Dracula himself) attack Renfield.

17. Quoted in John Gianvito, "An Inconsolable Darkness: The Reappearance and Redefinition of Gothic in Contemporary Cinema," in Christoph Grunenberg, ed. *Gothic: Transmutations of Horror in Late Twentieth Century Art* (Cambridge: MIT Press, 1997) 48.

18. Until the revolution begins, Lang's use of generic uniforms and strict, geometric patterns of choreography suggests a subsum-

ing of human individuality into the larger architecture of the underground space. Once the revolution begins, as we shall see, individuality is not recovered but rather is lost in a different manner, subsumed in a bacchic revelry against architecture. On Lang's use of choreography vis-à-vis architecture in the initial scenes, see esp. Eisner, *The Haunted Screen* 223–36.

19. Though invented to bring about violence and death among the workers, her initial public epiphany is as an erotic dancer on a stage in the Metropolis. At the same time, while she dances, Freder dreams blissfully of her. When he reaches out to touch her, however, his vision suddenly shifts to the cathedral statues of the Seven Deadly Sins coming to life and the Grim Reaper dancing before him, sickle in hand. Reminiscent of the machine becoming Moloch, this sequence shows the powerful attraction and repulsion of the robotic Maria.

20. The full text (in English translation) by Thea von Harbou, quoted before the opening scene, is: "This film is not of today or of the future. It tells of no place. It serves no tendency, party or class. It has a moral that grows on the pillar of understanding: 'The mediator between brain and muscle must be the heart.'" Maria concludes her sermon in the ancient catacombs with a variation on the same text: "Between the brain that plans and the hands that build there must be a mediator. It is the heart that must bring about an understanding between them." And in the last scene, as the foreman and Frederson face one another on the cathedral steps, Maria rephrases it once again to Freder in order to encourage him to join their two hands together: "There can be no understanding between the hands and the brain unless the heart acts as mediator."

21. Throughout the rise and fall of the Nazis, von Harbou maintained prominent standing in the film business, and was highly regarded by Joseph Goebbels, the lead propagandist of the Third Reich and a cinema aficionado. Goebbels also had great appreciation for Lang's films and for Lang himself, at least until he fled Germany in the summer of 1933 (also the year he and von Harbou divorced). Lang's own relation to the Nazis and Goebbels is unclear. Did Lang flee Germany because of his own growing anti-Nazi sentiments (as he often insisted, though with conflicting details, in interviews with American reporters), or out of profes-

sional and personal self-interest (he had Jewish background and was aware of the larger Nazi plan of genocide), or out of "hurt male pride," as a 1990 *Der Spiegel* article argues? Probably all of the above, as Patrick McGilligan, *Fritz Lang: The Nature of the Beast* (New York: St. Martin's Press, 1997) 171–85, suggests. Eisner, on the other hand, tends to attribute racist and classist orientations in Lang's films to his collaboration with von Harbou, whose "sentimentalism and deplorable taste for false grandeur were to make her lapse quickly into the darkness of Nazi ideology" (232–33; cf. Eisner, *Fritz Lang* [London: Secker & Warburg, 1976]). Whether or not Lang intended them to be, some of his films were amenable to the propaganda interests of emerging Nazism. In this regard, Siegfried Kracauer's *From Caligari to Hitler: A Psychological History of the German Film* (Princeton: Princeton University Press, 1947), remains convincing, especially his analysis of Lang's1924 German nationalist film *Die Nibelungen,* which was formative for the1934 official Nazi film *Triumph of the Will* (91–95). Also convincing is his analysis of *Metropolis* as a "youth film" that, in its final sham alliance between labor and capital, serves ultimately to "affirm fixation to authoritarian behavior" (162–64).

22. Kracauer 94–95, with regard to Lang's *Die Nibelungen.*

CHAPTER 11, ECOMONSTER

1. William L. Laurence, "Drama of the Atomic Bomb Found Climax in July 16 Test," *New York Times*, Sept. 26, 1945, 16. All subsequent quotations from Laurence are from page 16 of this article. Laurence had been detached for service by the War Department in order to explain the atomic bomb to the "lay public." He not only witnessed the first explosion in New Mexico, but also saw its use in war on Nagasaki.

2. Quoted in Laurence 16.

3. Statement of General Thomas Farrell, from the press release of the War Department on the New Mexico Test, July 16, 1945.

4. Donald Worster, *Nature's Economy: A History of Ecological Ideas* (second edition; Cambridge: Cambridge University Press, 1994), shows how nuclear technology inaugurated a new age of environmentalism "whose purpose was to use the insights of ecology to

restrain the use of modern science-based power over nature" (343–44). This new interdisciplinary field emphasized balance and order within ecological systems, and warned against the monstrously destructive potential of human technological intervention and industrial exploitation. Left to itself, they argued, nature tends toward a mature state of interdependence and harmony. Often this conception of ecological order was—and still is—expressed in explicitly religious terms, as sacred or even as divinely ordained. By the same token, ecological chaos, brought on by (sacrilegious) human intervention, was increasingly presented with a sense of urgency "bordering at times on apocalyptic fear" (353).

5. See also my article, "Behold Thou the Behemoth: Imagining the Unimaginable in Monster Movies," *Imag(in)ing Otherness: Filmic Visions of Living Together,* ed. S. Brent Plate and David Jasper (Atlanta: Scholars Press, 1999).

6. This sense of a monstrous subjectivity that sees without being seen is further heightened in many horror films by use of the unclaimed point of view shot, which identifies the viewer's point of view with that of the implied monster as it stalks its unaware victim. The viewer looks through the eyes of a monster. See esp. Isabel Cristina Pinedo, *Recreational Terror: Women and the Pleasures of Horror Film Viewing* (Albany: SUNY Press, 1997) 51–55.

7. The concept of suture was first developed not in film but in psychoanalytic discourse, by Jacques-Alain Miller, a student of Jacques Lacan. See esp. Kaja Silverman, *The Subject of Semiotics* (Oxford: Oxford University Press, 1983) 199–236.

8. Pinedo 56.

CHAPTER 12, OUR MONSTERS, OURSELVES

1. Shelley 10.

2. See esp. Huet 129–62.

3. "Bela Lugosi's Dead" was first released in 1979 on a12–inch single record, *Bauhaus: Bela Lugosi's Dead,* and has been re-released several times since. Cover art includes images of Bela Lugosi as Dracula in the movie and as Dracula in his coffin.

4. For bibliography and literary history of Lovecraft, and of his early interpreters and critics, see J. T. Joshi, *Lovecraft and Lovecraft*

Criticism: An Annotated Bibliography (Kent: Kent State University Press, 1981); and Chris Jarocha-Ernst, *A Cthulhu Mythos Bibliography and Concordance* (Seattle: Armitage House, 1999). Most of Lovecraft's Cthulhu Mythos stories are published in two collections: *The Dunwich Horror and Others*, ed. S. T. Joshi (Sauk City, WI: Arkham House, 1984); and *At the Mountains of Madness, and Other Novels*, ed. J. T. Joshi (Sauk City, WI: Arkham House, 1984). Also Joyce Carol Oates, ed., *Tales of H.P. Lovecraft* (Hopewell: Ecco Press, 1997).

5. Howard Phillips Lovecraft, *Supernatural Horror in Literature* (New York: Dover, 1973) 15– 16.

6. H. P. Lovecraft, "The Call of Cthulhu," *Tales of H.P. Lovecraft*, ed. Joyce Carol Oates (Hopewell: Ecco Press, 1997) 54.

7. "The Call of Cthulhu" 53–54.

8. H. P. Lovecraft, "The Dunwich Horror," *Tales of H.P. Lovecraft*, ed. Joyce Carol Oates (Hopewell: Ecco Press, 1997) 113.

9. "The Dunwich Horror" 113.

10. "The Dunwich Horror" 113.

11. "The Dunwich Horror" 128.

12. "The Shadow Out of Time" 308.

13. "The Dunwich Horror" 117.

14. "The Call of Cthulhu" 75.

15. Edward J. Ingebretson, *Maps of Heaven, Maps of Hell: Religious Terror as Memory from the Puritans to Stephen King* (New York: M.E. Sharpe, 1996), 133.

16. There are also numerous Lovecraftian and Cthulhian board, card, computer and role-playing games, including *Call of Cthulhu*, published by Chaosium, which is set in Lovecraft's world and which has remained popular since its release in 1981. Apparently Chaosium was able to acquire the gaming rights to Lovecraft's works, thereby keeping most other print-based role-playing game publishers out. Another popular print-based role-playing game is *Cthulhupunk* by Generic Universal Role Playing Games in cooperation with Chaosium (1995).

17. Quoted in *Clive Barker's A-Z of Horror*, ed. Stephen Jones (New York: HarperCollins, 1997) 47.

18. Robert M. Price, "Lovecraft's 'Artificial Mythology,'" *An Epicure for the Terrible: A Centennial Anthology of Essays in Honor of H.P.*

Lovecraft, ed. David E. Schultz and S. T. Joshi (London and Toronto: Associated University Press, 1991) 255–56.

19. Campus Crusade for Cthulhu has several chapters worldwide, but the largest website, and the source for the material discussed here is <*www.locksley.com/cthulhu*>, designed by Joe Bethancourt. The website for the Chaos Cult of Cthulhu is <*home.c2i.net/blinge*>. Many Lovecraftian and Cthulhian sites are given at <*www.cthulhu.org*>.

20. Mircea Eliade, "The Occult and the Modern World," *Occultism, Witchcraft, and Cultural Fashions: Essays in Comparative Religions* (Chicago: University of Chicago Press, 1976) 64–65.

21. Barbara A. Babcock, "Arrange Me into Disorder: Fragments and Reflections on Ritual Clowning," *Readings in Ritual Studies*, ed. Ronald J. Grimes (Upper Saddle River, NJ: Prentice Hall, 1996) 2, 15. First published in *Rite, Drama, Festival, Spectacle: Rehearsals Toward a Theory of Cultural Performance*, ed. John J. MacAloon (Philadelphia: Institute for the Study of Human Issues, 1984).

CONCLUSION

1. Shelley 28.

2. Although many earlier maps include images and warnings of various monsters in unfamiliar regions, it appears that the earliest known map to include the famous line the *Lenox Globe* (in the collection of the New York Public Library), which dates to the beginning of the sixteenth century. There the warning appears on the east coast of Asia.

INDEX

CPSIA information can be obtained
at www.ICGtesting.com
Printed in the USA
LVHW080054140919
631099LV00018B/185/P